BORN TO CLIMB

Zofia Reych

BORN TO CLIMB

FROM ROCK CLIMBING PIONEERS TO OLYMPIC ATHLETES

Vertebrate Publishing, Sheffield
www.adventurebooks.com

Zofia Reych
BORN TO CLIMB

First published in 2022 by Vertebrate Publishing.

Vertebrate Publishing
Omega Court, 352 Cemetery Road, Sheffield S11 8FT, United Kingdom.
www.adventurebooks.com

Copyright © Zofia Reych 2022.

Author photo copyright © Andy Day.
Front cover: Natalia Grossman in the IFSC World Cup semi-final in Briançon, France in 2021.
Photo copyright © Lena Drapella.
Back cover: Meta Brevoort, W.A.B. Coolidge and the Almer guides.
Photo copyright © Alpine Club Photo Library, London.
Other photography as credited.

Zofia Reych has asserted their rights under the Copyright, Designs and Patents Act 1988 to be identified as author of this work.

This book is a work of non-fiction. The author has stated to the publishers that, except in such minor respects not affecting the substantial accuracy of the work, the contents of the book are true.

A CIP catalogue record for this book is available from the British Library.

ISBN: 978-1-83981-152-4 (Hardback)
ISBN: 978-1-83981-154-8 (Ebook)
ISBN: 978-1-83981-155-5 (Audiobook)

10 9 8 7 6 5 4 3 2 1

All rights reserved. No part of this work covered by the copyright herein may be reproduced or used in any form or by any means – graphic, electronic, or mechanised, including photocopying, recording, taping or information storage and retrieval systems – without the written permission of the publisher.

Every effort has been made to obtain the necessary permissions with reference to copyright material, both illustrative and quoted. We apologise for any omissions in this respect and will be pleased to make the appropriate acknowledgements in any future edition.

Edited by Moira Hunter.
Cover design by Jane Beagley, production by Rosie Edwards, Vertebrate Publishing.
www.adventurebooks.com

Vertebrate Publishing is committed to printing on paper from sustainable sources.

Printed and bound in the UK by TJ Books Limited, Padstow, Cornwall.

CONTENTS

2017		1
Preface		4
1	First Steps	12
2	Mountain Gloom and Mountain Glory	17
3	Monty Python's Flying Circus	30
4	The Golden Age and Other Myths	38
5	The Descendants of Gods	54
6	London, 2011	62
7	Gymnasts on Rock	66
8	The Piton Dispute	83
9	A Rock Shelf High Above the Black Lake Valley	99
10	On Stolen Land	111
11	Hard Grit	127
12	Steel City, 2015	139
13	The Poetry of Mountaineering	155
14	Climbing Free	166
15	To Bolt or Not to Be	179
16	Switzerland, 2019	192
17	The Age of Plastic	208
18	The Rise of a Rock Star	219
19	'Agenda 2020'	228
20	Bleausarde with an E	238
Epilogue		246
Acknowledgements		253
Glossary		256
Acronyms		263
Grade Comparison Tables		264
Notes and References		267
Further Reading and Recommended Viewing		285
Index		289

2017

Dusk was falling fast and the narrow road to the Rila Monastery in Western Bulgaria climbed higher and higher. The plan was to arrive deep in the mountain forest early enough to set up camp in daylight, but driving past the monastery, I could barely make out its ornate cloisters and chunky tower – an odd combination that bore testimony to more than a thousand years of history. The GPS claimed that right behind the shrine there was a hotel and a restaurant, but I couldn't see a thing, not a soul in sight. I slowed down, wary of hitting an animal that could step out from the dense forest lining the road.

The tarmac came to an end and, just as the road disappeared from my map, the car started jolting on cobblestones. Then the trail forked and I chose the turn at random. I was meant to look for trail markers but, under a starless sky, the car's old headlamps weren't doing enough. I had no idea where I was and, resigned to my fate, I turned the engine off, stepped outside and squatted to pee. A sudden gust of wind brought fine and dense rain. Chilled to the bone, I crawled into the back of the car and wrapped myself in a sleeping bag. A still skinny but now very happy mongrel curled up next to me and we fell asleep, only slightly spooked by the impenetrable darkness enveloping the car.

I woke to the sound of bells and the gentle vibration of a growling dog. Groggy and stiff from sleeping in a boot that was too short even for me, I squinted, sat up and wiped the condensation off the window with the edge of my sleeve. There was a wet pine forest, a small meadow and an old firepit adorned with a scattering of soaked litter.

Cows grazed lazily right next to the car. One of them, with a big bell hanging from her neck, almost peeked in through the window.

Stefan's vibrations clearly showed what the dog thought of cattle; born and raised in a city of two million, I shared his sentiment. My distrust towards them could be irrational, but it helped me in making the decision to push on with my journey. On wet days the car liked to be moody, so I climbed into the driver's seat, praying for the engine to start without complaints. Luck was on my side.

After a little less than half an hour of jolting, we arrived at the end of the valley and a concrete-covered clearing with mountains rising steeply around it. To my right and left were dark, man-made openings. Facing one another, each led far into the depths of the mountain.

Uranium mines.

From the tunnel on my right flowed a small, clear stream – likely contaminated but still the only source of water in the area. Bulgaria's uranium-mining past made headlines at regular intervals, often surfacing with reports of tap water being unfit for human consumption. Nobody seemed to care, possibly because there was nothing that they could do about it.

The forest was still wet after the night's downpour but the birds were singing cheerfully. I was alone and I hadn't encountered anyone since driving out of Pastra, the last village before the monastery. Everybody who could be here must have checked the forecast more thoroughly than I did. Or maybe they were less eager. Either way, the forest would be dry by the evening and I was glad at the prospect of some company. The tunnels gave me a shiver each time I looked at them.

In the morning sun, steam was rising from the pine-covered mountains, and far in the north-west I could see a huge, vertical slab of granite towering over the slopes, perhaps the peak of Malyovitsa. But I wasn't there for the mountain.

I sat down, leaning against the car, and I lit the stove to brew some coffee. The dog made his rounds, wagging like a maniac, stopping at every tree to piss. Thankfully, he ignored the tunnels and we each tended to our own business. It wasn't even eight o'clock and it would be a while before the granite boulders, tucked away in the cool shade of the pines, were dry. Having tumbled from the cliffs above some twenty-five million years ago, they sat patiently.

I was more restless but there were hours to pass. Drinking coffee, walking around in the sun, waiting for the rocks to dry.

Waiting to climb.

PREFACE

Sport climbing was officially accepted as an Olympic discipline on 3 August 2016. The decision divided the community into those excited about the inclusion and those decidedly against it. Regardless, the International Federation of Sport Climbing (IFSC) agreed to the terms proposed by the International Olympic Committee (IOC) and, for better or worse, the discipline debuted at the postponed Olympic Games in Tokyo.

The main source of controversy was a competition format different from everything the sport had seen before. Over the last few decades of indoor climbing development, climbing has matured into three separate disciplines: lead, bouldering and speed. The competitions, now organised into an international circuit of around ten events per year, follow that division.

In lead climbing, competitors have a few minutes to observe a sequence of plastic holds before making one attempt to scale a fifteen-metre artificial wall. Most don't make it to the top and whoever gets the highest, wins. In case of a tie, time becomes a decisive factor. As with outdoor sport climbing, a rope is not used as aid for staying on the wall but only to catch a climber in the event of a fall.

In bouldering, the athletes are presented with four extremely physical problems: short climbs set on a 4.5-metre wall to test their strength and creativity. A climber can try each climb as many times as they want within a four-minute window. Ropes are swapped for thick mattresses which make the frequent falls relatively safe. The results are determined by the number of points awarded for reaching the top of the four problems, or for a less valuable midway point known as a zone.

In speed climbing, climbers compete on a standardised, fifteen-metre wall. To perfect the vertical sprint, they train on the exact same set of holds day in, day out, arguably making speed the most contrived of all the three disciplines. Incidentally, for a lay observer it is also the most exciting to watch. During competitions, the race is staged in duels with two athletes climbing side by side on identical tracks. The best get to the top in under six seconds.

Traditionally, competitive climbers excel in one, or at most two, of the three disciplines, with speed requiring a set of skills very different from the two others. However, as the IOC offered climbers only two gold medals in Tokyo, the IFSC was faced with a conundrum. After years of campaigning to include climbing in the Olympics, declining the offer altogether was unthinkable, but how could they divide one medal for men and one medal for women across three different disciplines?

After much deliberation, a new combined format was conceived: a kind of climbing triathlon in which athletes compete in all three disciplines to single out the best all-rounder. Aspiring Olympians suddenly found themselves in a difficult position: for a chance to compete at the Games, most of them would effectively have to learn an entirely new sport. Lead climbers had to pick up speed, speed climbers get into bouldering, boulderers into lead climbing.

Most competitors were plainly stunned by the decision, and the reaction of the international community was fierce. Everybody had something to say about the new format and none of it was good, but once the dust of controversy had settled, the climbing triathlon quietly came into being. It was first tested at the Youth World Championships in 2017, then in 2018 at the seniors' in Innsbruck. A year later, the combined World Championships in Hachioji became the first qualifying event for the 2020 Olympics.

In March 2020, the race to Tokyo was well under way. Tears of joy and disappointment, competitiveness and ambition overshadowed the community's doubts about the new format, but the sporting emotions were soon extinguished. A joint statement from the IOC and the Tokyo 2020 Organising Committee announced that the novel coronavirus pandemic necessitated the postponement of the Games by at least a year.

When the Olympic flame finally arrived in Tokyo in July 2021, the world – and all of us with it – was changed forever.

* * *

Despite the disruptions, climbing's ascension to Olympic glory coincided with an increase in mainstream interest on a scale that now warrants national media coverage. USA Climbing (a national federation) announced a multi-year agreement with ESPN to televise and live-stream national events, and the BBC reported on both British and international competitions. Images of climbers competing at the Olympics in August 2021 were broadcast around the world.

It could be easily assumed that the growth in popularity was a direct result of Olympic inclusion but, in reality, it was quite the opposite. Before the IOC even turned its eyes to climbing, the discipline had a well-established competition circuit especially impressive for a sport which didn't see its first event until 1986. World Cups and Championships regularly gather thousands of spectators in state-of-the-art arenas, with many more joining via the free live streams. For the IOC, well aware of the fading appeal of the Olympic Games, incorporating new and exciting sports was a move carefully calculated to attract a younger audience.

Climbing's appeal to the masses is twofold. Firstly, the colourful resin holds, screwed on to plywood walls in gyms around the world, mimic the holds that outdoor climbers' hands touch in the Alps and in Yosemite. The sport's roots go deep into the world of exploration, adventure and a countercultural disdain for the ordinary: values extremely appealing to those stuck in the daily routine of a nine-to-five. A new car and a mortgage might be exactly what they want, but by covering their hands in climbing chalk and pulling themselves up an indoor wall, they flirt with adventure. Blistered fingers and sore muscles are enough to find a new appreciation for the safety of the office cubicle. And, with around forty new climbing gyms opening in the US in 2015 alone, the plastic holds are much more accessible than Yosemite rock.

Secondly, indoor climbing offers an exciting alternative to tired, old fitness formats. To counterbalance the effects of a sedentary lifestyle, city dwellers spend hours on the treadmill, in Zumba classes or in a crossfit box. Indoor climbing is yet another way to beat rising obesity rates, diabetes, depression and a host of other ailments associated with sitting down in front of a glowing computer screen for ten hours at a time.

The added thrill of a potential fall and the exhilarating immediacy of success or failure augment the positive effects of physical activity. Climbing, even indoors, is fitness for the body and for the mind. It's an adventure packed neatly into a gym pass that sits in your wallet next to the Starbucks rewards card.

World-class competitors like Janja Garnbret and Akiyo Noguchi are relatable because they battle it out on walls deceptively similar to those at your local climbing gym. Watching climbing competitions, every spectator who has at least once in their life touched a climbing hold can become a pundit. Despite being a complex sport combining gymnastic ability with serious tactical skills, climbing is still just about grabbing the next hold and going higher, or faster, than your opponents. It would be hard to think of a discipline easier to follow by audiences in arenas and in front of their TVs, one which so perfectly fits the Olympic motto of 'faster, higher, stronger'.

Climbing's appeal to a young audience is also connected to the sport's more adventurous side; beyond what goes on in artificial climbing gyms, there is an entire exciting world of outdoor climbing.

Before the sport took athletes all over the world on the World Cup circuit, it had taken a few generations around the globe to test themselves on rocks. Still, many climbing Olympians excel on real rock or ice, with the best example being the Czech phenomenon Adam Ondra. In 2017, Ondra completed the world's hardest rock-climbing route (*Silence*, 9c), but he is also a five-time gold medallist at the World Championships and one of the best all-round competitors. (At the Olympics, and soon after outdoors, he was overshadowed by the stunning performances of Slovenian Janja Garnbret.)

While differences in climbing disciplines and styles are fairly obvious to any participant, for a lay observer the subtleties may be not only confusing but also seemingly insignificant. At the same time, one very specific type of climbing ignites the mainstream imagination. The news of Ondra's or Garnbret's records doesn't reach far beyond specialist press, but for a few years their climbing peers from a different discipline have been making major headlines.

In 2015, Tommy Caldwell and Kevin Jorgeson captured the attention of the entire world with their ascent of the *Dawn Wall* on Yosemite's iconic El Capitan. Their epic nineteen-day effort, as well as the drama of one climber holding the other one back, made for perfect TV. Journalists flocked to Yosemite Valley to point their lenses towards the 914-metre vertical slab of granite and zoom in on two men trying to achieve their life's dream. When after a harrowing battle they finally pulled themselves over the edge of El Cap, they were cheered on by the whole world. Caldwell has since written a best-selling autobiography, and a feature film documenting the *Dawn Wall* ascent has made over $1 million at US box offices alone. It might not be as impressive as the latest *Star Wars* (over $1 billion), but considering that *Dawn Wall* is a movie about a niche adventure sport, it's impressive that it made it to major theatres in the first place, and has since found its way on to Netflix.

Just over two years later, thirty-two-year-old Alex Honnold changed the game forever, and in more ways than one. For the climbing world, the big news was his completion of the first solo ascent of El Capitan via *Freerider*, a route put up by Alex Huber in 1998.[1] The big difference was the style of the climb; Honnold scaled the enormous rock face with no ropes and no other equipment but his climbing shoes and a chalk bag. Just one misstep at any point of the climb – from its start at the bottom of Yosemite Valley to its end more than 914 metres above – would have meant a fall to his death.

The next milestone came about as a result of Honnold inviting his long-time friend Jimmy Chin to document the climb. A climbing filmmaker and a high-class mountaineer in his own right, Chin took on the task with serious reservations. After all, he could be agreeing to film Honnold's death. Again, the drama and tension made for the perfect mass-audience content and, in the end, Honnold's vast experience and meticulous preparations made for a happy ending. Bringing together Chin's cinematography and director Elizabeth Chai Vasarhelyi's storytelling skills, the documentary was a major hit. The box office sales exceeded $5 million, and in February 2019, *Free Solo* won the Academy Award for Best Documentary Feature.

Circling back to Ondra, the Czech proved his exceptional versatility by repeating the *Dawn Wall* only a year after Caldwell and Jorgeson. The ascent was a feat of athleticism executed with surgical precision but, beyond a piece in *National Geographic*, it didn't attract any mainstream attention. It appears that what the general public craves is not only a story of success, but one of unlikely success, a grand undertaking with an uncertain outcome. In other words, what they want is adventure.

While the vertical granite slabs of El Capitan may seem quite far removed from the plywood climbing gyms and competition arenas, their connection is undeniable. Although very different if observed at this particular moment in their history, they stem from the same exploratory tradition of mountaineering that set young minds on fire as early as the eighteenth century. In addition, the elation of a nine-to-five office worker pulling on plastic holds at their local climbing gym is the same elation that a professional, cutting-edge climber experiences in their outdoor exploits. The skill level and scale of investment might be completely different, but the emotions remain the same.

Combining the media appeal of climbing competition, the sport's roots in adventure and its enduring image as a countercultural activity, it is no wonder that the IOC picked it for the Olympic roster.

Campaigning for the sport's inclusion, the IFSC estimated in 2015 that there were thirty-five million climbers worldwide – most of them recreationally visiting their local climbing wall. Since then, facilities have continued to spring up at an astonishing rate and, although no official metrics are available at this moment, the Olympics undoubtedly brought climbing into the consciousness of millions more. Yet most of them – both recreational climbing gym patrons and fans watching the competition on screens – will have a very fragmented image of the sport: a snapshot of a discipline born out of two centuries of tradition and the contrived, arbitrary IOC format.

This book is an attempt at painting a more accurate picture. It is intended as a portrait of sorts but not a full historical record, whose scale would be far beyond these pages. In addition, timelines and chronicles rarely make for good reads, and history, although it claims to deal only in facts, tends to be more of a construct than an exact science. I'd rather throw the notion of an objective truth right out of the window and offer the reader *a story* instead.

It is the story of the defining moments, historical circumstances and iconic figures that have shaped the sport of climbing to become what it is today. Hopefully, some readers will find in it a reflection of their own experiences and an insight into how climbing's past has shaped them. For those coming to the climbing culture afresh, it can serve as a guidebook to climbing's myriad idiosyncrasies. To avoid breaking the flow of storytelling, climbing-specific slang and specialist lingo are explained in a glossary which is followed by grade comparison tables (pages 256 and 264 respectively).

My personal endeavours on plastic and rock are included as a counterweight to the tales of exceptional greatness associated with the likes of Tommy Caldwell and many others before him. Climbing's past is too often seen through newspaper headlines – the great successes and the tragic accidents. As much as climbing's present is usually portrayed through the very same lens, it is not necessarily an accurate one.

I remember my first steps in the sport as an adult, having devoured climbing magazines for some ten years. They developed in me an incredibly false idea that every climber was as athletic as British Olympian Shauna Coxsey, and I expected a similar prowess of myself. But climbing – even professional climbing – is ninety-nine per cent failure. Beyond the ascents, the medals and the goals, there are sacrifices and lifestyle choices incomprehensible to anybody from outside the community, along with injuries and doubts.

Through mixing the stories of the past and present greats with my own very typical climbing story, I hope to paint an accurate and full image of a sport that in recent years has captivated the world like no other. I hope you will enjoy it and, perhaps, find even more appreciation for a passing hobby that made you pick up this book, or maybe the great passion that has shaped – or will shape – your entire life.

CHAPTER 1

FIRST STEPS

*'Lying here on the fragrant meadow, on a glorious July day,
I felt a sensation so strange to the lowland dwellers:
a feeling of inhibited freedom.'*
Mieczysław Karłowicz (1876–1909), Polish composer
and conductor, died in an avalanche

I don't remember the beginning of my love affair with the mountains. As soon as I could walk, my mother packed her walking boots, a huge bag full of things apparently necessary for toddlers, our dog and my three-year-old self, and headed to the Warsaw Central railway station to board the train south. It was 1989. The Berlin Wall still stood, but the fall of the Polish communist regime was about to send ripples throughout the Eastern Bloc.

If the communists can be credited with doing anything positive, it would be the support that the state provided for elite mountaineers. Their achievements in the Himalaya, including many ascents completed in the dead of winter, were ammunition for one of the many fronts of the Cold War. But few climbers cared for politics. What they cared for were the passports and money necessary to go abroad. In the Himalaya, the Karakoram and Pamir, they were free.[1]

Many of them, like Wojciech Kurtyka, excelled not only in the greater ranges but also on the limestone outcrops of southern Poland.[2] While the international climbing community regards Kurtyka predominantly as a mountaineer, among the Poles he's also known for his incredible solo of a VI.5 graded route.[3] In 1993, probably the only other climber capable of such boldness was the celebrated Frenchman Patrick Edlinger.

The small Polish community of elite climbers was incredibly insular. While their achievements in the greater ranges were widely commented on in the media, they were seen as superhuman feats completely out of reach of a layperson. At the same time, no rock climbing made it into the mainstream consciousness, in part because discretion was deeply ingrained in the Polish climbing culture. Displaying a coiled rope, or any other climbing gear, on top of a backpack was seen as a great *faux pas*. The culprit would be ridiculed and no longer taken seriously by their peers.

As a result, non-climbers were hard-pressed for a glimpse into the sport, and the only form of climbing my mother could dream of was hiking. Much more mainstream at the time, it could also involve scrambling and exposure, and my mother revelled in the rare moments of balancing along a granite ridge. As a single working mother, she sneaked them into her busy life only during the summer holidays and, without a passport, she would choose between the two home ranges of Sudety and Karpaty. The latter would always win, luring her with the alpine peaks of the High Tatras.

In the few years between getting pregnant and my first wobbly steps, the one thing on her mind was to be back among the grey rocks, running up and down the trails, closing her hands on the chains of the *via ferrata*, and spending the evenings in the dark common rooms of the shelters, the air thick with the scent of sweat, goulash and tales of adventure.

Perhaps if life had left my mother with more freedom than the reality of post-communist Poland allowed, her passion for the mountains would have taken her much further than the Tatras, but in times of economic scarcity and no benefits for a single parent, the Tatras were far enough.

The smell and the sounds of the train departing from Warsaw Central station at 7.20 a.m. for Zakopane, already then a busy tourist town at the foothills of the mountains, are forever ingrained in my memory as a synonym for adventure. In a child's mind, the seven-hour journey south was a pilgrimage on the grandest scale. We passed the time drinking hot tea from a flask, peeling hard-boiled eggs and trying to count grazing cows before they disappeared out of sight.

We stayed in a house owned by an elderly couple: a six-foot-tall highlander with straight back and white hair, and his little wife with rosy cheeks wrinkled like an old apple. He was a retired forester, and the whole house was filled with horned hunting trophies, taxidermied owls and squirrels arranged in lifelike poses over every bed. In the evenings, his wife would fry us wild mushrooms served from a hot, butter-filled pan with only salt to taste and fresh bread to mop up the juices. There'd be stories of folklore heroes, encounters with bears, and of running up the mountains with no shoes 'because shoes were only for church'. I absorbed them like the bread absorbed melted butter, and studied the gullies and ridges of our hosts' weathered faces.

The morning after our train arrived at the old Zakopane railway station, my mother packed a backpack and we set off for the trails for the first time. (Back then the road by our hosts' house was not yet paved.) After walking through town, we followed the beautiful and appropriately named Path Under the Firs. The flat trail runs between a steep, forest-covered hillside above and a rolling meadow below, where sheep grazed lazily, guarded by huge dogs and sometimes the occasional shepherd. Some of the men still wore the traditional, ornate highlander's outfit. Every couple of miles there was a small bale hut with a triangular hole below the roof to let out the smoke from the open fire inside.[4]

After what seemed like an eternity to a toddler, but was just a short walk for an adult, we left the cool shade of the firs and took a path leading uphill and towards the Little Meadow Valley, a place impressively grand despite its modest name. The vast expanse of the meadow, incomprehensible to my three-year-old eyes, was beautifully described by a keen climber, Maria Steczkowska, around the year 1850:

> 'Soon a sight so charming and surprising comes before our eyes that for a moment we stand as if intoxicated, unable to comprehend whether what we look at is but a dream, or if indeed, on the background of dark forests and rocky peaks, a delightful meadow blossoms in semblance of a bonnie flower.'

Steczkowska was one of the first independent tourists in the Tatras, not only exploring the valleys and ridges on her own, but also guiding friends up peaks more than 2,000 metres high. Apart from the fact that she was a schoolteacher, there's very little known about the woman who in 1858 anonymously authored a popular mountain memoir. Her book became one of the first guidebooks in Poland, but most details about Steczkowska's life have fallen into obscurity.[5]

I played in the tall grasses of the Little Meadow, noticing with fascination the scores of minute creatures around me, all busying themselves with staying alive and passing on their genes. Beetles climbing up thin straws, grasshoppers jumping here and there, ants, bees, flies and mosquitos – they absorbed all of my attention. My mother took out a cotton hat from the backpack and carefully placed it over my head to protect it from the early morning sun. The valley, shaped like a giant cauldron, trapped the heat so that even the gentle breeze, so cool among the trees, felt like a blast of hot air.

Three white boards attached to a wooden post signalled the direction of walking trails going beyond the valley. My mother looked longingly towards them as she prepared us a light lunch. The trails led steeply through forest-covered slopes, then up into more open terrain where the dwarf mountain pine rarely grows above head height. From there, the rocky trail would turn into a series of stones weaving through steep scree, neatly arranged but still threatening a broken leg to anybody keen to take a hasty step. As I looked up from there, the sheer walls of granite and the rugged peaks of the High Tatras seemed within reach.

Mum wiped the crumbs off my face and clothing and packed away the tea flask. It was time to go back, but my little legs were already exhausted, and I was keen to stay among the grasses until I fell asleep. A sneaky promise of spotting rabbits on the way back was enough bait to get me going, but I spent a good portion of the journey in my mother's arms.

I don't remember any of it, but in the evening of the same day my mother spotted that my eyes were glassy and my forehead was burning. Just as she put me to bed, a nosebleed sprayed everything around me with red. Panicking and nearly certain she had killed her only child with too much walking, my mother promised herself never to take me on a mountain trip again, ready to give up anything for my recovery. Even after I finally fell asleep, she stayed up a long time, watching, praying and worrying in the way that only a mother can.

By the morning of the next day I was completely recovered and, although to this day my mother is certain I fell ill because of exertion, I'd blame packing my dirty fingers into my mouth.

During the same trip, Mum discovered that by getting up long before dawn, she could cram in relatively long excursions, run through the trails at breakneck speed, and be back in our room before I even opened my three-year-old eyes to demand breakfast. But despite the eager promises and prayers of the nosebleed night, she always took me along whenever it seemed like I could manage, and by the time I was sixteen we had walked and scrambled together through every single tourist trail in the Polish Tatra National Park – and many more than once.

The spell had been cast.

CHAPTER 2

MOUNTAIN GLOOM AND MOUNTAIN GLORY

'History is a series of lies upon which we agree.'
Napoleon (1769–1821)

At 1,912 metres tall, Mont Ventoux in Provence isn't a particularly beautiful mountain and only the flattering light of sunrise or sunset adorns it in mystery. There's a white chapel on the summit and an asphalt road zigzagging its way there – a popular challenge for keen cyclists.

In 1336 things were quite different. It took the extraordinary mind of a man now regarded as the father of modern humanism to come up with the outlandish idea of climbing this otherwise unremarkable peak.

The endeavour required certain preparations, and Francisco Petrarch took his time when choosing the right partner for the ascent. Not concerned with the technical difficulties of the climb (the route to the peak is more of a walk, even by fourteenth-century standards), he nonetheless wanted to ensure pleasant companionship. In the end, he settled on inviting his younger brother and, joined by their servants, the two noblemen set off from their home in Avignon on a fine April morning.

After a night spent in the village of Malaucène, the party encountered an old shepherd who confessed to having reached the summit some fifty years earlier, but assured Petrarch that no other ascents had been made. Ignoring the shepherd's warnings about how arduous the climb would be ('his counsels increased rather than diminished our desire to proceed, since youth is suspicious of warnings'), he saw his plan through, soon standing on the very summit of Mont Ventoux, albeit not without some strain and having to overcome what he himself described as 'laziness'. The view from the peak, from the outset the main reason for the climb, did not disappoint.

> *'At first, owing to the unaccustomed quality of the air and the effect of the great sweep of view spread out before me, I stood like one dazed. I beheld the clouds under our feet, and what I had read of Athos and Olympus seemed less incredible as I myself witnessed the same things from a mountain of less fame.'*[1]

Further, the scholar reflects on his ascent, oscillating between awe at the grandeur of the natural world and near guilt in allowing himself this hedonistic experience. An intellectual man deeply rooted in the tradition of medieval mysticism, he grapples with the pull of his inner world and its predominant interest in matters of the soul and the Christian God. The detailed account of the ascent and the thoughts that accompanied it, combined with the author's position among the world's greatest thinkers, have made a lasting impression on the generations that followed.

Contrary to the old shepherd's revelations, it is now known that Francisco Petrarch was not the first nobleman to scale Mont Ventoux – if the ascent was not fictional altogether – but philosophers and historians have bestowed upon this moment a special significance: a transition between epochs; an end to the Middle Ages and the beginning of modernity. The ascent is also often cited as being pivotal in the history of mountaineering, allegedly marking the moment when for the first time mountains were seen not just as an obstacle but also as a source of pleasure.

Although not all humans share Petrarch's urge to climb a mountain, most of us would agree that soaring peaks, snowy couloirs and rocky outcrops hold at once some kind of mystery and promise. If beauty were to be a universal value, it should then follow that the love of wild places – mountains in particular – is a universal feeling shared by all people and at all times. But, when it comes to appreciation of landscape, our tastes are subject to the same instability as those, for example, in fashion or design. Somewhat unbelievably, mountains, now cherished in arts and sports, and so desirable as a place of leisure, were long described as ugly.

Despite that, in 2021 athletes from all over the world for the first time competed in sport climbing elevated to the rank of an Olympic discipline. Their vertical playing field was riddled with colourful pieces of resin – handholds and footholds – moulded to reflect the surface of real rock as found on crags and in the mountains.

Our current views on nature and wilderness, including the need to represent nature in our creations, are a result of major cultural changes that have intensified in the last 200 years. Without them, a society that climbs for sport could not exist.

* * *

In times when human survival depended on cultivating the land and farming, mountains, unsuitable for agriculture, were a hostile environment. Rife with dangers, they became a symbol of nature's uncontrollable power, the abode of the supernatural and the gods.

Still, the ancient Greeks must have felt some underlying appreciation for Mount Olympus given that it was home to Zeus and his divine family, and the nine Muses, patrons of the arts and culture, were believed to live at its feet.[2] All throughout antiquity, shrines and altars were commonly placed on hilltops and in majestic outdoor settings.[3]

After the divide of the Roman Empire marked the end of classical antiquity, the newly dominant Judeo–Christian ethics emphasised man's command over nature. A seminal quote from Genesis 1:28 leaves no doubt as to the relationship between humans and our environment:

> 'Be fruitful and multiply and fill the earth and subdue it, and have dominion over the fish of the sea and over the birds of the heavens and over every living thing that moves on the earth.'

What was cultivated, fertile and orderly was seen as beautiful, as it provided food and presented no danger. Mountains were mere wastelands, aberrations on the surface of the otherwise flat and ploughable Earth; an obstacle to agriculture which became not only a matter of day-to-day survival but an act of fulfilling God's will.

An appreciation of landscapes carefully shaped by the human hand is fundamental to the very concept of a Christian paradise.[4] It wasn't by coincidence that Adam and Eve were exiled from the Garden of Eden, and not, say, an untamed forest full of wild beasts and with a rugged Alpine ridgeline in the background. Even as recently as the seventeenth century, English author John Milton, in his magnum opus *Paradise Lost*, depicted Eden as a golden city complete with 'Pavement that like a Sea of Jasper shon'.

Technological progress and urbanisation gave us hope first for keeping wild animals and diseases at bay, and then for easing the struggle of working the land. Human desires, distilled into fantasies of the ultimate reward in the afterlife, were almost a direct antithesis of nature. We dreamed not of the wild but of the cultivated and urbanised.

If the wilderness was hostile and ugly, then mountains were wilderness at its worst. Authors travelling for military or trade purposes were often filled with contempt for infertile landscapes, describing mountains as 'uncouth, huge, monstrous Excrescences of

Nature, bearing nothing but craggy stones', or, perhaps less eloquently, as 'deformities' and 'warts'.[5]

In his 2003 best-selling book *Mountains of the Mind*, Robert Macfarlane argues that it wasn't until the early eighteenth century that the heights were looked at with a little more favour.[6] It was the arrival of natural theology, writes Macfarlane, that brought about a new interest in the world and all of its aspects. Nature, once seen as an enemy to be conquered, was for the first time conceptualised as God's gift to humanity; 'a universal and public manuscript' from which everyone could learn about His might. Thus, the study of nature became a form of worship.

Huge scientific advances, including in geology and glaciology, were made. Young scholars, hungry for knowledge, travelled further and further afield, undertaking greater risks and inconveniences for the sake of their natural studies.

Meanwhile, the progression of industrialisation accounted for an unprecedented growth of European cities. In 1801, Greater London became the first Western metropolis with a population of more than one million inhabitants, only to surpass two million within another five decades. Disillusionment came fast: instead of being the promised land, cities were ripe with poverty, disease and pollution. While the rising bourgeoisie lived in relative comfort, factory workers toiled six days a week, sixteen hours a day. Soon, the unsustainable growth of the industrialised city was a burden not only to the poorest inhabitants of the slum, but an inescapable reality for all, including the rich.

Nothing could epitomise the situation better than the Great Stink of London. In summer 1858, the outdated sewer system could no longer cope with the growing population. In a period of unusually hot weather, water in the Thames fell low, turning into a 'monster soup' of human and industrial waste.[7] In the Houses of Parliament the smell was so bad that there was talk of temporarily moving government business to a different location. Yet the odour was only a minor inconvenience compared to the regular outbreaks of waterborne illnesses such as cholera, which could claim thousands of lives in one, far-from-clean, sweep.

The challenges of urbanisation caused many to look more favourably upon the great outdoors. Suddenly, nature could not only act as a tantalising laboratory for the curious scientist, but also offer relief from the strains of modern city life. Shady forests, windswept beaches and – yes! – majestic mountains had never been as appealing as in the mid-nineteenth century.

* * *

The expansionist policies of the British Empire, advances in science and industry and, perhaps most of all, a burgeoning economy built on exploitation were all necessary components in the creation of a new aesthetic category: the sublime.

The concept was still unheard of in 1672 when a youthful Charles Paulet left the shores of England for his grand tour of Europe.[8] A few decades earlier, the grand tour had become a permanent fixture in the education of young gentlemen of certain status and means. To make the most of this extravagant rite of passage, aristocrats would often be assisted by servants, and almost always chaperoned by a tutor. The eleven-year-old Charles Paulet, 2nd Duke of Bolton and Earl of Wiltshire, set off in the company of one Thomas Burnet.

A Cambridge fellow and already a respected scholar, Burnet took what was meant to be a sabbatical but became a whole decade chaperoning a long list of young aristocrats back and forth between England and the Mediterranean. Charles Paulet's tour was Burnet's first expedition to the continent and, consequently, the first time he saw the mountains. The Alpine crossing through the Simplon Pass was as arduous as could be expected in 1672, but for Burnet it was also the beginning of a much bigger theological journey which would lead to great discoveries long after his lifetime.

His revolutionary theories, developed as a direct result of his experiences in the mountains, were first published in Latin in 1681, and two years later in English as *The Sacred Theory of the Earth*. Before Burnet, most scientific opinions as to the natural history of the Earth took biblical genesis word for word. It was believed that since the seven days of creation, not much had changed. Burnet was the first to suggest that the appearance of the Earth as we know it was the effect of more godly tinkering than just that one initial week of effort.

The idea stirred a lot of controversy and was widely opposed, but it began to erode the firm beliefs of contemporary scholars that the Earth's appearance was, forgive the pun, set in stone. Suddenly, debating the Earth's history became very fashionable. As early geological theories advanced, so did an understanding of time. Never before had human brains been exposed to the vastness of prehistory. For the first time, it was possible that the biblical days were in fact only metaphors for unimaginably long epochs.

The realisation that mountains were not, as it was believed before, a permanent fixture on the horizon, but rather the most striking evidence of transformative processes of unimaginable scale, brought a new and exciting dimension to how they were perceived. The early to mid-nineteenth century was the time when natural sciences were hotly discussed among intellectual circles.

By that time, the grand tour was already somewhat democratised by the advent of relatively cheap steam travel. But before the custom could become *passé*, many a young aristocrat and artist painstakingly trekked the length of Europe and back, exposing themselves – and through their accounts also the wider public – not only to the monuments of civilisation but also the grandeur of the Alps.

By the mid-eighteenth century, travellers were keen to experience mountainous landscapes differently from their predecessors. The 1732 poem *'Die Alpen'*, by Swiss naturalist Albrecht von Haller, had popularised the idea of the Alps as the archetypal idyll and an antidote for the moral decay of city life. Soon after, Jean-Jacques Rousseau's theorising on 'primitive' cultures gave rise to the idea of the noble savage, whereby the savage was not only wild and uncivilised, but also brave, honest and, in the desirable sense of the word, simple.

For the early Romantics, untamed nature – not necessarily beautiful in the classicist sense of the word but admirable and grand nonetheless – was a reflection of the turbulent internal states of their souls. It isn't without reason that the German proto-Romantic movement (of which Goethe was one of the greatest figures) is known to this day as *sturm und drang* – storm and stress.⁹ At roughly the same time, Rousseau wrote of his desire for 'torrents, rocks, pines, dead forest, mountains, rugged paths to go up and down, precipices beside me to frighten me'.¹⁰

However, when Horace Walpole, the son of a prime minister, and Thomas Gray, the poet, embarked together on their grand tour in 1739, they were both decidedly unsure about the allure of the Alpine crossing – especially after Walpole's beloved spaniel was eaten by a wolf. At the same time, there must have been something in the landscape that spoke to his poetic sensibility and gloomy disposition, for he noted in a letter:

> 'Precipices, mountains, torrents, wolves, rumblings, Salvator Rosa – the pomp of our park and the meekness of our palace! Here we are, the lonely lords of glorious desolate prospects.'¹¹

Only three decades elapsed between this passage written in an Alpine inn and Gray's *Journal of the Lakes*, which became a hugely popular guide to the English Lake District. In the meantime, philosopher Edmund Burke published his treaty, *A Philosophical Enquiry into the Origin of Our Ideas of the Sublime and Beautiful*, defining the new, modern aesthetic category. Beauty was to be found, according to Burke, in what's light, delicate and regular, inspiring the comfortable feelings of love. Sublimity, on the other hand, resides in the rugged, the grand and the gloomy – and also the terror-inducing. The Lake District, as heralded by Thomas Gray, fitted this description exceedingly well. After the publication of his *Journal*, scores of tourists flocked from the cities to the Lakes to experience the sublime for themselves. Very likely, without his early experiences in the Alps, Gray would not have found his love for the rugged landscape of the Lake District and would never have passed it on to a wider audience.

From its early stages, the perception of risk was an integral part of the love affair with the sublime. 'The odd thing about my liking for precipitous places', confessed Rousseau, 'is that they make me giddy, and I enjoy this giddiness greatly, provided that I am safely placed.' In the twenty-first century, with hundreds of horror movies produced every year and bungee jumping available as a tourist attraction, it seems hardly a revelation that the slight tingling of fear can be fun. Three hundred years ago it was a major novelty, arriving at roughly the same time as the idea of outdoor recreation for the sake of leisure.

In his *Philosophical Enquiry*, Edmund Burke elaborated:

> 'When danger or pain press too nearly, they are incapable of giving any delight, and are simply terrible; but at certain distances, and with certain modifications, they may be, and they are delightful. [...] Terror is a passion which always produces delight when it does not press too close.'[12]

Before these ideas could become the very foundation of adventure travel and, later, adventure sports, they quickly found their place in literature. Shortly before Thomas Gray published his *Journal*, his grand tour companion of old, Horace Walpole, produced *The Castle of Otranto* (1764), now recognised as the first Gothic novel and a precursor to many Victorian classics, including Shelley's *Frankenstein* (1818) and Stoker's *Dracula* (1897). Blending death and romance for literary effect is perhaps not too dissimilar to blending relaxation with thrill-seeking for leisure.

It is no coincidence that the early explorers of the sublime – Romantic writers and climbers – were often one and the same person. Among the Lake District poets, named so because of their long-time residency in the region, was Samuel Coleridge. In 1800, the twenty-seven-year-old writer moved with his family to Keswick to live near his lifelong friend William Wordsworth. By this time, Coleridge's abuse of laudanum had already taken its toll on both his body and his mind, but despite the addiction, both poets frequently visited one another on foot, sometimes making the round trip of over twenty-five miles within one day.

It was not only the two poets, now credited with founding English Romanticism, who enjoyed the Lakes' scenery. Their whole literary circle, composed of both men and women, were prolific walkers. Wordsworth's sister Dorothy was also a writer, and although unpublished in her lifetime, she became hugely influential over her brother's work, which included almost direct quotations from her journals. She frequently walked in the hills and was not shy about her outdoor prowess. Aged forty-six, she wrote to a friend:

> 'I can walk 16 miles in four hours and three quarters, with short rests between, on a blustering cold day, without having felt any fatigue.'[13]

Only a few months later, in October 1818, Dorothy made an ascent of the highest mountain in England, Scafell Pike, accompanied by a friend, Mary Baker. At a time when women rarely left their homes unchaperoned, and mountaineering was still in its infancy, Wordsworth's and Baker's independent tourism was not only a sporting achievement, but a cultural precedent.

The brand of climbing practised by both Wordsworths and their friends was what is now commonly referred to as fell or hill walking, a sport still hugely popular in Britain. In the early nineteenth century, ascending a peak even by the tamest of slopes was considered climbing, though the description of one outing by Samuel Coleridge is, even by contemporary standards, an account of rock climbing proper – perhaps the first in history.

On 1 August 1802, Coleridge had just set off from his home in Keswick for a solitary tour of the Lakes. Armed only with a walking stick and a knapsack, he reached the slopes of Scafell Pike after three days. As he stood on the 978-metre peak (the same later ascended by Dorothy), a storm began to brew. Coleridge then turned to what he called 'a new kind of gambling' in which, instead of searching for the safest descent path, he'd choose at random to see where fate might cast him.[14] On Scafell Pike, this daring strategy got him into severe trouble – or, to put it in the rock-climbing lingo of today, he had a total epic.

Following his nose and unaware of what lay ahead, Coleridge decided to descend on the north-east side of the mountain. While all the other slopes are relatively gentle, this direction was the one to avoid, with the precipitous drop of Broad Stand's giant rock steps forming a formidable obstacle even by today's standards. (It claimed the life of a tourist as recently as in 2017.) Considering that going down is always harder than going up, Coleridge maintained an astonishingly light-hearted, if rather romantically affected, attitude to the near-fatal experience:

> *'I began to suspect that I ought not to go on, but then unfortunately tho' I could with ease drop down a smooth Rock 7 feet high, I could not climb it, so go on I must and on I went. The next 3 drops were not half a Foot, at least not a foot more than my own height, but every Drop increased the Palsy of my Limbs – I shook all over, Heaven knows without the least influence of Fear, and now I had only two more to drop down, to return was impossible – but of these two the first was tremendous, it was twice my own height, and the Ledge at the bottom was so exceedingly narrow, that if I dropt down upon it I must of necessity have fallen backwards and of course killed myself. My Limbs were all in a tremble – I lay upon my Back to rest myself, and was beginning according to my Custom to laugh at myself for a Madman, when the sight of the Crags above me on each side, and the impetuous Clouds just over them, posting so*

> luridly and so rapidly northward, overawed me. I lay in a state of almost prophetic Trance and Delight [...].'[15]

Had Coleridge attempted to continue downward, he would most likely have died on that stormy August day. Instead, on the left side of the shelf to which he was confined, he noticed a narrow gap in the rock. Known today as *Fat Man's Agony*, the crevice forced Coleridge to remove his knapsack in order to squeeze through. On its other side, a less prohibitive, grassy slope led him to safety and allowed him to live another twenty-three years before he passed away of drug-induced heart failure.

* * *

Over two centuries later, Scafell Pike is an extremely popular tourist destination; a central attraction of the Lake District National Park which receives as many as fifteen million visitors a year. Scores of walkers follow in Coleridge's footsteps and squeeze through the narrow passage that saved his life, documenting their adventures on mobile phones and uploading videos to social media.

Recreating in the English countryside has since become an egalitarian activity, seemingly accessible to all in equal measure. However, statistics show that while the gender gap in recreational walking has been all but closed, the same can't be said for ethnicity and income, as the bulk of walkers is made up of white professionals. And the more technically advanced the activity, the starker the social stratification. As a result, most participants are still affluent white males.

Despite many falsely believing that climbing has working-class roots, elitism is deeply ingrained in the identity of the sport. As the generation of Wordsworth and Coleridge created the foundations of the discipline, they also infused it with ideas of class and intellectual superiority, and it was perhaps at that time when the false dichotomy of 'before us' and 'after us' came into being.

Modernity, with all of its opportunities, ideas and flaws, was a prerequisite for the sport of climbing to come into being, but it would be wrong to assume that never before had a human admired a mountain or found pleasure in the effort necessary to overcome it. However, these instances were certainly not the norm, and most of them went unrecorded, with only rare accounts gaining status as groundbreaking moments.

The idea of a sharp transition between the pre-modern period of mountain gloom and the modern era of mountain glory dates back to the time when climbing emerged as a leisure activity of the cultured classes. The story of this transition was written down in a 1959 monograph by American literary scholar Marjorie Hope Nicolson. *Mountain Gloom and Mountain Glory: The Genealogy of an Idea* became the cornerstone of knowledge about the history of our relationship with high places, informing the following sixty years of research and influencing climbing writers.

Recently, scholars have called for a more nuanced narrative, pointing out that the theory of mountain gloom and glory is more symptomatic of the time in which it was created than the era it seeks to explain, but now the path is clear for new research to bring fresh perspectives into the field.[16]

CHAPTER 3

MONTY PYTHON'S FLYING CIRCUS

'The Grépon has disappeared. Of course, there are still some rocks standing there, but as a climb it no longer exists. Now that it has been done by two women alone, no self-respecting man can undertake it.'
Étienne Bruhl (1898–1973), French alpinist

Rising steeply from green valleys and gorges, the rocks of the Polish Jura are often white like a bone, similar to the ruined castles which overlook the grassy plains of the region. The walls of limestone are riddled with one-finger pockets just like those that make the German Frankenjura a world-class sport-climbing destination. Smaller than its German counterpart and with fewer long and hard routes, the Polish Jura remains one of the best-kept climbing secrets in central Europe.

Before stepping between the soaring outcrops in the very heart of the Jura, I had no idea about their existence less than 200 miles south of home. At sixteen, I could hardly wrap my head around the view which boggled my mind almost as much as the fact that my mother had agreed to the trip.

A couple of years earlier, I had realised that there was more to the

Tatra mountains than hiking; that the granite walls could actually be scaled upwards and not simply walked around. First, I learned to make out climbing parties in the distance, noticeable only by the colour of their helmets, the occasional gleam of their gear or the echoes that carried their commands. I could rarely make out the words, but sometimes a clear 'watch me!' or 'off belay!' would carry in the still, crisp air of the morning.

Then, despite their best attempts at hiding their identity, I learned to discern climbers from what I called 'common tourists'. With heavy backpacks, they walked uphill faster, the trail being merely a path which led to a much grander challenge. Here and there, a telltale sign: a coiled rope under a backpack that didn't quite want to close properly; fingers gnarled by years of pulling on small holds; or boots that were designed for scrambling rather than long days on a trail. Pieced together, they marked someone as a rock climber. I looked at them in awe, but had absolutely no idea how to rectify my own status of being a common tourist.

Things picked up when a new school friend announced that her father was himself a climber and that she planned on joining a beginner course. In the early 2000s, the Polish climbing community was still gripped by institutionalism, a hangover from the times when, for the state, mountaineering was a matter of politics. While in the British community skill-passage relied, and still largely does, on informal mentorship, in Poland a six-day course was regarded as the first mandatory step in a climber's education. Following a set curriculum and conducted by a certified instructor, it ended with a practical exam. Assuming a pass, the newbie was then qualified to take a centralised theoretical exam provided by the Polish Mountaineering Association. A positive result earned a green laminated card known as the Rock Climbing Licence, which entitled them to climb independently.[1]

Usually a year or two later, and not before completing a certain number of routes, you could join a two-week-long mountaineering course in the High Tatras with the hope of getting yet another obligatory accreditation. It was that accreditation – the Tatra Climbing Licence – that was my sole objective. Still, the first stop along the way had to be the Jura. I signed up for the course with two friends and, to make up two climbing parties of two, we were matched with another woman we had not met before.

Our instructor's name was Robert, a cheerful, stocky man who within minutes announced that he had never taught climbing to a group of four girls. One female on the course, yes, that had happened a few times. Two, he wasn't sure. But never, ever in his career had he seen a course of four women.

To Robert's surprise, we learned fast. In keeping with stereotypes, we were more focused, orderly and keen to listen, eager to show we could do anything a boy could. It was then decided that, after covering the regular curriculum faster than expected, we could have a go at skills usually only taught on the longer mountaineering course.

On the last day before our exam, I was learning to build a top-hanging belay suitable for a multi-pitch climb. Although the outcrops of Jura are rarely tall enough to warrant this technique, in the mountains it's a fairly common scenario in which the leader climbs for the whole length of the rope and stops to bring up their belayer. The latter then continues upwards for the next pitch, and so they alternate until they reach the summit.

Hanging in my harness halfway up a light grey rock face, I was fiddling with gear, carefully recreating a scheme I had seen in a yellow-paged textbook the day before. Getting ready to bring my belayer up, I cast one last look at the anchor, at the carabiners, wires, slings and the rope tied to the thin, oh-so-thin, loop of my harness. I had learned earlier that it could withstand fifteen kilonewtons of force, amounting to roughly three Asian elephants dangling off it. But there were no elephants around, just me and a drop of more than eighteen metres straight down to the ground. I tried to stand up but my feet could find no purchase on the slick limestone. I was helplessly suspended by the very gear I had just placed, connected to a medley of webbing and shrapnel only with the offending loop. 'It is too thin,' I said to myself. Panic seized me by the throat and I started hyperventilating. 'It's too thin!' The scream came out as a squeak and I suddenly *needed* to be back down by the fastest means possible. And the fastest way happened to be by untying the rope connected to the loop of my harness.

I didn't think that far ahead, but this method would get me to the ground at the speed of more than forty-two miles per hour and in less than two seconds.

Perhaps to prevent exactly this kind of vertigo-induced madness from killing people, the knot connecting me to my anchor was a figure of eight, complete with an additional stopper knot. It takes a good couple of minutes to tie with an unpractised hand. After being loaded with weight, the knot tightens, making it even harder to undo.

Hanging in his own belay some four metres to the right of me, Robert noticed my frantic fight with the rope.

'Whaddya doin' there, luv?' His calm voice came from some faraway place, or was it that I had cotton wool in my ears?

'WHAT-ARE-YOU-DOING?' came again, but my answer was completely unintelligible through the sobs that shook my body.

'What??!!'

'The belay … loop … The loop is going to break!'

This shocking revelation was surely going to set Robert ablaze with efforts to save me. In fact, it most certainly did – apart from working as an instructor, he was also a member of the elite Tatra Volunteer Search and Rescue, but nothing in his movements indicated urgency.[2]

'In the case of a lass your age,' he said in a bored voice under his breath, while already halfway between his original position and me, 'there's only one thing that's sure to break fairly soon.'

The rudeness of his words immediately found its way through the cotton wool and right into my brain. Even faster than it began, the panic was over. I burst out laughing and blew out quite a lot of snot.

'Piss off, will you?' I snorted.

Robert didn't move any further but looked intently at my harness and the rope attached to it. My figure of eight was intact. My fingers, stiffened with fear, had only managed to undo the stopper.

'You've got it now?' he asked seriously, knowing that my wits had returned.

'I've got it,' I nodded, wiping snot off my face with the top of my dusty hand.

* * *

I vaguely remember that we may have misled our parents into thinking that the course lasted two weeks. In reality, after six days of learning with Robert, the three of us stayed on for another week, planning to climb in all the valleys we could reach on foot, as none of us could drive.

We had a rope and a set of quickdraws, bought with our pocket money ahead of the trip, as well as an insatiable appetite for alcohol, which we tried to buy in every shop we encountered. When finally one cashier forgot to check my age, I swiftly became a proud owner of two bottles of cheap Merlot.

One thing I now believe they should teach all teenagers is that heat and dehydration lower your tolerance for alcohol. I would certainly have drunk more water had I known that alcohol poisoning could deprive me of two good days of climbing.

Finally recovered from violent bouts of vomiting and a monstrous headache, I was determined to catch up with my friends and get up as much rock as possible. Poring over guidebooks, we found every single route easier than V and went after them, but quickly there was nothing left for us to climb other than fives.[3] And, after just a few days of practice, fives scared the shit out of us.

It was late afternoon on our last day of climbing and the heat had eased off a little. I was already tired, perhaps more from walking with a backpack than from actual climbing, but I wanted to do one more route before sundown. In the guidebook we found a short line with only four bolts – perfect for a quick go. My knees felt a little shaky when I casually asserted that, yeah, for sure I could lead a V+.

The sun was low, casting long shadows and filling the air with liquid gold. Our intended route had been in sight when we passed by another rock with three climbers sitting at its base, sharing a beer after the day's effort. We waved at them self-consciously. We couldn't make out what they were saying, but it was obvious who was the subject of the talk. Then, one of them theatrically raised his voice to make sure that we heard, 'Look! Monty Python's Flying Circus is in town to climb!'

We walked on as his mates started laughing, the sort of vile laugh typical of a bully's sidekick. I bit my tongue to stop myself shouting back obscenities, but ignoring the guys was the only way to show that we didn't think the remark was about us. Suddenly there was sand in my eyes and I felt both very angry and very sorry for myself.

During those few days spent in the valley, we couldn't help but notice that we were not only the youngest, but also the only all-female party around. Aside from us, we hadn't seen anybody but males leading routes, and the one girl we met each day was pacing back and forth under a rock, her phone glued to her ear as her boyfriend climbed with friends. We were aware of the existence of some strong female climbers in the wider community – the likes of Ola Taistra and Kinga Ociepka, both of them in the then incredibly elite 8c club – but the excitement the magazines showed for their achievements was in no way reflected by the demography of the community as we got to know it.

Most evenings were spent sharing a bonfire and some beers with guys met during the day. Nearly all of them were university students, older than us by a good few years and so much more grown up than our high-school friends. The majority were also much better climbers than us and we felt *so cool* just hanging out with them, listening to the stories of the day and telling our own. And although we were collectively smitten with all of them, their ripped muscles frequently the topic of our private conversations, anything more than a flirt was the last thing on our minds. We cared only for climbing.

Thinking back to that time from the perspective of two extra decades of experience, my instincts tell me that the situation could have quickly turned very wrong. But the reality was that it had never even crossed our minds that we could have been in any way unsafe. In our naivety, we felt equal among equals, sharing camaraderie and booze. And suddenly one ill-intentioned remark shattered that feeling into very small pieces.

None of us had any doubts that the sole reason for the mockery was that we were girls. We felt betrayed. Had we not proven ourselves, climbing and drinking as hard as we could? We stood in silence as my friend flicked the rope, running all of its length through her hands to ensure no knots would get in the way of belaying. I pulled my harness on and then racked up with five quickdraws (four for the bolts and one spare), two screwgate carabiners, two regular ones, two slings and a prusik cord, as per the textbook we had studied religiously the week before. As my partner tightened her harness and put the rope through a belay device, I dipped my hands in chalk while she carefully examined the figure of eight I had just tied. We didn't exchange any words apart from the ceremony of climbing commands, enacted to the letter. 'Can I go?' I asked in a quiet voice. 'You can go,' she replied. 'Climbing,' I said, and my fingers touched the rock.[4]

Until then, we were spellbound to silence, our lips closed tight for fear of all the words that could flow out. Maybe I'd even cry. In our childish minds, probably way more naive than any sixteen-year-olds today, my climb had just become a matter of our girlish pride, a sure way to redeem our souls from the sin of girlhood. It was so serious that until I clipped the first bolt, some three metres off the deck, I forgot to be scared. Only the act of hanging my quickdraw and putting the rope through reminded me of the immediacy of a possible fall. I also realised that the sun had set behind the horizon and that dusk was rapidly falling over the valley. And if the darkness progressed fast, I certainly climbed slow.

I'm not sure if my memory of what followed is at all correct, or if

I created the story in my head on the way back home from the Jura. What I know is that I completed the climb, albeit in darkness, for we definitely didn't take any falls on that first climbing trip. I'm not certain, however, if the three beer-drinking climbers really walked up to us and pointed their torches at me, shouting words of encouragement. I'm not certain if our grit and commitment were enough to prove that they had wronged us. That, girls or not, we were worthy of their respect.

CHAPTER 4

THE GOLDEN AGE AND OTHER MYTHS

> 'He is a true apprentice of the craft only when he can say from a full heart **Labor ipse voluptas** *[labour is pleasure].*'
> Sir Frederick Pollock (1845–1937), 3rd Baronet, English aristocrat and intellectual, member of the Alpine Club

'You must imagine your lake put in agitation by a strong wind, all frozen at once,' wrote William Windham Sr in 1741 upon seeing the great glacial tongue of Montenvers reaching towards Chamonix.[1]

At the time, he was living in Geneva – indulging in a prolonged stopover during his grand tour of the continent – where he had become a pivotal member of a dining society of British expatriates who met for book reading, staging theatrical plays and other entertainment. It's possible that the atmosphere of the City Republic of Geneva was too sombre for their liking, as most of the Calvinist Genevans were of a strict Protestant disposition. And, despite the stunning view of the mountains surrounding the city, for the most part the locals had little or no interest in the distant peaks.

The few exploration attempts had been made by early eighteenth-century scientists, and some of them even reported encountering dragons.² Such frivolities were of little interest to most Genevans but the expat community was more inclined towards adventure. The arrival of an experienced traveller, Richard Pococke, provided the perfect opportunity for Windham to organise an expedition. Their objective became the mysterious region of Savoy and the village of Chamonix.

The heavily laden and well-armed party set off from Geneva, displaying – in keeping with the times – ostensibly scientific ambitions. Apart from an array of 'mathematical instruments', including thermometers, barometers and a quadrant, they carried an ample supply of wine, and the whole endeavour, however pioneering, was of a decidedly touristic character.

After three days of arduous travel, the group arrived in Chamonix only to discover that while the glacier was visible from the village, it was not accessible. Despite being warned by 'the peasants' that a further journey would be extremely tiresome and only worth it for the chamois hunters or crystal collectors, the intrepid tourists decided to press onwards.

The following day they hired local men for guides and walked for five hours uphill to Montenvers, from where they could have a close-up view of the glacier and tread directly on the ice. After raising a toast to the successes of the British Army, they turned back down.

Having completed his grand tour, Windham returned to London, where he spent time editing his travel letters to produce a pamphlet in support of his candidature to the Royal Society. The sixty-page booklet became hugely popular in elegant circles and, beyond securing Windham's election to the Society, it had the unexpected side effect of putting glaciers on everybody's lips. Their popularity grew so quickly that already in 1779 Scottish physician Dr John Moore was spouting:

'One could hardly mention anything curious or singular, without being told by some of those travellers, with an air of cool contempt,

"Dear sir, that is pretty well; but, take my word for it, it is nothing to the glaciers of Savoy."[3]

Although Moore's lamentations make it seem as if a kind of mass tourism was already happening in Chamonix in the eighteenth century, it was still only the members of the most privileged circles who could afford it. Admittedly, the first inn, named L'Hôtel d'Angleterre in honour of Windham and Pococke, was opened as early as 1770, and by 1783 up to 1,500 visitors visited Chamonix every summer.[4] But the road network of pre-Napoleonic Europe was still very poor and stagecoaches were expensive and tiresome: the journey from London to Geneva could take as long as two weeks.

In Geneva itself, a newfound interest in the natural world drew more and more scientists to the region. For many, Mont Blanc became an obsession; despite its rounded silhouette (if observed from the French side), it was known to be the highest point in all of Europe. To stand on the summit would be not only to gain fame but to greatly advance scientific knowledge.[5] In 1786, after over a decade-long race for the first ascent, Chamonix doctor Michel-Gabriel Paccard and guide Jacques Balmat finally stood on the summit. The competition for the laurels of the first ascensionist was fierce not only between various parties, but also between Paccard and Balmat themselves. As a result, most of Chamonix and indeed the whole of Europe's intellectual circles became divided into two factions – pro-Paccard and pro-Balmat – fighting over who was the real hero of the ascent. Certainly, Paccard was the scientist, but Balmat was the guide and the porter burdened with most of the load of the scientific equipment that Paccard wanted to take to the summit. He also led Paccard down after the doctor was struck by snow blindness. The competition between the two men got out of hand to the point that they had a public fight at an inn in Chamonix, and for a while Paccard became a wholly unpopular figure due to vicious gossip spread by another jealous rival.

Paccard's involvement in the first ascent was soon forgotten by the public when, one year later, a prominent scientist, Horace Bénédict de Saussure, made another ascent followed by a great deal of scientific publicity. In the meantime, Balmat became an in-demand guide and his statue, standing next to de Saussure's, was raised in 1887.

The conflict between Paccard and Balmat was finally settled and the doctor went on to marry the guide's sister. Chamonix honoured Michel-Gabriel Paccard, erecting a statue in his own right in 1986.

* * *

The turn of the century saw a massive acceleration in exploration: while there were only fifteen first ascents in the fifty years prior, by the mid-nineteenth century much of the Alpine terrain was mapped by the locals. Nearly forty peaks were climbed within half a century, but soon the aftermath of the French Revolution gripped continental Europe in a political and religious turmoil which didn't allow for much travel.[6] Meanwhile, Britain was left with but one enemy in Europe: distant Russia, soon to be defeated in the Crimean War. The empire was slowly but steadily on its way to the height of its power; a result of nearly 300 years of mercantilist colonisation which, depriving the conquered lands of their resources, fattened the British purse.

While the sun never set over the empire, at home Victorian Britain seems to have somewhat lacked in terms of entertainment. A hundred years later, the *Alpine Journal* was as humorous as it was merciless in its depictions of opportunities for amusement in mid-nineteenth-century London. According to an article, the audiences had no choice but to be content with dull scientific demonstrations – 'charcoal being burnt in bottles of oxygen, and hearing the physiology of the eye explained by diagrams' – with only 'the hippopotamus at Regent's Park' providing any real excitement among the 'fustian', suffocating alternatives.[7]

Enter Albert Smith, the son of a respectable surgeon and a doctor himself who gave up medicine to pursue the far less respectable profession of satire journalism. From early childhood, Smith was obsessed with Chamonix, and at the age of thirty-five he finally realised his dream of visiting the Alps and scaling Mont Blanc. It was the fortieth ascent of the mountain and, together with another three English gentlemen, the party was led by sixteen local guides. The provisions carried by the porters included eleven large fowl, thirty-five small fowl and ninety bottles of wine.[8] The Chamonix guides had already perfected their upselling skills to mercilessly rip off their gullible, wealthy clients.

Forty-six fowl aside, the ascent was markedly unremarkable, but it went on to make Smith a wealthy man and put the Alps in the minds of the middle classes.

Combining his love of travel with a passion for showmanship, Albert Smith self-published a book and produced a show that was promptly scheduled for an extended run at the Egyptian Hall in Piccadilly. Complete with chalet-style decorations, two chamois, a pack of St Bernard dogs and a pair of good-looking barmaids in regional costume, it easily overshadowed the sad hippopotamus in Regent's Park. Audiences were mesmerised by the vividly painted backgrounds changing on a scrolling screen, and the story of Smith's ascent remained on stage for seven years – more than 2,000 performances – cut short only by the entertainer's premature death.

The well-to-do Victorian middle class was now 'gripped with Mont Blanc mania' and soon the final obstacle that lay between them and Chamonix, over 6,000 miles of poor roads, had been removed by the arrival of the railway.[9] Geneva became accessible from London in two days and, at just £2, the journey was now ten times cheaper.[10]

A young and affluent judge by the name of Alfred Wills – the same who later presided over Oscar Wilde's trial and sentenced the writer for gross indecency – had already made several trips to Chamonix which, including numerous stopovers in substandard inns, were tiresome and wholly unsuitable for a lady. The development of the railway in 1854 became the first opportunity for Wills to take his wife for an Alpine honeymoon and share with her his love for the Alps. In a subsequent account, he recollected how Lucy accompanied him on long excursions and even partook in an overnight bivouac, though special preparations were made to ensure appropriate lodgings.[11]

Wills' *Wanderings Among the High Alps*, partially written as a guide for anybody who wanted to follow in his footsteps, became a great success and one of the earliest accounts of alpinism as a sporting activity.[12]

* * *

Although Wills' attitude to the mountains and his admiration for nature were deeply rooted in the Romantic tradition of the sublime, in another passage from *Wanderings*, he marvelled at the proud and strong posture of one of his guides, signalling the cult of masculinity which would soon become synonymous with mountaineering.

> *'I could not help admiring Lauener's figure, as he stood there, straight as an arrow, more than six feet high, spare, muscular and active, health and vigour glowing in his open and manly countenance, his clear blue eye sparkling with vivacity and good temper, a slight dash of rough and careless swagger in his attitude and manner, which suited well with the wild scenery around, and made him look like the genius of the place.'*[13]

The Victorian era saw a reinvention of manliness which was closely related to the Muscular Christianity movement championed by one Charles Kingsley, a Broad Church priest and a man of many contradictions. He was a friend to Darwin and an author of numerous novels, including *The Water Babies*, a children's tale, a century later turned into a feature-length cartoon. The term 'Muscular Christianity' was coined to describe the athletic characters in another one of Kingsley's novels and, in the hugely homophobic atmosphere of the era, quickly gained popularity.[14] It was believed that 'a man's body is given him to be trained and brought into subjection and then used for the protection of the weak, the advancement of all righteous causes'.[15] Sporting pursuits were to be a 'counterbalance' to 'education and bookishness', and 'manliness' was 'an antidote to the poison of effeminacy'.

The prosperity of Britain and the prolonged peace had apparently added to the disgraceful softening of Britain's boys and men. It followed that physical hardship and team sports could be used for building character, a doctrine which was enthusiastically adopted in public schools, subsequently becoming one of the defining characteristics of sporting culture for the next 150 years.

Engaging in a form of 'vicarious imperialism', young men attempted to prove themselves through travel.[16] Arctic exploration in particular was igniting many imaginations, but few had the opportunity to roam that far. If the North Pole was wholly inaccessible, the Alps were the next best thing. Their glaciers were now only a short train journey away, and £2 was a sum that many an ambitious young man could scrape together.

The British began flocking to the Alps in numbers greater than ever, and local guides quickly professionalised to facilitate the first ascents by foreign gentlemen willing to pay. Not only modern mountaineering, but also rock climbing and, to a degree, competition climbing all stem in a straight line from the ideals and ethics that were born in the Alps in the nineteenth century.

The newly popularised pastime lost its innocence on one momentous day in July 1865 – on the first ascent of the Matterhorn, regarded back then as the last great Alpine challenge to be conquered. Four Englishmen and three Zermatt guides made it to the top in a close race between two parties. (The other party, upon seeing their opponents on the summit, retreated without bothering with a second ascent.) Tragedy struck on their descent. The least experienced slipped on the snow and fell, pulling down with him three others. They disappeared into the abyss right before the eyes of their companions. The two survivors owed their lives to an old rope which broke, allowing them to hold on to their stances instead of perishing with the others.

News of the accident spread around the world, making this climb the most publicised ascent to date. Two issues were enraging the public: firstly, the nascent sport of mountaineering was condemned as an unreasonable way to risk one's life, a theme which regularly comes up in the press and literature to this day. Secondly, it was suggested that perhaps the rope was not broken but cut by the guide Peter Taugwalder in order to save himself and his client, Edward Whymper. This lie was fuelled by the gossip of the guides from Chamonix looking to discredit their rivals from Zermatt.[17]

Despite the tragedy, no amount of bad publicity could dampen the enthusiasm of those few whose passions were now tightly tied to the Alps. As the outrage following the accident subsided, Whymper published his popular *Scrambles Amongst the Alps* in 1872. Soon the public, living vicariously through the tales of adventure, was ready again to cheer for those risking their lives in this new and dangerous game.

From the early days, climbers produced a great body of literature. Combining the public's thirst for travel accounts with the initially very narrow social stratum of participants, climbing might traditionally be the most 'literary' of all sports. Well-educated members of the professional classes fulfilled their intellectual ambitions by turning their adventures into memoirs, articles and lectures. One of them was W.A.B. Coolidge, a New Yorker by birth who nonetheless became one of the great apostles of Victorian mountaineering.

Coolidge's climbing career began in 1876 with the first ascent of Piz Badile, and it was he who retrospectively coined the term the 'Golden Age of Alpinism' – a decade of British dominance in the Alps. He chose the Matterhorn tragedy as the Golden Age's closing date, and the ascent of Wetterhorn by Alfred Wills, despite not being a first, came to be known as its beginning. This curious choice can only be explained in terms of national pride – all previous ascents of note were made by continental climbers – and the somewhat pretentious notion of good taste. Albert Smith's fortieth ascent of Mont Blanc happened three years prior to Wills' Wetterhorn and equally resulted in the great popularisation of alpinism. However, due to Smith's passion for showmanship and satire, he was simply not respectable enough to open the gentlemanly Golden Age.

* * *

In 1857, in London, twenty friends formed the Alpine Club. Conceived as a gentlemen's society and lacking formal rules of membership, the club was composed entirely of upper-middle-class professionals of certain repute. Of course, Judge Alfred Wills was among the founding members and, although not without some sideways glances, so was Albert Smith.

Around Europe, similar organisations followed suit, many of them much more egalitarian. For example, the Austrian Alpine Club, formed in 1862, was never an exclusively male enterprise, while its predecessor did not open its membership to women until 1974. However, despite initially catering only to a very small minority, the high social standing and the prolific writing of the Alpine Club members allowed it to become a dominant voice in the discourse around mountain exploration.

The somewhat self-congratulatory character of the Club and its satellites had a profound effect on climbing's emerging culture, as much of the writing produced by the early members carried a distinct flavour of exceptionalism. For example, in 1871 Leslie Stephen, the fourth president of the Club, published his *Playground of Europe* and in the opening essay recalled a conversation with a guide who expressed his preference for the London cityscape over the view from the summit of Mont Blanc. Prompted by Stephen, the Swiss guide elaborated:

'"Ah, sir," was his pathetic reply, "it is far finer!" This frank avowal set me thinking. Were my most cherished prejudices folly, or was my favourite guide a fool?'[18]

Stephen believed the love for the mountains to be an acquired, highbrow taste shared only by gentlemen. In addition, he credited none other than the climbers of the Golden Age with the invention of that taste, a common theme in the writings and discussions of the Alpine Club, often tainted with a note of nationalism. Member C.E. Matthews referred to the year 1855 as the 'earliest infancy' of mountaineering and went on to note that 'the English' had been 'the first to carry off the honours', with others merely allowed 'to follow our example'.[19]

According to an opinion popular among AC members, scientific motivations did not make a mountaineer, nor did even lowlier professional reasons such hunting, crystal collecting, or, for that matter, guiding. In other words, a mountaineer had to be an amateur – a man of sufficient means to be able to afford extensive travel for pleasure. 'He is a true apprentice of the craft only when he can say from a full heart *Labor ipse voluptas*,' wrote Sir Frederick Pollock in his preface to *Mountaineering*, a popular volume published in 1885. There can't perhaps be a more classist remark than one with its Latin sentence translating to 'labour is pleasure'.

But the Alpine Club was not without its critics. Among them was John Ruskin, a prominent art patron and one of the most versatile intellectuals of the Victorian era. He had a great admiration for the mountains, yet not much admiration for those who climbed them. He chastised mountaineers for the vanity and self-centredness that fuelled their desire for first ascents. Having received a strict upbringing and education, he could not help but despise self-congratulatory fellows such as Albert Smith, and it is perhaps Smith's triumphant return from Mont Blanc that inspired the following passage:

'You have made race-courses of the cathedrals of the earth [...] the Alps themselves, which your own poets used to love so reverently, you look upon as soaped poles in a bear-garden, which you set yourselves to climb, and slide down again with "shrieks of delight". When you are past shrieking, having no human articulate voice to say you are glad with, you fill the quietude of their valleys with gunpowder blasts, and rush home, red with cutaneous eruption of conceit, and voluble with convulsive hiccough of self-satisfaction.'[20]

It is no wonder that Ruskin is remembered as the anti-mountaineer, a representative of the so-called aesthetic tradition, as opposed to its heroic counterpart. The aesthetes sought the mountains for their beauty and the spiritual experience, abhorring notions of conquest and personal achievement. The discussion between the two schools is an ongoing theme in the climbing community even today, often resurfacing when it comes to the professionalisation of athletes and the publicity necessary to sustain their relationship with sponsors.

Yet even Ruskin, with his spite for what he saw as the vulgarisation of the mountains, was not impervious to the allure of masculinity and the rapidly changing attitudes to risk.[21] A letter to his father clearly reflects Rousseau's romantic ideas, adding a Victorian touch of Muscular Christianity and machismo:

'If you come to a dangerous place and turn back from it, though it may have been perfectly right and wise to do so, your character has suffered some slight deterioration; you are to that extent weaker, more lifeless, more effeminate [...]. But if you go through it, wrong and foolish as it may be, you come out a stronger and better person, fitter for every sort of work and trial, and nothing but danger produces this effect.'[22]

Passages like the above came to define how we think of mountaineering and rock climbing, making both appear even more male dominated than they ever were and considerably slowing the process of opening them up to other genders. Female climbers referenced in mountaineering's early texts were either presented as anomalies or, at best, addendums to the male protagonists. In addition, 'true women' wouldn't dare go against the medical advice of the time, which recommended ample amounts of rest due to the plight of menstruation. Therefore, female climbers were often termed 'new women', a disparaging label which could describe attributes from independence to promiscuity.[23]

Luckily, new research that focuses on reviewing primary sources, such as expedition records, diaries, letters, visitor books and personal notes, reveals that women in the mountains were not such an anomaly as many came to believe, nor were they uniformly adhering to some kind of archetype. They were certainly all well-educated members of the upper middle classes, confident and interested in discovering the world. But like the men, early female climbers had their distinct characters, motives and attitudes. Their ranks include Mrs Hamilton, the first British woman to scale Mont Blanc, and later Mabel Neruda, Isabella Charlet-Straton, Maud Meyer, Gertrude Bell, Lucy Walker, Anna and Ellen Pigeon, and many others. Each of them still awaits as much historical and literary attention as was given to their male peers.

The history of mountaineering was written about by men and for men, but the reality was often different. It's increasingly apparent that Victorian society's rigid ideals of acceptability did not always accurately reflect real life. For example, we came to believe that nineteenth-century women did not exercise in order to preserve their supposedly delicate reproductive systems, and not to scandalise. While the majority certainly followed this guidance, many rightly distrusted contemporary medical knowledge and *convenance*, and chose to follow their own instincts. Towards the turn of the century, men gradually stopped advising against women's physical activity, probably because too many simply ignored them, engaging in outrageous activities such as cycling or venturing into the mountains.

However, the myth of female frailty lingers in society to this day. It prevented women from officially running marathons until 1967 and from high-level ski jumping until 2004. In fact, some still believe that the latter could cause female reproductive organs to … fall out.

Even in the early days of mountaineering, women willing to ignore societal conventions exerted themselves in the mountains on a par with men. In 1887, after summiting Täschhorn (4,491 metres), Mary Mummery completed the first descent of a route now known as the *Arête du Diable*, then described as the 'embodiment of inaccessibility'. The whole expedition took twenty-eight hours, including an emergency bivvy on the mountain. In a similar vein were the adventures of the Pigeon sisters, whose detailed climbing diaries reveal that they certainly did not take days off from climbing during their periods. This went against all medical knowledge of the time, when men stipulated that menstruation was a disease which, if not handled properly, could result in madness.[24]

While Muscular Christianity was redefining masculinity, femininity was not subjected to the same revolution. Despite the arrival of gentle sports in girls' public schools, excessive exercise for women was seen as harmful and, perhaps worse than that, vulgar. It is no surprise that when in 1874 a group of female friends decided on a tour of the Alps, their initial plan was to enjoy the scenery, landscape painting and walks – that was until they happened upon another female party descending from Mont Blanc and got the bold idea to bid for the summit themselves.

They promptly put together an expedition and saw their plan through, making it from Chamonix to the peak and back again in a continuous push of twenty-one hours. As by Victorian standards guides didn't count, they became the first all-female party to scale Mont Blanc. Being described by a male American tourist as 'very plucky to go about without gentlemen', they sassily replied that 'amongst the mountains, particularly the glaciers, guides were much more useful than gentlemen' and, upon returning home, they published a volume entitled *Swiss Notes* under the joint pen name of 'Five Ladies'.

Despite such successes, women in the mountains were certainly the minority. Fewer of them went on to publicise their ascents, and those accounts that were made could not rival in popularity those made by men because women operated on a different cultural plane to their male counterparts. As admitted by Leslie Stephen in *The Playground of Europe*, men climbed to achieve recognition and the glory of being immortalised in history. Lacking such options, women likely did it simply because they enjoyed it, and then went back home to take care of households and bear children. Still, it didn't stop them from reaching most Alpine summits by the mid-1870s.

Adventurer Frances Havergal wrote of joy and liberation, and a 'delicious freedom and sense of leisure' experienced in the mountains:

'How we spied grand points of view from rocks above and (having no one to consult, or to keep waiting, or to fidget about us) stormed them with our alpenstocks and scrambled and leaped and laughed and raced as if we were not girls again but downright boys!'[25]

* * *

It was the summer of 2015 when a historic heatwave swept across France. In Paris, the temperature reached over forty degrees Celsius and 15,000 people died nationwide due to the hot weather. In the Alps, the Goûter Route up Mont Blanc had to be closed because an excess of melting snow threatened the safety of climbers.

I had not long moved to Chamonix and, hiking up to Montenvers in the early afternoon, I felt like I was attempting a cardio workout in a sauna.

I was still glad to avoid the little cogwheel train that takes tourists to the upper Montenvers station for the extortionate price of thirty-five euros, but I cursed myself for not waiting to make my hike in the cooler days of autumn. Salty sweat was pouring over my eyes and lips, and my feet were burning in a pair of cheap Decathlon shoes. I took them off and trod gently on the warm stones. Even when the trail wound into the shade of tall spruces, the temperature barely dropped and the still air didn't have the usual alpine freshness. At least the granite stones now felt pleasantly cold beneath my bare feet.

Had I read it earlier, the account by William Windham would surely have popped into my mind:

> 'We were quickly at the Foot of the Mountain, and began to ascend by a very steep Path through a Wood of Firs and Larche Trees. We made many Halts to refresh ourselves, and take breath, but we kept on at a good Rate. After we had passed the Wood, we came to a kind of Meadow, full of large Stones, and Pieces of Rocks, that were broke off, and fallen down from the Mountain; the Ascent was so steep that we were obliged sometimes to cling to them with our Hands, and make use of Sticks, with sharp Irons at the End, to support ourselves.'[26]

Like mine, Windham's journey took place at the end of June, but he spoke of 'avalanches of snow' and was disappointed at not being able to explore the place where the crystal hunters mined their treasures. 'The season was not enough advanced' and in 1741, snow was still making the trail inaccessible.

Drenched in sweat and with my face burning like a furnace, I finally got to the viewpoint. Over the tips of trees I saw a deep valley with steep slopes falling sharply on either side towards its bottom and, in the background, two rows of ragged granite peaks. For a moment I thought I had hiked the wrong path, but soon the curious shape of the valley and a mass of scree deposited within it made me understand. The riverbed-like shape was where the glacier used to be in 1741, in the times of Windham and Pococke. Today, the sea of ice has retreated even higher, and every year it is melting faster and faster.

The frozen waves visible higher in the gorge were grey and dirty, nothing like a great 'lake put in agitation by strong wind', and recognisable as a glacier only because I knew it was there. In the unrelenting heat of the afternoon, the mighty Mer de Glace seemed no more than an ice cone left by a child to melt before being remembered.

In the distance, nestled on the western slope of the glacial valley was the sturdy edifice of Refuge du Montenvers, built in 1890, a fortress of stone designed to stand against the harsh Alpine weather. Originally a shelter for the early mountaineers, it is now a luxury restaurant and hotel offering dormitory beds for the bargain price of 100 euros a night. It seemed a dark joke that the refuge should stand unwavering while La Mer de Glace was recoiling, shying away from the heat and humans.

As much as the early glaciologists and geologists had been exposed to the depths of time that shaped the surface of Earth, suddenly I felt naked and exposed in the face of the undeniable truth that within just a few years the Montenvers glacier will likely be gone.[27]

Washed over by a profound sense of the end of times, cheated from my encounter with the Sea of Ice, I turned on my heel and dragged myself back towards Chamonix.

CHAPTER 5

THE DESCENDANTS OF GODS

'Mens sana in corpore sano.'
Decimus Junius Juvenalis, second century AD

Located in the county of Shropshire, on the A458 between Shrewsbury and Bridgnorth, Much Wenlock is an archetypal English town. With charming narrow streets, neatly trimmed lawns and a sixteenth-century guildhall, it resembles a movie set – one which every year becomes an unusual backdrop for the town's very own Olympian Games.

The tradition dates back to the mid-nineteenth century and precedes the 'official' Games by nearly three decades. It began when a Much-Wenlock-born philanthropist, Dr William Penny Brookes, became concerned with the living conditions faced by the working class. He decided that the best way to elevate them from poverty, ill health and petty crime was through education; he promptly established an 'open to every grade of man' society for the promotion of art and science – which, in practice, taught people how to read and write. Embracing the spirit of Muscular Christianity, and drawing inspiration from Brookes' interest in ancient Greece, the society's curriculum was soon expanded by an 'Olympic Class' which provided physical games and contests.

In 1858, Dr Brookes happened upon a curious mention in his local newspaper: the ancient Greek Olympiad was to be revived in Athens, instantly striking a chord with the good doctor. The following year saw the first annual 'Wenlock Olympian Games', a very local but successful affair. Greater plans were soon afoot and Brookes founded the National Olympian Committee (NOA), tasked with staging a country-wide event. The general mission of the NOA was defined as 'the encouragement and reward of skill and strength in *manly* exercises and of literary and fine art attainments'.[1]

Purpose-built for the 1851 Great Exhibition, London's Crystal Palace was chosen as the main location of the first National Olympic Games, which welcomed 10,000 spectators. The disciplines included fencing, gymnastics, swimming (in the River Thames), hurdles and rope climbing. The event seemed like the beginning of a movement which could provide opportunities for the underprivileged classes.

But in 1866 Britain, sport was not meant to be egalitarian. A rival organisation was set up under the name of the Amateur Athletic Club (AAC) and its upper- and middle-class members were gravely offended by the idea of competing against working people. Putting an emphasis on amateurism (not receiving financial compensation for participating in sports), the AAC effectively excluded anybody without sufficient means to exercise for leisure. Pushing the excusatory ideas to the point of absurdity, any man receiving wages for physical labour – a builder, cobbler, blacksmith, and so forth – was deemed a professional athlete and therefore ineligible.

Despite their differences, the NOA and the AAC could have coexisted in harmony if not for the conceited attitudes of the Amateurs. A new AAC rule stated that any gentleman athlete who entered a competition against 'professionals' would be banned from all AAC events in the country, leading to a complete boycott of Brookes' Games. Wielding much greater financial and social influence, the Amateurs effectively forced Dr Brookes to abandon his project.

* * *

If the original Olympic Games were not more egalitarian, they were certainly more bloody. Held every four years over the course of a millennium, the ancient Games grew in importance to become the pinnacle of the social, religious, political and athletic life of the Greeks.

During the competition, warring city-states obeyed an Olympic Truce which allowed the athletes from the farthest regions to gather in Olympia. The event was staged for the glory of Zeus, and the disciplines closely mimicked the skills required of a warrior: running, chariot racing, long jump, javelin and discus throwing, as well as boxing, wrestling and a brutal mixture of the two, the pankration. It is unclear how many attendees would descend upon Olympia at the height of the Games' popularity but sources speak of some events attracting as many as 45,000 spectators.[2]

The ideals of the ancient Olympics were somewhat different from the modern Games and it was not unusual for athletes to die in chariot crashes or in hand-to-hand combat. There was no glory in participation and no glory in coming second; what mattered was to win and, in doing so, to acquire a near-divine status. The laurel wreaths bestowed upon the heads of champions were the symbols of the gods' favour. The winners, basking in their glory, were the ancient equivalent of modern sports celebrities in the vein of Michael Phelps or Simone Biles.

The Roman conquest of Greece marked the beginning of a new era and set in motion a slow decline of the Games. Finally, in AD 394 Theodosius the Great, the first Roman emperor to convert to Christianity, outlawed pagan festivals: the Olympic Games, held for the glory of Zeus for more than a millennium, were bound for extinction.

It wasn't until the European Renaissance that intellectuals looked back at the Hellenic period with renewed interest. Neoclassicism involved a rediscovery of both ancient Greek and Roman cultures, with many Romantic poets looking towards Athens for aesthetic inspiration. This coincided with numerous influential thinkers advocating for the independence of contemporary Greece, which had remained in the hands of the Ottoman Empire since the mid-fifteenth century.

When in 1832 Greece was finally established as a sovereign state, it was a shadow of the largest empire of European antiquity. Controlled by foreign powers, it lacked a strong government and modern infrastructure, and the weight of former glory rested heavy on the shoulders of Greek intellectuals. Instead of playing catch-up with Western Europe, they decided to rebuild their national pride by looking to the past.

Thanks to fervent lobbying by artists and financial backing from powerful businessmen, the first modern Greek Olympiad was held in Athens in 1859 but, with no international guests, no appropriate venue, untrained participants and no cohesive idea to bind it all together, the event couldn't command the attention of the masses.

Soon afterwards, the death of its wealthiest benefactor halted the movement; while back in England, frustrated by the elites, William Brookes was forced to give up on his own Olympics. Instead, he turned his attention to popularising physical education in schools, a topic igniting many intellectuals across Europe – among them a young and wealthy Frenchman: Charles Pierre de Frédy, Baron de Coubertin.

In 1883, Coubertin's research took him across the English Channel to Rugby School for boys, which had given rise to the eponymous discipline. Upon witnessing the physical games played by the pupils, Coubertin duly noted that 'organised sport can create moral and social strength'.[3] Reaching out to Brookes, Coubertin visited Much Wenlock for a special edition of the local Olympiad held in his honour. Brookes also described to him the 1859 event in Greece, as well as the London Games of 1866.

After returning to France, the baron was initially very critical of the Olympic revival and it is unclear what then led him to completely change his mind. The somewhat ugly fact remains that when he began enthusiastically promoting the resurrection of the Games, he attributed the idea to himself and himself only, failing to mention the contribution from Brookes or anyone else.

In 1894, the Sorbonne Congress to Revive the Olympic Games was an elegant three-day affair staged by the baron, with entertainment, gourmet dining and fine wine provided for the representatives of twenty-four French and thirteen foreign sports organisations. During the course of the event, the first International Olympic Committee was established with fourteen members, all of whom were white males from the very upper crust of society and with sufficient means to get the IOC off the ground. Athens was designated as the host of the first international Olympics to be held two years later. Despite its strong association with the elites, sport was to have a much wider appeal and another vital role to play: that of *controlling* the masses.

* * *

Rugby School became famous for its experiment with sports shortly after the student rebellion of 1797. The boys vandalised much of the school's property, held staff hostage at sword-point and eventually were pacified by soldiers. Physical education was introduced as a new preventive measure which provided a convenient means of disciplining the pupils and allowing their frustrations to vent. It was quickly understood that the same tool could likely be used in other social contexts.

The French Revolution brought forward the dangerous idea that *the people* deserved rights and, if sufficiently displeased with the ruling class, they could reach not only for the crown but also for the head upon which it rested. This in itself created an urgent need for new means of control. In addition, the successes of Napoleon gave rise to nationalism which quickly spread across Europe and beyond. It facilitated the now-ubiquitous nation state, allowing for the validation of a new world order and for the creation of previously unimaginable military powers. Physical education turned out to be just the right vehicle for instilling both control and a sense of national pride.

For the middle classes, sport was a means of differentiating themselves from labourers, as for the first time in history, leisure wasn't solely the domain of the aristocracy. Despite great internal stratification, the newly emerged bourgeoisie was almost universally concerned with notions of respectability and the need for self-betterment. Physical exercise and travelling abroad – especially to fashionable destinations such as the Alps – were both ways to express the first and achieve the latter. Travel was seen as education, and sports had the benefit of teaching the future elites teamwork, leadership and rivalry (the latter soon to define the spirit of capitalist society).

Somewhat paradoxically, while seeking to distinguish themselves through leisure, the middle classes also looked to sport as a means of improving the lives of the poor whose situation had also changed rapidly but not for the better. The Industrial Revolution resulted in scores of farmworkers moving to the cities where they ended up living in degrading conditions. The social structure of their previous lives had been eroded and the rhythm dictated by the seasonality of working the land suddenly lost. Long hours in factories, low pay and poor sanitary conditions contributed to high crime rates and soaring mortality. Something had to be done and, much like William Brookes, other middle-class philanthropists decided to act through the promotion of sport.

With virtually no social mobility, physical exercise was used to teach working people a different set of values from those taught to the elite: here the emphasis was on discipline and obedience. As with pupils in Rugby, factory workers were granted an avenue for venting their frustrations while gaining a sense of agency, individuality and self-worth – those precise values that tedious work in factories had stripped away.[4] The additional benefit of having the working men run around a football pitch was that their improved health resulted in more efficient and reliable employees.

This twofold social context was what resulted in the idea of 'amateurism', which allowed for a clear division between gentlemen and plebs and came to define much of the later history of sport.[5] Meanwhile, similar movements were taking root around the world. In Germany, Belgium and Sweden, gymnastics – accessible because it required little or no equipment – became a popular means of boosting citizens' health and building national identity. In France, the defeat in the war with Prussia in 1870, just one year after gymnastics was introduced in schools, further convinced the authorities of the need to physically strengthen the male populace, boost the people's morale and rebuild a sense of national pride.

The growing popularity of sports quickly went beyond schools; gymnastics and foot races were soon joined by ball games, and by the end of the century most of France was already hopelessly in love with *cyclisme*. Clearly, Baron de Coubertin did not operate in a cultural void; the historical moment was ripe for the creation of a sports movement which would feed off national identities while transcending state borders. However, despite the narrative relentlessly promoted by the IOC for more than a century, Coubertin was not the noble philanthropist we came to imagine. Very much a product of his time and environment, he believed that 'the theory of equal rights for all human races leads to a political line contrary to any colonial progress'.[6] The Anthropology Days held at the 1904 Olympic Games in St Louis were perhaps the epitome of this belief. One hundred indigenous men were recruited from the concurrent World Fair's human zoo to compete in disciplines for which they were completely untrained. Ten thousand spectators ridiculed the unprepared contestants, shattering the romantic myth of the naturally athletic 'noble savage' and replacing it with even greater contempt for anybody who was not white.

The baron's views on female participation in sports, only thinly veiled by chivalry, matched his rampant racism, but a search for the more shocking quotations in the official compilations, available on the IOC's website, would be in vain.[7] Only digging through the digitised originals of some of the baron's writings lays bare that diversity, in both sports and society, is a very recent concept.

Addressing the inequalities that lie in the foundations of the modern Olympic movement will not happen unless they are openly reckoned with. For now, a Disneyfied version of history continues to be served up to audiences still largely enchanted with the grandeur of the spectacle and its lofty ideals. But until the public demands that the IOC's values and ethics are put under closer scrutiny, the self-governing body is unlikely to step forward with a critical self-evaluation.

* * *

People have climbed mountains all throughout history – with some eccentrics even doing it for pleasure – but the founders of the Alpine Club were right in arguing that mountaineering could only become a modern sport in the nineteenth century, simply because sports did not previously exist. Perhaps in a sense, Britain did become the birthplace of mountaineering but, given time, any other post-industrial, affluent society would have done the same. With its colonial wealth and the spirit of imperialism, London just happened to be the first.

Even though mountaineering was not yet referred to as *sport*, its ethics and culture formed around the same period that brought about modern sports in general. Both required the same conditions: money, an interest in physical exercise and a certain amount of free time. Early climbing and modern organised sports were both grown from the same soil, making them unlikely but nonetheless close relatives. Perhaps this explains Coubertin's decision to include mountaineering as one of the original Olympic disciplines in 1894.

As history likes to play out differently than intended, medals for *alpinisme* were awarded only four times before being dropped entirely in 1946. For nearly a century, mountaineering and the Olympics grew further and further apart. The next time they converged, the world was a very different place – and climbing was a very different discipline.

CHAPTER 6

LONDON, 2011

'It is not the mountain we conquer but ourselves.'
Sir Edmund Hillary (1919–2008), New Zealand
mountain climber and Antarctic explorer

The flat we rented off Portobello Road was one of those bright, high-ceiling apartments that should have a crystal chandelier hanging in the lobby. Instead, there was a bare light bulb and a lack of basic furniture, and my Polish roommate and I shared the rent with six Italians I had never met in my life before.

One winter morning, I reluctantly got out of bed to put on my crinkled work T-shirt with the big word 'STAFF' written on its back. The night before I had stayed up late, finishing an article for my series of essays on the upcoming Olympics. Juggling the writing commitment with my day job in a cycling shop was starting to wear me down. The need for some form of relaxation – for anything other than trying to make rent or have a career – was even more desperate than the need for a good night's sleep.

Without any time for breakfast, I grabbed my bag and my bike and left for work. I would eat something behind the counter during the slow hours of the morning and then, if I got lucky, grab a quick nap in the workshop during my lunch break. Empty delivery boxes made for an excellent bed.

The previous night while putting off writing, I'd googled London's climbing walls. The first result was Mile End Climbing Wall in the East End. I checked the ticket price (higher than I expected) and made up my mind to give it a go. After a whole day of fidgeting in the shop, barely able to focus on my customers, I finally clocked out, hopped on my bike and cycled across town along Regent's Canal.

* * *

Walking through the heavy blue double doors of the indoor climbing gym, my heart was pounding and my stomach was full of butterflies. It wasn't because climbing walls in the UK were about twenty times bigger than any of those I'd climbed at in Poland. Instead, it was because I hadn't done any sport for years. I felt deeply embarrassed of how incapable I'd be.

And there was more. Before moving to London, I'd gone to Rodellar in northern Spain for my second or third ever climbing trip. I was eighteen, had climbed for just over a year and imagined myself flying up orange Spanish limestone just like my idols. In reality, I was confronted with cliffs that were far beyond me, and tonsillitis from hell.

In the third week of the trip I slipped off a foothold while clipping a draw far above my head. I was still only three runners above the ground and my belayer had to give me a sharp catch.[1] The slack rope rapidly became tight and the impact jolted my body towards a fat tufa sticking out from the overhanging wall. First to come in contact with it was my left ankle – the one that, following another accident, a surgeon had painstakingly put back together just over a year earlier.

Before I was lowered to the ground, I noticed two things: painful throbbing in the joint and rapid swelling. My heart sank even lower than at the moment I fell. I untied the shoe and took out a foot which was going numb worryingly fast. While my belayer ran ahead to find me a ride to the hospital, I dragged myself to the campsite, most of the way on my butt, the palms of my hands bleeding from putting them repeatedly on the stony ground.

Later that day, a Spanish doctor put my leg in a cast that ended just under my knee. I took it off the same evening with the help of a camping wood saw. The X-rays showed no broken bones and the foot didn't feel limp as it did when I needed the surgery.

After a couple of days off, I took the laces out of my climbing shoe and packed my swollen foot inside. To secure the shoe in place, I strapped it with finger tape to my ankle. Then I put my harness on, tied in and started climbing up a 6b face. I'm not sure if I was feverish from the random bout of tonsillitis or the inflammation in my foot, but I moved up in a stupor.

Suddenly, I became aware of the paralysing pain in my leg. My mouth was parched and my throat was on fire. I stopped next to a runner and started crying. My belayer shouted to ask if I wanted to come down. I shouted 'no' but continued to sob. I was in so much pain. I was terrified of the height. I wanted to be back on the ground. Back home.

At the same time, being up there – eighteen metres off the ground on a slab of orange limestone – was what I wanted more than anything else in the world.

The two opposing needs couldn't coexist in my brain. Tears kept rolling down my cheeks as the calf of my one good leg was getting increasingly shaky from standing on a small foothold.

After what felt like forever (but was probably no longer than a few minutes), I finally agreed to be lowered. The shame of leaving a quickdraw in the route was already burning, but I had to get down. I was young and overambitious. I pushed myself too far. I felt defeated and broken, and I had nobody to tell me otherwise. Nobody to tell me that sprained ankles were par for the course. Nobody to tell me to chill and drink sangria in the sun. I stacked the stakes too high and it all crumbled down, together with my determination and self-confidence.

That day was the last time I climbed. I came back from Spain to Warsaw, finished my degree, travelled, then ended up an immigrant in London, trying to make some money and take off as a journalist.

When my situation became stable enough to afford some free time, I began to think about self-care other than cigarettes and booze. I needed to lower my stress levels and I needed to move. (The parallel with a Victorian factory worker escaped me back then.) I had been daydreaming about climbing for a while, but each and every time a new, crippling sensation would creep up on me. A fear of heights.

But the pull of climbing was too strong to ignore. I found myself walking through the heavy blue doors of Mile End Climbing Wall with sweaty palms and a pounding heart. I bought a day pass and completed a safety assessment at the counter. My long-unused climbing shoes felt stiff and tight. I looked at the colourful blobs of resin stuck to the plywood, dipped my hands in a chalk bag and started going up. One hold, second hold, up and up. Then I looked at the blue mats just over a metre below me.

Suddenly, I was standing on the orange limestone cliff, my foot throbbing with pain and my head spinning with vertigo. I looked down again. My heart was still in my throat, but this time there was only a metre of height between me and solid ground, and I had nothing to prove. Perhaps climbing was simply not my thing. Or, more likely, I wasn't right for climbing.

Terrified, I got back down the wall as quickly and carefully as possible, took my shoes off and left, with the heavy double doors swinging shut behind me.

CHAPTER 7

GYMNASTS ON ROCK

'But a line must be drawn somewhere to separate the possible and the impossible, and some try to draw it by their own experience. They constitute what is called the ultra-gymnastic school of climbing.'

Owen Glynne Jones (1867–1899), Welsh rock and mountain climber, perished in the Alps

By the end of the nineteenth century, rock climbing had begun to develop simultaneously in a few independent hotspots around the world – the result of a host of sociopolitical changes playing out at an unprecedented rate.

Beginning in the Enlightenment, an interest in natural sciences saw academics and amateurs heading into the wilderness in the pursuit of knowledge. As the Romantic movement created and popularised its own take on sublimity, these wild places acquired a new allure, inspiring artists to portray their beauty in literature and on canvas.

In addition, the Industrial Revolution and the rapid expansion of cities quickly put an end to the myth of paradise as an orderly environment built by man; the world's biggest metropolises were plagued by pollution, disease and poverty, laying bare the shortcomings of unplanned, spontaneous urbanisation. Technological progress created both a new class of disempowered, penurious factory workers, as well as the bourgeoisie: a vastly stratified group ranging from clerks and small-time merchants to clergy, military men and even prominent entrepreneurs whose wealth might have surpassed that of the aristocracy. In Victorian England, the bourgeoisie, or the middle classes, constituted about fifteen per cent of society, and they increasingly sought solace and leisure outside the city boundaries; a practice previously reserved for aristocrats was now open to affluent professionals keen to elevate their status. Soon the development of railways, and later the enterprise of one Thomas Cook, made international travel much more accessible. For anyone who couldn't quite afford to go overseas, destinations closer to home offered a less costly alternative. Travel became a middle-class staple and an expression of upward social mobility.

As these changes took place, the rapid emergence of the nation state in post-Napoleonic Europe led many thinkers and educators to search for a way to instil a cohesive sense of identity among citizens. One solution was formal physical exercise, which had the additional benefit of being a versatile tool in the education of both the rulers and the ruled, with leadership and obedience taught respectively to the members of each social group.

This new interest in physical education coincided with the popularisation of print media following innovations in printing – the arrival of steam-powered presses and double-sided printing – resulting in a symbiotic relationship between the media and sports, and with both growing exponentially. Many spectator sports quickly institutionalised, with some also professionalising, while mountaineering, and soon after rock climbing, remained amateur disciplines which nonetheless gained in popularity thanks to enthusiastic reporting and the popularisation of photography.

By the end of the nineteenth century, the stage was set for rock climbing to emerge into a pre-globalised world. Nascent rock-climbing communities grew independently, often producing charismatic individuals at the centre of close-knit groups. Without any written rules or formal competitions, the pioneers frequently clashed with their closest rivals about the use of gear, ethics and objectives, and many professed to be the inventors and guardians of the one true form of rock climbing. Perhaps without these fierce rivalries and passions, climbing would lack a certain depth which, from the outset, singled it out from many other disciplines, making it not only a sport but, as will be seen, most of all a lifestyle.

* * *

Nearly half a century after William Wordsworth and his sister took up residence in the quaint, almost austere Dove Cottage in the Lake District, a new development was threatening their sublime peace. A proposed railway extension would see public transport reach all the way to the glacial lake of Windermere, only six miles from Wordsworth's new marital home in Rydal. Appalled at the prospect, the poet sent a series of outraged letters to the *Morning Post* in London. He argued that the idea of '[placing] the beauties of the Lake District within easier reach of those who cannot afford to pay for ordinary conveyances' was altogether flawed, opining that 'the perception of what has acquired the name of picturesque and romantic scenery is so far from being intuitive, that it can be produced only by a slow and gradual process of culture'.

In other words, Wordsworth believed that there was no point in making his beloved Lakes accessible to uneducated, working people. His reluctance to share the District with scores of tourists was no doubt rooted in wanting to preserve its wilderness, but the Industrial Revolution could not be stopped, and technological and social change was imminent. In spite of Wordsworth's vehement protests, the Kendal and Windermere Railway opened in 1847.

Visitors from across the country flocked to the Lakes, and it is somewhat ironic that many were certainly encouraged by no fewer than five editions of Wordsworth's own *Guide Through the District of the Lakes.* Soon after, mountaineers from the newly formed Alpine Club also caught wind of the region's potential but, much like Wordsworth, they wanted nothing to do with the crowds. Perched at the foot of Scafell Pike and over ten miles from the nearest train station, the Wasdale Head Inn became their preferred meeting point, offering room and board to those who could make it to the remote location. Initially, it was a tight-knit collection of the same weathered faces that could often be seen in Zermatt or Chamonix, but inevitably more and more newcomers found their way to the inn.

It was 1880 when a young Oxford student by the name of Walter Parry Haskett Smith reserved rooms at Wasdale for a summer reading trip. Little did he know that the hills of the Lake District would preoccupy him much more than Plato, and he began returning to Wasdale every year, where, under the tutelage of older mountaineers, he steadily progressed from fellwalking to scrambling and, finally, to rock climbing proper. Unlike the previous generation of climbers, for Haskett Smith the Lakeland crags were not merely a training ground for the Alps; by contrast, it's likely that he was the first to see them as an end in themselves.

During one of his early trips, a soaring rock tower protruding from an outcrop known as Napes Needle caught Haskett Smith's attention. Although the rock tower was located only two miles from the inn and is now regarded as the birthplace of British rock climbing, 'in those days climbers had never really looked at the Napes. The vast slopes of cruel scree below them not only kept explorers away, but gave the impression that the whole mass was dangerously rotten.'[1]

After a few days of bad weather the rain had cleared, but clouds and thick mist were still chased by a terrible gale. Haskett Smith ventured out for a walk, heading towards Lingmell, a lesser peak standing in the shadow and shelter of Scafell Pike. Many years afterwards, he described what happened next:

> 'Suddenly [...] the mist grew thinner, and it became just possible to locate the Napes. Then they were swallowed up again, but a moment later the outermost curtain of mist seemed to be drawn aside and one of the fitful gleams of sunshine fell on a slender pinnacle of rock, standing out against the background of cloud without a sign of any other rock near it and appearing to shoot up for 200–300 feet. The vision did not last more than a minute or two [...].'[2]

Enchanted by the sight, Haskett Smith searched for the pinnacle a few days later, but amidst the bad weather it was impossible to find. The fickle English summer then came to an end and a few years went by before he returned to Wasdale to find the needle. This time, together with a friend, he traversed the Napes and had a good look at the elusive tower. It turned out that at the first sighting the perspective and poor visibility exaggerated its height: in reality it was some eighteen metres tall. Still extremely steep and exposed, it still was an obstacle that the climbers did not dare to attempt.

Another two years passed and the summer of 1886 was sunny and dry. Back at Wasdale, Haskett Smith ventured alone towards the Napes, walking stick in hand and no intention to climb anything, but, by the time he stood in full view of his pinnacle, he couldn't resist examining the climb.

> 'A deep crack offered a very obvious route for the first stage, but the middle portion of this crack was decidedly difficult, being at that time blocked with stones and turf, all of which has since been cleared away. Many capable climbers were afterwards turned back when trying to make the second ascent not by the sensational upper part but by this lower and (under present conditions) very simple piece.
>
> From the top of the crack there is no trouble to reach the shoulder, whence the final stage may be studied at ease. [...] My first care was to get two or three stones and test the flatness of the summit by seeing whether anything thrown-up could be induced to lodge.

If it did, that would be an indication of a moderately flat top, and would hold out hopes of the edge being found not too much rounded to afford a good grip for the fingers. Out of three missiles one consented to stay, and thereby encouraged me to start, feeling as small as a mouse climbing a milestone.

*Between the upper and lower blocks, about five feet up, there is a ragged horizontal chink large enough to admit the toes, but the trouble is to raise the body without intermediate footholds. It seemed best to work up at the extreme right, where the corner projects a little, though the fact that you are hanging over the deep gap makes it rather a "nervy" proceeding. For anyone in a standing position at the corner it is easy to shuffle the feet sideways to the other end of the chink, where it is found that the side of the top block facing outwards is decidedly less vertical. Moreover, at the foot of this side there appeared to my great joy a protuberance which, being covered with a lichenous growth, looked as if it might prove slippery, but was placed in the precise spot where it would be most useful in shortening the formidable stretch up to the top edge. Gently and cautiously transferring my weight, I reached up with my right hand and at last was able to feel the edge and prove it to be, not smooth and rounded as it might have been, but a flat and satisfactory grip. My first thought on reaching the top was one of regret that my friends should have missed by a few hours such a day's climbing [...]; my next was one of wonder whether getting down again would not prove far more awkward than getting up!'*³

Over 130 years later, Napes Needle remains an iconic climb, with two pitches now graded HS in the British adjective scale. The impressive shape of the thin pinnacle with a prohibiting overhang near the top (climbed for the first time in 2002 and weighing in at E3 5c) became the subject of many photographs taken not long after the first ascent, contributing to the recognition of the new sport of rock climbing, and the Lakes as its birthplace.

Both Haskett Smith's bold ascent and its style – solo and with no protection whatsoever – caught the attention of the Alpine Club establishment, and not in a good way; it seems that the mountaineers of old felt threatened. An article in the *Alpine Journal* encouraged members to explore the British crags so as '[not to] be beaten on our own fells by outsiders, some of whom consider ice axes and ropes to be "illegitimate"', but climbers of the new school were soon to cause even more outcry among the old-timers.

At Wasdale Head Inn, the rift between the AC establishment and the neophytes was obvious enough: the smoking room remained the domain of the older generation, with Haskett Smith pledging his allegiance there perhaps due to his Eton and Oxford pedigree, while the youth took over the billiards room, quickly transforming it into a rowdy party den. Much like twenty-first-century climbers, they amused themselves with booze and outrageous challenges involving feats of strength and gymnastic agility. The classic table traverse, in which a climber has to pass over and under a table without touching the floor, was likely invented there during the dark, rainy days of cabin fever. Another game, called 'the billiard fives', involved hand-throwing the balls to score points by aiming for the pockets. Often bouncing off the table, the balls would fly all around the room, with everybody ducking to avoid a hit, and an innocent window often being smashed in the process.

The wild spirit of the billiards room's antics was no doubt influenced by a change in the social mix of the Wasdale visitors; unlike the original members of the AC, many younger climbers did not hail from London's high society. Not only were the Lakes now accessible by train, but also many working people had both the means and aspirations to engage in outdoor pursuits. Climbing on British rock was far more egalitarian than the Alps could ever be, and Owen Glynne Jones, the son of a humble Welsh builder, was one of the first to benefit. In return, he redefined the sport with his athleticism and a very modern approach to developing new routes – and all with a flair for publicity. He was also a firm believer that 'all men should climb and they would be better for it'.[4]

Born in London in 1867, Jones spent his summers with his family in Wales. Rambling around the Welsh crags as a boy, he developed a love for climbing long before knowing that the sport existed beyond his childhood adventures. Back in London, he continued developing his skills on urban ascents which included 'several London church towers, Cleopatra's Needle and a complete traverse of the Common Room at the City of London School' where he was an assistant in the Mechanical Department.[5] Inevitably, he soon made his first pilgrimage to the Wasdale Head Inn and there, on the Lakeland rock, he excelled like no one before him. His approach to climbing performance was surprisingly similar to the direction the sport took nearly a century later. In the view of Haskett Smith, only six years his senior, Jones 'studied his own physical powers as a chauffeur studies a car and for that reason he talked a great deal about himself'.[6]

The crown jewel in Jones' Lakeland achievements was the forty-three-metre off-width *Kern Knotts Crack* completed in 1896. First doing it on a top rope, Jones proceeded to learn the moves so that he could go up the route and then down the adjacent gully in seven minutes. The photographs of Jones, taken by brothers George and Ashley Abraham, with whom he often roped up, made his exploits famous far and wide, and together the three climbers produced a hugely successful guidebook titled *Rock Climbing in the English Lake District*. However, Jones' tactics and popularity didn't sit well with some of his contemporaries, with Cambridge-educated Aleister Crowley scoffing in his *Confessions*:

> 'Jones obtained the reputation of being the most brilliant rock climber of his time by persistent self-advertisement. He was never a first-rate climber, because he was never a safe climber. If a handhold was out of his reach he would jump at it, and he had met with several serious accidents before the final smash. But his reputation

is founded principally on climbs which he did not make at all, in the proper sense of the word. He used to go out with a couple of photographers and have himself lowered up and down a climb repeatedly until he had learnt its peculiarities, and then make the "first ascent" before a crowd of admirers.'[7]

The disdain for promoting one's climbing achievement was often found among the older AC members. In his youth, Crowley was a brilliant climber himself, known for his impressive technique on rock honed under the tutelage of another of mountaineering and rock climbing's giants, Oscar Eckenstein (1859–1921). Apart from many technical gear innovations, Eckenstein can be credited as the first person in the UK to give any serious attention to bouldering, significantly advancing climbing technique. Exploring his abilities on low, relatively safe blocks, he was able to go beyond big holds, previously paramount to any upwards progress, and develop skills based around balancing and friction.

* * *

At the turn of the century, further social and technological changes continued to diversify climbing, and the ageing Victorian mountaineers bemoaned the arrival of the new school, characterised – in their view – by petty competition, self-promotion and an unhealthy desire for distinguishing oneself. Even the adjectival grading system, created in large by Jones and accepted as the standard in British trad climbing today, seemed a heresy invented to highlight one's achievements. Continuing in the tradition of John Ruskin, the great aesthete who earlier chastised Alpinists for '[making] race-courses of the cathedrals of the earth', they belittled the climbers of the new wave, referring to them derogatively as 'gymnasts' and, with a particular reference to the newly formed Climbers' Club, 'chimney sweeps'.

Contrary to this opinion, formed in 1989, the Climbers' Club was initially centred around the figure of Geoffrey Winthrop Young, who brought with him the aesthetic, gentlemanly tradition of mountaineering. Many figures gathering at his infamous Pen-y-Pass meets were representatives of the very elite of British society, and they themselves were rather concerned with the imminent popularisation of climbing.

Photographed in 1898, Winthrop Young's serious, handsome face is adorned with a coiffured moustache and framed with a Wertheresque wide collar and a white scarf. He cuts the perfect image of a Romantic poet and a gentleman mountaineer. It's hard to reconcile this intellectual and sombre portrait of an artist and aristocrat with Winthrop Young's tongue-in-cheek booklets written during his time at Cambridge. *The Roof-Climber's Guide to Trinity* (1899) and *Wall and Roof Climbing* (1905) list a number of routes soloed by Winthrop Young and friends on the university campus under the cover of night. The subversive nature of the activity aside, Winthrop Young's writing is an evident mockery of nineteenth-century mountaineering guides, and includes 'illuminating appendices on furniture, tree and haystack climbing'.

Beyond his university antics, the aristocratic climber and founder of the British Mountaineering Club had another, much better-kept secret. In a time when homosexuality was still an offence against the law, Winthrop Young was gay. According to biographer Alan Hankinson, one of his most enduring crushes was none other than George Mallory and he was likely sacked from his teaching job at Eton due to suspicions about his sexuality. Nearly a century later, Geoffrey Winthrop Young's portrait (this time a dashing, middle-aged gentleman with a pipe at his lip) appeared on the cover of *The Summit*, the British Mountaineering Club's publication, in celebration of LGBTQ+ History Month. With an impressive list of first ascents in the Alps and in the UK, as well as his work in outdoor education, including his involvement with establishing The Duke of Edinburgh's Award, Winthrop Young remains one of the most interesting and complex figures in the history of British climbing.

* * *

It was 1848 in Saxony, and eighteen-year-old Sebastian Abratzky was looking for work. He headed for Königstein where he could find employment laying railway tracks for the new Saxon–Bohemian line, today one of the oldest and most important connections in Germany.

With no money and nothing to do on a Sunday, Abratzky wandered about town in search of a distraction from hunger. He soon happened upon the imposing, impenetrable Königstein Fortress, the largest mountain castle in Europe, spreading over a plateau guarded by a sandstone cliff up to forty-three metres tall. Fascinated by the sight, Abratzky wanted to get in but was turned away at the gate where an entry fee of one thaler was required. Disappointed, he walked around the fortress until a curious feature of one of the cliffs caught his attention, bringing to mind a conversation he had overheard during his apprenticeship as a chimney sweep. His master had been arguing with a colleague about whether the famous Königstein Fortress could be breached if assaulted by a skilled climber – and chimney sweeps were famed for their agility. And now here he was, with an inviting, chimney-like rock formation leading to the top of the cliff. He thought about it for a moment and then concluded that if his prank was successful, perhaps he'd be rewarded with applause, something to eat or even a few coins from impressed spectators.

He pressed his back to one side of the chimney and his knees to another, much like he had done during his apprenticeship time, and quickly gained height. Halfway up, the climbing got harder and Abratzky began to lose his strength but, as he boasted later, he 'knew fear only by its name'.[8] Arriving at the top of the cliff, he then had to navigate the smooth blocks of the castle wall and found it possible to wedge his toes and fingers into the cracks between them. Abratzky's account of the climb, given on many occasions to anybody willing to listen in the years that followed, was nothing short of cliffhanger suspense.

Jumping down from the wall into the fortress, the chimney sweep cut open his foot, but that was the least of his problems. A guard approached out of nowhere, immediately arrested the intruder and escorted him to prison. This resulted in at least one of Abratzky's wishes being granted, as he was soon well fed, but nonetheless he spent a day chained up in a cell.

Although not a climber in the sporting sense of the word, Abratzky became a local celebrity. He is also often referenced as the first of Saxony's rock climbers and his ascent was very much ahead of its time.

It is one of the more amusing ironies of sport's history that while the British mountaineering establishment turned up their noses at the 'ultra-gymnastic school of climbing', at the same time in Saxony, actual working-class gymnasts – and one bold chimney sweep – were laying the foundations for the new discipline of rock climbing with a strict set of ethics that remains virtually unchanged to this day.

* * *

When Napoleon rose to power first as First Consul, and soon after as Emperor of the French, his zeal for expanding his territory led to the creation of an empire that at its peak spanned everything from the eastern border of Portugal to the western border of Russia, including the many territories previously united under the Holy Roman Empire which now fell under French occupation. Oppressed by a foreign power, their inhabitants needed something that would bring them together. They found it in the German language, which soon gave rise to the notion of a shared national identity. Physical exercise, promoted by educators since the late eighteenth century, became an unlikely ally in the creation of a loyal, physically and mentally strong German citizen who could fight against the French.[9]

Early nationalist Friedrich Ludwig Jahn proposed a programme of gymnastic training involving many pieces of apparatus similar to those used in modern sports, as well as tall wooden structures for drilling both strength and bravery. Ladders and ropes up to twelve metres high were climbed, often with only one hand or upside down.[10] Before Jahn's ideas were used a century later in support of Nazism, they became the cornerstone of the German gymnastic movement, which included hundreds of grassroots associations – one of them in the Saxon town of Schandau, today known as Bad Schandau and located on the edge of the Saxon Switzerland National Park.

Today one of the most popular climbing destinations in Germany, the extraordinary region offers 21,000 climbing routes spread over 1,000 free-standing sandstone spires. The otherworldly landscape began attracting tourists as early as 1804 and, although back then the rock summits were deemed unattainable, the region was increasingly recommended as a leisure destination, with Der Falkenstein, its tallest sandstone outcrop, dramatically towering nearly ninety-two metres over the thick forest canopy.[11] In January 1864, the imposing outcrop attracted the attention of the athletes from the Schandau gymnastic club, who rallied at its base to plot an ascent. After three months of route-searching and work which incorporated ladders and ropes similar to those often used at contemporary gymnastic facilities, they finally stood on the summit.

It is commonly believed that the ascent of Der Falkenstein, by master carpenter Gustav Tröger, master saddler August Hering, travel agent Ernst Fischer, bricklayer Johannes Wähnert and carpenter Heinrich Frenzel, was the first rock climb completed for purely sporting reasons, even if the Schandau gymnasts used all manner of aids to reach the summit.

The next milestone came a decade later and again at the hands of local gymnasts hailing from the working class: stonemasons Otto Ewald Ufer and Hermann Johannes Frick climbed the spire of Der Mönch without the use of artificial aids. (Over a century later, their route remains a popular climb graded III on the local scale.) Even though the yellowish sandstone towers of the region continued to gain popularity among the members of the gymnastic clubs from the nearby towns of Schandau and Pirna, free ascents did not become the norm and the gymnasts' brand of aid climbing was practised until the end of the century.

Much like their English counterparts, continental climbers were predominantly interested in snow-covered mountain summits before turning their eyes to rocky outcrops. One of them was Oscar Schuster, a son of a successful instrument maker born in the Saxon town of Markneukirchen in 1873.[12] Due to his poor health, young Oscar was sent to attend a *gymnasium* in Davos – surrounded by the Swiss Alps, the school was a specialist facility where boys suffering from lung diseases could learn and recuperate thanks to the mountain air commonly prescribed as a remedy for respiratory ailments.

The stay in Davos not only helped Oscar recuperate but also made him fall in love with the peaks surrounding the school. Not long after completing his first excursion to the nearby pass of Diavolezza at the age of sixteen, he joined the Davos section of the Swiss Alpine Club, founded in 1863, and continued exploring the peaks of the Central Eastern Alps. When Schuster moved back home to Saxony, a longing for the Swiss mountains soon led him to explore the next best thing available close to home: the sandstone towers of the Elbe Valley in Saxon Switzerland, and he pioneered the use of soft, hemp-soled shoes on the Saxon rock.

Unlike the working-class gymnasts pioneering Saxon climbing until then, Schuster inherited enough money to give climbing his undivided attention and soon he began pushing the standards of difficulty. He was also the first to describe the Saxon sandstone in mountaineering literature, introducing the region in 1894 in the communications of the German and Austrian Alpine Club, and later contributing a series of articles to the journal of the Saxon Switzerland Mountain Association. Although Schuster climbed in Saxony mainly in spring and autumn, devoting his summers to alpinism, he was the first to recognise its sandstone towers not only as a training ground for mountaineering but also as a significant climbing region in its own right.

In September 1892, together with a school friend, Martin Klimmer, Schuster opened the second route leading up the Falkenstein, this time on its more prohibitive eastern flank. Although they used a ladder to overcome the most difficult section of the climb, the route was a notch harder than anything else done in Saxony before and, graded IV, it remains a popular classic of the region.

The outbreak of World War I interrupted Schuster and his climbing partner on an expedition in the Caucasus. Arrested and moved between various internment camps in Russia for three years, Schuster became ill, deteriorating quickly, and he died of typhoid in 1917.

Schuster had pushed the standards of Saxon climbing to the fifth level, as well as developing an ethic against the use of artificial aids. He was planning on publishing a guidebook to the region, but in the end left the task to his protégé, Dresden attorney Rudolf Fehrmann. The guidebook went to print in 1908 and included around two hundred rock spires and twice as many open routes. In an updated version of the guide five years later, Fehrmann included a chapter on rock-climbing ethics, most likely the first of its kind in history, clearly stating the rules which, with minor changes, continue to apply in Saxon Switzerland today. In the decades which followed, they came to define free climbing around the world. Fehrmann clearly stated that no artificial aids could be used to make a valid ascent, and allowed for no alterations to the rock surface. Drilling permanent bolts for protection, equivalent to hammering in pitons but more suited to the soft nature of the Saxon sandstone, was allowed only for the first ascensionist and it was paramount that only the most exposed sections of routes warranted the practice. This resulted in the very run-out, bold character of Saxon climbing, including a technique of protection used only in the region: instead of metal nuts, knots of rope are wedged in the cracks of the rock to create attachments for the rope used for protection. The soft knots do not cause damage to the soft sandstone. Another decade later, in 1923, the next update of the guidebook brought the total number of climbing routes to more than a thousand.

Perhaps inspired by the tradition of the gymnastic clubs, Saxon climbers formed the first association, the Mountaineering Club Rustig, in 1879 in Schandau. This was soon followed by the Falkensteiner in 1895, Wanderlust in Dresden in 1896, Mönchsteiner in Pirna in 1898 and Edelweiss in Neustadt in 1905, as well as many others, each identified by a unique, often humoristic badge. They soon united under the Saxon Climbers' Federation, which consisted of forty-four sections and 3,500 individual members, and printed its own journal.

As levels of difficulty steadily increased and climbers were able to go beyond well-defined holds to friction-based climbing on slopers and smears, Fehrmann proposed the idea of 'great lines', perhaps unwittingly echoed in 2008 in the title of an iconic movie about Chris Sharma, *King Lines*.[13] Sharma explains the concept at the start of the movie, driving home how much of a visionary Fehrmann was when he had introduced the idea a century earlier:

> 'I've always been dreaming of finding the biggest, most bad-ass line you can imagine; a line that's just calling out to you, beckoning to be climbed. That's the king line.'[14]

Finding the most striking, uncompromising routes was Fehrmann's speciality. His greatest ascents were realised with an unlikely partner in Oliver Perry-Smith, a tall, young American who had moved to Dresden and attended the same school as Fehrmann. If Fehrmann was the visionary, then Perry-Smith was the prodigy. Friends from America recollected that 'he had the most extraordinary sense of balance, and used to walk like a monkey across four-inch beams in a building under construction, that were over fifty feet above the ground'. Fehrmann praised his 'bear-like strength', as well as his endearing, if sometimes difficult, character:

> 'Perry-Smith was the strongest individual personality I have ever known. He had a flair for the super-monumental, whether it was to find new routes on rock or ice, to drive his Bugatti racing car along the highways by night, or in friendly carousal to lift many a glass.'[15]

Perry-Smith was the first in Saxony to leave cracks and chimneys behind and venture on to open rock faces. He also was the first to open the sixth level of difficulty, probably then the most advanced in the world, although at that time the ethics of free climbing still allowed for standing on the partner's shoulders to overcome the most challenging sections of rock. This obscure method of climbing fell into oblivion likely only because on harder ascents it soon became completely impractical.

After about a decade of intense activity in Saxon Switzerland, Perry-Smith turned his full attention to skiing, but he remains an iconic figure responsible for much of the spirited and sometimes whimsical character of Saxon climbing.

Fehrmann continued pushing the envelope of difficulty and promoting Saxon climbing until the outbreak of the war. Not able to afford losing precious army recruits to potential injuries, the authorities issued a ban on rock climbing which Fehrmann was able to lift in the interwar period. Unfortunately, his considerable influence was a result of his membership in the National Socialist Party, which was soon to unleash the horrors of the Holocaust during World War II. After the Nazis were defeated and Saxony fell under Soviet occupation, Fehrmann was considered a war criminal and held in an internment camp until his death in 1948.

CHAPTER 8

THE PITON DISPUTE

'I do not understand at all how a person could be so cruel as to want to constrain rock-climbing within limits.'
Tita Piaz (1879–1948), outstanding Dolomites climber and guide

It was 1903 when newly widowed Lina Preuss decided to move from Vienna to Altaussee, a charming spa town in the Eastern Alps. Both Preusses loved the mountains and passed this passion on to their children. When Lina's husband succumbed to a deadly throat infection, which quickly spread to the rest of his body, there was nothing to keep her in the city.

In the mountains, the three Preuss children were given a lot of freedom. Paul was the youngest and, introduced to hiking by his father, continued to explore the mountains, often accompanied by one of his sisters. Aged eleven, escaping under the cover of night from a locked room, he graduated to rock climbing proper, summiting the highest peak in the local Gosaukamm range. Perhaps it was losing his father at an early age, combined with his own experience of illness – as a small child he suffered temporarily from polio-induced paralysis – which made him very inclined to risk-taking. It was as if through bravery and skill, he sought to affirm life itself.[1]

* * *

From the early days of alpinism, the Western Alps – mostly the peaks surrounding Chamonix and Zermatt – were the main focus of exploration. Everything east of the Splügen Pass, including the mighty Dolomites, was viewed with mild disregard for its lower altitude and 'a slightly rushed, subservient look'. Only occasionally, a more observant visitor would appreciate the distinct character of limestone peaks. Paul Grohmann wrote:

> 'The fantastic Dolomite mountains towered all around me in shapes more like dreams than sober realities; they recall quaint Eastern architecture, whose daring pinnacles derive their charm from a studied defiance of the sober principles of stability. The Chamonix aiguilles [...] remind one of Gothic cathedrals but in their most daring moments they appear to be massive, immovable and eternal. The Dolomites are strange adventurous experiments, which one can scarcely believe to be formed of ordinary rock.'[2]

In the late 1850s, the Viennese student and soon-to-be pioneering mountaineer discovered the potential of the region, established the world's second mountaineering club (the Austrian Alpenklub) and published a book which gave rise to the Dolomites' popularity.[3] By the time Paul Preuss moved to Vienna for university, the city had a small but dedicated climbing scene and an ethos different from that which developed in the Western Alps. The soaring limestone pinnacles favoured gymnastic ability and bravery, and instead of focusing only on first ascents, Viennese climbers searched for more demanding routes leading to the same peak. As few mountains were permanently covered in snow and ice, they inevitably became specialists in rock – much more advanced than their Western Alps counterparts.

Although in the first years of the twentieth century the Eastern Alps fell within the borders of the Austro–Hungarian Empire, the most accomplished climber of the region was Tita Piaz, later known as the Devil of the Dolomites, an Italian speaker hailing from the Fassa Valley. His solo ascent of the Winkler Tower, famously first summited with the aid of a grappling hook, brought him enough attention to begin a career as a guide despite having earlier failed his guiding exam, which he described as an 'exercise in servitude'.

Preuss served his apprenticeship repeating some of the hardest of Piaz's routes but, unlike the great Italian, he disapproved of the recently invented piton, which allowed climbers to hammer a metal point of protection into the rock. Soon, an abseil technique invented by Hans Dülfer (or possibly by Piaz but history can't quite settle the dispute) – and thus known as the Dülfersitz – provided a means of descending from walls without having to downclimb. The use of pitons was made even safer by the carabiner, making it possible to thread a rope through without having to untie. Preuss saw all this as excessive use of safety equipment.

Brought up without a father and with two older sisters, he naturally gravitated towards women. The Austrian climbing scene suffered no shortage of exceptional female mountaineers, but Preuss preferred to be the stronger of the party, always leading, always in the position of the mentor. Emmy Eisenberg was the only female partner who admitted to also having a romantic relationship with him, and she praised his attitude, which she described as encouraging but never patronising. Contrary to that, Preuss often spoke of female climbers with disregard, belittling their achievements and even penning an article entitled 'Climbing with Women', a sexist exercise intent on amusing his male colleagues in an attempt to justify his frequent rock partnerships with women.

Preuss himself was no stranger to discrimination. As a Jew, despite his already significant climbing achievements and converting to Protestantism, he was barred from joining the Austrian Alpenklub. The Munich Academic Alpine Section accepted only 'academically educated gentlemen of germanic ancestry', but somehow, after moving from Vienna to Munich for his postgraduate studies, Preuss was accepted.

At the time, Munich was the urban capital of the continental mountaineering world. In 1899, the German General Sports Exhibition featured a whole section dedicated to *Bergsport*, or mountain sports, which proved to be one of the most popular attractions. Soon climbers from all social classes were meeting frequently at the rocks of Buchenhain, only fifteen kilometres from Munich city centre, where they prepared for their mountain adventures. Some began to visit Buchenhain with no aspirations beyond scaling a few cliffs. To distinguish this new activity from mountaineering, they called it *Klettersport* – outcrop climbing.

Much like the Elbe pioneers, the Buchenhain climbers did away with nailed mountaineering boots and swapped them for light canvas shoes with a rope sole. The rock 'no longer succumbed to the iron-click of your boot nail'. The climbing shoe allowed one to listen to the rock's 'temperamental beauty' and, despite shunning other equipment as unsporting, Preuss quickly adopted its use.[4]

By 1911, he was likely the most skilled rock climber on the continent. Soloing Tita Piaz's route on the Totenkirchl in the Kaisergebirge was a statement which clearly marked him as being in a class of his own. Piaz himself hailed him 'Lord of the Abyss' and the press loved him. Preuss responded with a kind of double-sided humility: he climbed without ropes, so his style and skills were not better but different. Like many high achievers, he hid self-doubt behind boastfulness, and there is no better way to boast than by being overly modest.

While for others his superiority was obvious, for Preuss it was not enough. The ultimate test was still ahead of him: soloing a hard line and one that had never been climbed before. This would involve not only technical skill and a cool head, but also expert route-finding.

Four days after the Totenkirchl, Preuss, his sister Mina and friend Relly took the train to the Dolomites to tackle Campanile Basso via the moderate Via Normale. The thin limestone spire, 300 metres tall and vertical on each side, had some eighty ascents through the Via Normale and the harder Fehrmann's Dihedral. The sheer, east face remained unclimbed and was widely considered impossible.

After the first section of the Via Normale, Paul, Relly and Mina stopped on a ledge. Here Preuss revealed his real objective and asked Relly for a belay so he could have a peek at the east face. Mina asked him what he could see and he jokingly replied, 'not very much'. He then proceeded to untie from the rope and ventured alone on to the 110-metre-tall unclimbed face. His pace was much slower than on the Totenkirchl, attesting to the difficulty of the route and the challenge of finding the line on a first ascent. At the summit, Preuss signed the register, adding a succinct note, 'alone', next to his entry.

The climb sent shockwaves through the climbing community. It was not only one of the hardest routes climbed to date, but it was climbed onsight – which in today's climbing lingo means first go and without any knowledge of the wall – and solo. As if that wasn't enough, instead of abseiling, Preuss then *reversed the route*.

Even being used to Preuss' uncompromising climbing style, Mina and Relly must have been relieved to see him alive and unharmed. And they had happy news of their own: while waiting, they had got engaged. Relly had a small, hand-held camera with him, one of the kind which greatly added to the popularisation of climbing at the beginning of the century. He snapped a photo of Preuss before he set off on the east face, and a second after his return when he was belaying Mina back on the Via Normale. The latter shows him in a relaxed pose, completely at ease despite having just completed the most daring ascent to date.

Shortly afterwards, Preuss expressed his opinions on climbing ethics in an article entitled 'Artificial Aids on Alpine Routes', commissioned by the German *Alpine Times*. As much as climbers loved the rock and the mountains, they also loved their press, with many living vicariously through print when they couldn't escape the routine of urban life. The annual magazine of the German and Austrian Alpine Club was 700 pages long and consumed half of the organisation's budget, and many other commercial titles, not affiliated with clubs, catered to the interests of the climbing community. A century ago, climbers were already a market sector and the capitalist race for their money was well under way. Commissioning Preuss' article, the publisher of the *Alpine Times* hoped for controversy that would increase the sales – and controversy he got.

Preuss' article summarised his approach to climbing and compelled others to follow suit. He renounced all aid, believing that if a climber could not go up and down the same route, they were not ready to tackle it at all. Rope, pitons and a hammer could be carried as emergency backup only, but their use would invalidate the ascent, which should be done cleanly, without any aid or protection, and descended in the same manner. Using gear for protection reduced climbing to 'gymnastics on a steep wall with absolute safety' and therefore could not be seen as a worthy accomplishment. Preuss' idea of 'sport' incorporated not only physical ability but also a gentlemanly readiness to face danger.

Yet even Preuss saw his claims more as food for thought than rules to be followed by all. He himself referred to them as a 'crazy notion', but his self-righteous tone of being the defender of the one true spirit of climbing was met with vehement resistance. Franz Nieberl, a pioneer of the limestone Alps, author of seminal book *Das Klettern im Fels* (1909) and a patriarch of the German climbing community who lived to ninety-four, resorted to thinly veiled antisemitism to discredit Preuss' opinions. Tita Piaz joined in to debate the type of emergency that would justify the use of a piton. The editorial exchanges involving Preuss versus the most prominent figures of climbing grew to over thirty articles before the publisher decided to draw a line under them. An in-person debate was organised for all interested parties where, with a little diplomacy and a dose of his natural charm, Preuss emerged victorious. The ideal of free climbing, although much stricter than how we define it today, was born.

* * *

In 1913, Preuss' attention was turned to the north ridge of the Mandlkogel, a peak at his local range of Gosaukamm. At the time, it was the greatest remaining challenge of the region. However, before he could make an attempt, Preuss was called to Vienna to fulfil a speaking commitment and he returned to Altaussee with a serious case of angina. He was ill with an ailment similar to that which led to his father's demise.

Impatient and perhaps feeling that he had just escaped a close brush with death, Preuss decided to push on with his climbing season. It was already late September and snow would soon force him to postpone the Mandlkogel ridge to the following year. On 3 October, with heavy clouds already rolling over the sky and only a week after the doctor had instructed him to rest, Preuss set off for his ascent.

Another week later, when the first flakes of snow turned into a fully fledged snowstorm, his friends organised a search party. In the time before mobile phones, it wasn't unusual for climbers to return late without giving due warning, held up by bad weather or simply prolonging their trips, but with the conditions turning so abruptly it was clear that Preuss had to be in trouble. The hope was that he was simply trapped by the snow and, if he had not succumbed to hypothermia, was still awaiting rescue.

When the rescuers arrived at the foot of the Mandlkogel, they found Preuss' body enshrouded by a metre of fresh snow. His injuries were serious and it was clear that he was killed in a fall. Perhaps if not for his illness or for the change in conditions, he would have made it safely to the summit and back, continued with his brilliant climbing career and made soloing a much more mainstream part of the sport. Or, like many of his contemporaries, he'd live only to be swept away by a much greater storm brewing in Europe.

* * *

From the second half of the nineteenth century, the border between Italy and the Austro–Hungarian Empire ran through the peaks and valleys of the Alps and the Dolomites, following the line from the Alpine region of Trentino to the port of Trieste on the north coast of the Adriatic. Italy was the first country to officially introduce mountain infantry into the army. The *Alpini*, recruited from the local rural population to defend the northern frontier of the new nation state, knew their valleys and peaks better than any invader, but in Austria, specialist troops were also deployed to defend the border. On the Italian side alone, 3,000 kilometres of trenches were cut into the mountainsides. Both armies used dynamite and miners to build tunnels which provided some protection for the troops on the mountains exposed to artillery and sniper fire. In one month alone, 10,000 soldiers were killed by avalanches which occurred both naturally and triggered by troops intent on burying their enemy.

The population of the occupied port of Trieste, with its Italian majority, refused to fight on the Austro–Hungarian side and eagerly awaited liberation by the Italian Army. The port town was on the edge of starvation throughout the war and many of its inhabitants were sent off to the front, but thirteen-year-old Emilio Comici, short, plump and late to show signs of puberty, was too young to fight. Two years after the war's outbreak, he left school to work at the docks and also decided to join the Trieste Gymnastic Society.[5]

Soon, the Austro–Hungarian capitulation increased the nationalist atmosphere in Trieste, giving rise to Italian fascism. The emphasis on physical training intensified; the re-establishment of the Roman Empire – the utopian vision of the leaders – required raising a strong, physically capable nation. Newly formed in Trieste, the XXX Ottobre society organised hikes, climbs and caving outings. Comici, now nearly twenty years old and an athletic young man, became an enthusiastic member.

Right-wing intellectuals came to view climbing as an extension of the *Alpini* tradition, the troops having been drafted from the sturdy, local highland folk and credited with the reunification of Italy. Although they were often seen as intellectually inferior, their resilience, bravery and masculinity were a blueprint for the new 'spiritual-athletic' school of climbing that was to succeed the old 'bourgeois-sentimental' tradition. Comici displayed great climbing talent, quickly introducing his own advancements to the sport. Instead of carefully weighing at least three points of contact with the rock, he developed a semi-dynamic, daring style of movement. Where free climbing was impossible, he relied on ropework and resorted to his own novel aid-climbing techniques. The new methods were soon copied by others throughout the Alps.

* * *

After the end of the war, with the Dolomites again a part of Italy, Austrian and German successes in the mountains were seen as an affront to Italian national pride. When in 1925, two Munich climbers made the first ascent of the Civetta via the 1,200-metre north-west face, it was a groundbreaking achievement which pushed the Italians to step up.[6] It was a beautiful and uncompromising line, leading through technical rock as well as snow and ice, and it was graded VI (5.9), the highest number on the newly developed scaling system. Not long beforehand, in the times of Preuss, climbers had no unified way to express the difficulty of routes. Now, with little Roman numbers, later followed by a plus or minus, appearing by the name of new routes, the grading system fuelled the rivalry between nations.

Emilio Comici was searching for a new route that would allow him to surpass the Germans. In the Julian Alps, Cima di Riofreddo had an unclimbed north face which, like all groundbreaking climbs, had been hailed as impossible. In 1926, Comici made an attempt but quickly backed off. Two more parties tried to make an ascent and a friend of Comici, young Ricardo Spinotti, paid the highest price for his effort. Bad weather slowed him and his partner down, forcing them to bivouac overnight on the wall. At first light, they retreated, but

Spinotti was hypothermic. At the base of the climb, just as it seemed they were safe, he died of exhaustion.

Comici was undeterred; to give up would be to betray Spinotti. The fascist ethos encouraged an unwavering, heroic attitude even in the face of death, but beyond that Comici also had his own reasoning. Like many climbers of the time, venturing into the vertical realm and making possible what was not long ago seen as impossible, he had a curious understanding of the supernatural, blurring the line between reality and dream. Whether it was only figurative or actually spiritual, throughout his climb on the Riofreddo he reported feeling the guiding presence of his deceased friend watching over him and his partner Fabjan.

The pair overcame the hardest part of the route using Emilio's innovative aid-climbing techniques. Where it wasn't absolutely necessary to rely on aid, they free climbed. Using only hands and feet for upwards motion and not pulling on gear for assistance saves precious time spent on hammering in pitons and enables climbers to cover more ground within a day. Passing the point from which Spinotti retreated, they learned that the difficulties eased only a few metres above. Had Spinotti pushed on, he may have still been alive. Without time to dwell, Comici and Fabjan reached the summit before sunset. Knowing there was still a technical descent ahead of them, they decided to bivvy and rest. With good conditions, they were not at risk of falling victim to the cold. On their way home, they stopped at a small village cemetery and laid flowers on Spinotti's grave.

Their success brought a lot of press attention to Comici, even though Riofreddo turned out to be a grade easier than the route led by the Germans on Civetta. The authorities noticed Comici's potential and that of climbing as a vector for propaganda. The new style of combining gymnastic free climbing with liberal use of the piton proudly became the Italian style, and the Rosandra Valley school of rock climbing, where Comici and his peers honed their skills, was endorsed by the regime as the national school of alpinism.

Unfortunately for the climbers, the fascists were keen to share the glory of the sportsmen but not keen to support them financially, and Comici struggled for money. Becoming a guide was his best option for making a living far from the docks of Trieste.

Meanwhile, the distrust of the guides hailing from the mountain valleys towards Trieste climbers intensified after the latter were backed by the government. For the highlanders, many of whom belonged to the Ladin ethnic minority, Rome was as distant as Vienna. Nationalism was not a sentiment they shared, and their loyalties lay with a family, a parish and the lands where they grazed their livestock. They rarely established hard new routes, and saw guiding as the same hard work as farming. The most prolific of the guides, Tita Piaz, was soon interned for his anarchist opinions.

Despite Comici's successes, he had a hard time finding guiding clients. The traditional guiding families were doing whatever possible to keep him out of business. It was a surprising turn of events when for his next great climb, Comici shared the rope with Giuseppe and Angelo Dimai, two Ladin climber-guides from Cortina d'Ampezzo.

The obsession of all cutting-edge climbers of the interwar period was the so-called six great north faces. Among them was Cima Grande di Lavaredo, the tallest of the three phantasmagoric peaks called the Tre Cime (or, in German, Drei Zinnen). It had been regularly attacked by the best climbers of the period from both sides of the Italian–German border. Often, attempts were made without the intention of reaching the summit but only to achieve a high point. In 1931, Emilio held the record and left a red handkerchief to mark the place from which he retreated. Hot on his heels were the Dimai brothers, wanting to establish their superiority over Comici and snag a high-profile ascent to create publicity for their guiding business. However, after a few attempts and some scheming to prevent Comici from making another attempt of his own, the Dimai brothers realised that to stand on the summit of Cima Grande via its north face, they would have to team up with another climber who at least matched their skill and experience. They had no choice but to join forces with Comici.

On their first joint attempt they were stopped by water running down the rock cracks after a recent downpour. A day later, with the ropes still saturated and heavy, they tried again. Comici was leading, but at the crux, the weight and drag of the rope proved too much. He decided to stop, build an anchor and bring the Dimai brothers to him. Giuseppe took the lead and later on claimed that he stepped in where even the great Comici could not manage.

After the crux, the party bivvied on the wall before finishing it through a few easy pitches the day after. It was yet another groundbreaking ascent, perhaps the biggest one since the north face of the Matterhorn, and their contemporaries weren't able to grasp its significance. The climbing scale was not yet open-ended, with VI being the highest notch. The new route was then called a VI, but today it is widely regarded as the first alpine VII.

The Italian press was jubilant and most of the climbing community was ecstatic, but Julius Kugy, over seventy years old and a patriarch of Italian climbing, ruled that 'the north face of the Cima Grande remains unclimbed'. For him, as for Paul Preuss, the new aid-climbing techniques and the popularisation of the piton were a disgrace. Equally critical of the ascent were the German Alpine Club and the Brits who, in keeping with their ways of expressing the highest disgust in the most taciturn way, abstained from comment.

Soon after, Venice-born alpinist Domenico Rudatis published his *Das Letzte im Fels*, or *The Latest in Rock Climbing*. The book fully embraced the spirit of the new Italian style, with its grade-fuelled competition, liberal use of the piton, and aid climbing. A bitterly negative review in the *American Alpine Journal* followed:

> 'There have always been those who, for good or bad reasons, wished to grade climbs according to their difficulty. [It will] always fail, since the many variable factors remain uncontrolled. Second grade may become sixth grade when a storm breaks,

or seem so merely as a result of a dietary indiscretion. And what will the author think of the sixth grade, one day when a tractor with suction grips, loaded with first-grade climbers, comes steaming past him, as he blacksmiths his way up walls that once were best left alone?'[7]

Ironically, soon after, the very ethics that this article raged against, along with the dreaded piton, were imported from the Alps to proliferate on the great walls of Yosemite.

After the Cima Grande and before being drafted for his compulsory military service, Comici had time to complete a few other firsts. Perhaps the most impressive of them was *Spigolo Giallo* (VI+) on Cima Piccola, the smallest of the Tre Cime. His partner was Mary Varale, one of the strongest climbers of the period and a member of an elite group who could lead the sixth grade.

Despite her outstanding rock abilities, complemented with a head for soloing, Varale constantly battled the era's unrelenting machismo. A year after climbing with Comici, she opened another extreme line. Although it was one of many in her career, the southwest face of Cimon della Pala, known because of its shape as the Matterhorn of the Dolomites, was a climb of particular difficulty and significance. The leader of the successful team of three, Anvise Andrich, was proposed for the gold medal for athletic excellence by the Italian Alpine Club. Later, he was rejected. Rumours spread that it was because of Andrich's rope partnership with Varale – a woman.

Furious, she penned a letter to the president of her section, describing its members as 'clowns', 'hypocrites' and 'buffoons'. She then famously quit the Alpine Club, explaining that she did not want her future achievements to 'honor the club' whose decisions left her 'disgusted'. The signed letter, dated 1935, is held at the Civic Library in Belluno, a stark testimony to the obstacles faced by women in a sport dominated by men.

* * *

Comici's rock star status meant that he ended up with an unusual job in the army, guiding officials during their lavish mountain breaks in the guise of alpine training.

The level of discipline among the high-level fascist military was questionable, and one day Comici was stuck at a *rifugio* waiting for a party of officers who were fashionably late. Suddenly overcome with a desire to climb the *Fehrmann Dihedral* (IV+) on the nearby Campanile Basso, he left the mountain hut and headed for the pinnacle. Reaching the top, he picked up the summit register to log his climb and, paging through the booklet, came across the neat handwriting of Paul Preuss. His entry after completing the east-face climb was finished off with the German word *allein*. Alone. This struck a chord in Comici and he quickly downclimbed the Via Normale to the ledge where in 1911 Preuss had left his sister Mina and his friend Relly to wait for him. Like Preuss, Comici peeked over the rock bend obstructing the east face from view, and then set off on the climb. Unlike Preuss, he placed a piton for safety, but new desires were stirred nonetheless.

By that time, the Cima Grande di Lavaredo had seen some thirty ascents, but nobody had ever soloed the sixth grade. On a crisp day in September 1937, Comici packed a small rack and set off for the Tre Cime.

Four years earlier, together with the Dimai brothers, he had left some thirty pitons on the crux section of the climb. This time a hundred in-situ pitons lined the pitch, all left by the parties that came after them, making the climb both safer and easier. Deciding to climb solo, Comici was ready to tackle the difficulties as he remembered them, but he welcomed the new pitons. Still, it was with sadness that he realised that the precedent of driving them into the rock had brought about a practice of seemingly uncapped hammering.

On a ledge, Comici happened upon a roped party. The two climbers looked on in horror as Comici threw his well-organised rack down the wall. He no longer had need of it and didn't want its weight to spoil his pleasure. They must have thought him a madman.

With the others still resting, Comici set off again and soon stood on a small shelf. Without warning, the entirety of it collapsed. He frantically searched for something to hold on to and for a moment his feet skidded helplessly in the dusty scar left on the broken rock. As suddenly as the crisis unfolded, it was over. Comici held on and, safe again, looked down. He learned with relief that the avalanche of stones had missed the ledge below him, leaving the others unharmed.

Despite the drama, Comici continued on, making his climb the hardest solo ascent to date.

* * *

Unlike Paul Preuss, who died pursuing another one of his hard ascents, Emilio Comici passed away following a common climbing accident that could have easily been avoided. After two heartbreaks, the first when the prodigy climber Bruna Bernardini took a fatal fall, and the second when his long-term girlfriend left him due to his unstable lifestyle, Comici's friends set him up to meet a young woman at a group lunch. He didn't plan to climb that day and, instead of his climbing rack, he brought a guitar. After food and a few songs, his date asked him to show her some rocks. Rummaging through everything they had with them, they managed to haphazardly put together a bunch of gear and headed for the cliffs.

On top of their route, Emilio was setting up the rope to tie his date in for an abseil. When a friend on a nearby climb shouted for advice, Comici pressed his feet into the rock and leaned back to see better. As he had done many times before, he held the old rope with both his hands. It snapped without warning and Comici plummeted thirty metres down. Blood gushed from a gruesome head wound. He immediately stood up, took a wobbly step and fell down again.

The rope, clasped tightly in his dead fist, was rotten through to the core.

* * *

In a time when death while climbing or on one of the fronts of World War I was not uncommon, one of the few who lived to an old age was Tita Piaz. An old-style guide born and bred in the Alps, a member of the Ladin minority and a prolific first ascensionist, Piaz lived through not one but two world wars and died an old man in the village where he was born.

CHAPTER 9

A ROCK SHELF HIGH ABOVE THE BLACK LAKE VALLEY

'I am determined and this gives me a sense of freedom. I am free from everything which is not The Mountain or myself, free from fear and apprehension – because I have no choice left.'
Wanda Rutkiewicz (1943–1992), the first woman to reach the summit of K2, died during an attempt on Kangchenjunga

The rock shelf wasn't too narrow, and the drop wasn't so steep that we would tumble all the way down to the beautiful Gąsienicowa Valley floor, some 800 metres below us – but it still was steep enough. We built a solid anchor, tied in, and proceeded to find the most comfortable sitting position on our coiled ropes. Unsurprisingly, none felt too luxurious.

The first stars were out, but it wasn't completely dark yet. Even in the dusk, the clear air still sharpened the details of every rock bend, couloir and crack. I looked around us, calculating the hours left until sunrise. Too many. I looked to the stars and thought that with a little bit of luck we could stay dry. The next thought was less optimistic. I tried pushing it away but a sudden gust of wind made it impossible.

Clear mountain nights are the coldest.

* * *

It was two years after I had regularly started climbing at Mile End Climbing Wall, and a year after I applied for a job there. Hopeful, I left my CV at the counter, but the good-looking shift supervisor failed to keep his mouth shut and blurted to his boss that we had started dating. The management didn't want any romantic drama and, to my great surprise, I didn't get the job. I did, however, get the supervisor.

He was a bit older, well spoken and could pull hard on plastic. I considered him an expert on all things climbing, so when he offered to take me to the Peak District, I was beside myself. I packed my climbing shoes, a chalk bag and my hip-length version of the classic trench coat. Luckily, a spare down jacket and gloves, offered by friends in Sheffield, saved me from freezing in the merciless wind lashing against the Peak. I fell in love with the harsh weather and the abrasive rock that made my fingertips bleed in less than an hour. And I fell in love with Andy.

Wanting to return the favour of being shown around, I offered to introduce him to my favourite place, the Polish Tatra mountains. He claimed to have had some trad experience and was a qualified outdoor instructor – to my naive mind, a perfect candidate to share my lifelong dream of climbing in the Tatras. I would organise the trip and he'd lead the trad, multi-pitch routes on the dark granite. The plan seemed bombproof.

We bought a brand-new double rope, the sort that protects a mountaineer should it get cut by a falling rock or detach from its anchor points. I hadn't climbed with a rope since my Spanish mishap, and I hadn't climbed with a double rope ever, so we practised our gear skills in Andy's lounge in Hackney. Then, a cheap flight from Stansted carried us to Poland.

Even though the dining car's menu had changed, the long-distance train to Zakopane smelled and looked the same as it did when I was a child, but the town itself had changed much more and the quiet, rural atmosphere of old was all but gone.

The main drag had always been a magnet for tourists and snobbery. Even in 1889, when the town's population counted 3,000, there were some 600 guest rooms available.[1] When the railway extended to Zakopane only fifteen years later, it seemed that the craze began for good, but the two world wars prevented the resort from developing in the same way as Chamonix or Zermatt. Even a century later, there were still dirt roads, farmers driving horse and cart, full pigsties and fat hens lazily pecking for worms.

The twenty-first century brought high-street shops and hundreds of restaurants, luxurious villas at thousands of euros per night, and a total of three million tourists per year. Finding the town as it was even two decades earlier became nearly impossible. Only a determined researcher could find traces of the notorious outlaw culture that had shaped the region from the sixteenth century onwards. A commercialised version of history is sold in every shop window and at every street stall.

Arriving at the station, we swung our gear-filled backpacks on and bypassed the crowds to hide in the shade of the firs protected within the bounds of the National Park. The well-known trail led through windswept meadows – the cattle grazing lands of old – and along rounded ridges of the lower parts of the mountains. Our first stop was the Polish Alpine Association's hut, open to members and all climbers affiliated with other national governing bodies. Built in the 1920s, the wooden cottage sleeps thirty in two impossibly crowded rooms with one shared bathroom and no kitchen. For years I had dreamed of being admitted.

We proudly displayed our British Mountaineering Club cards to the hut's manager, and he reluctantly typed our names on his tired computer, taking the payment for our bunks in cash. On the wall behind him, a large poster depicted a naked woman with curly blond hair and impressive breast implants. With a climbing rope wrapped around her thigh and back, she was abseiling using the antiquated Dülfersitz. A kind of historical joke, I presumed.

The next day we woke up before dawn and hiked up the steep trail leading from the Black Lake, a fifty-metre-deep glacial pond, to the Karb Pass. Located between two pointy peaks, the pass is a meeting point of two official, marked paths: one leading down the other side, another leading up the higher peak of Kościelec. But there is a third peak, almost as tall, hiding behind the one visible in plain sight. A faint path scoots around Kościelec and leads to that third summit, guarded by a solemn wooden sign. Intended for tourists and not the much smaller population of climbers, it reads:

> 'Do not leave the marked trail. Do not make shortcuts. Do not make noise. Do not destroy anything. You are within the bounds of a National Park.'

We walked right past the notice and soon started climbing, choosing our footing carefully and even more carefully choosing the placements for our protection. I had placed my own gear only once before, as a teenager during my climbing course, but I had full faith in Andy's ability. It didn't occur to me that his confidence was only a result of not knowing what lay ahead.

An hour of random zigzagging later, unable to match the hand-drawn scheme of our route with the rocky reality in front of us, we were completely, undeniably lost. As I had seen countless times before, a storm was approaching fast from the Slovakian side of the range. It quickly turned out that weathering a storm while climbing was not quite the same as waiting it out on a trail.

Within minutes, I was alone, leading our second pitch in a mist that obscured not only Andy some twenty metres below me, but everything further than my arm's length. The mist, or perhaps the cloud, seemed to muffle everything apart from the rapidly nearing thunder. I placed a nut and tried pulling the rope up to clip it to the quickdraw but, searching for my route, I changed the direction too many times, putting too many kinks in the rope and preventing it from sliding easily through all its attachment points. It was noticeably pulling me down and I couldn't pull up enough of it to clip. I shouted, 'SLACK!', but my voice disappeared, absorbed by the cotton candy around me. I shouted again. Nothing. We had forgotten to agree on rope pull signals to use in this very scenario. The mist again soaked up my swear words like a sponge.

The terrain below me felt easy, so I climbed down and unclipped my previous quickdraw. The little hexagonal nut wedged in the crack was stuck. I wasted even more time trying to get it out, then climbed back up, trying not to think how far below me I had left my last runner. I passed my high point accompanied by the rolling, never-ending thunder that seemed to make the whole mountain tremble.

Soon the rope drag was terrible again and I had to stop, bring Andy up and let him take over the lead. Standing comfortably on a wide step, I stared blankly at the rock in front of me. It was dark grey with slivers of crystal and a greenish-white lichen pattern. I looked at the gear left on my harness, and then back at the rock.

Hail pounding on my helmet rapidly brought me back to thinking mode. I had to build an anchor – but how? My mind was empty like a student's during an exam and I was beginning to panic. Then I felt a sharp tug on the rope. And another one. Holy shit. Immediately, the emergency response system of fight or flight kicked in.

Andy was about to start climbing. I had led a pitch that was way too long, used way too much rope on needless zigzagging and taken forever to get to where I was. Without any means to communicate, he thought I was done, had built an anchor and was ready for him to come up. He must have started climbing, removing the points of protection that were now the only thing attaching us to the rock in case he fell. No anchor, no belay.

With hands red and numb from the hail, I built an anchor at a speed that could be recorded in the Guinness book of world records. Then I pulled out the slack until I was absolutely sure that the resistance on the rope was nothing else but Andy, probably going mad over me needlessly jolting him with the pulls. He took no time to join me.

'What on earth was that?' he asked grumpily as soon as we could see one another.

'Umm, I took my time placing gear,' I replied bashfully, worried that Andy hated me, that our mountain date was going horribly wrong, and that he wouldn't want to climb with me – or go out with me – ever again.

'I can tell!' He seemed really pissed off. 'Half of the pieces were stuck. And why were you pulling me?'

There was a crash of thunder seemingly right next to us and we instinctively rolled up our shoulders, recoiling and shivering. The hail had turned to rain and tiny streams of water were flowing down the rock everywhere around us. My misery was complete.

'I'm sorry,' I mumbled, sure that I had screwed up, but Andy gave me a sharp pat on both shoulders and a delighted smile bloomed on his face.

'Hey, chin up! Type two fun! You having fun?'

'Oh, yeah! Sure!' I answered with relief, completely ignoring the fact that if we killed ourselves on the easy climb, the date would not be entirely successful. But we organised our gear, coiled the ropes, ate a piece of chocolate and, as Andy set off on his lead in the pissing rain, were in very high spirits.

After two more pitches and a rappel through the impenetrable mist, we were physically and mentally exhausted. At one point Andy might have suggested that we were in way over our heads, but somehow we reached the conclusion that the only reason we had taken three times longer than expected was the adverse conditions. It did not cross my mind that an experienced party would know how to read their map, how to place gear fast, how to manage the two ever-tangling ropes and how to bail in case of a biblical rainstorm. Forgetting about all our difficulties, I was delighted with our progress and hungry for more.

The next day the weather cleared and we rested, sunbathing on the fragrant meadow that surrounded the Association's hut, drinking beer and plotting our next excursion. Looking through the guidebook, I found a beautiful nine-pitch climb leading up a prominent rib feature to the top of Skrajny Granat. Graded IV on the local scale, it was about 5.6 in American money, or 4+ in French – in other words, more of a scramble than a climb, but for a novice party the difficulties would lie in route-finding and gear. With a great weather forecast, I was sure we were up to it.

Much like on our previous climb, we made every single mistake possible. On a third or fourth pitch, I wanted nothing more than to bail. I was desperately grabbing on to grass growing out between loose rock, my legs skidding on choss, and sending down little avalanches of stones and soil. The only point of protection between me and Andy was a sling looped around a spike some ten metres below me. When I had pulled on it to check it, it moved ominously and I pondered if I should bother at all. If I fell, and the spike with me, it would miss Andy by a good two metres, so with clenched jaws, I had slung the loop of blue tape around it and clipped one of my ropes through a carabiner. Psychological gear.

Coming up second, Andy climbed fast, not even changing his approach shoes for climbing ones. His every lead was also much faster than mine, making up for all the time we spent untangling our ropes, my painstaking gear placements and – most of all – continuously getting lost. Once again, we took nearly three times longer on the route than the guidebook's estimate. After pitch five, we looked around for a supposedly easy walk off to our right and saw nothing but an impossibly steep, grassy slope that looked way more dangerous than the rock above us.

Pitch eleven was meant to be the last one and relatively easy, and it was my lead again. Above us, we'd find a faint path leading to the summit, where we'd meet with the trail traversing all of the 4.5 kilometres of the ridge. Not finding the walk-off route made me suspicious, but I tried to ignore the growing anxiety and focus on the beauty around me. As I looked up, the sky changed from blue to shades of peach and orange, and little birds – the Alpine accentors – were flying past, busying themselves with their evening chores. I was nearly at the end of the ropes, but the summit still seemed quite far away. Mentally surrendering to what had been on my mind throughout the pitch, I felt a sense of relief, but I wasn't sure how Andy would take it. Finally, I stopped and built a sturdy anchor on a comfortable, wide shelf. I shouted the call announcing I was safe, pulled the very little remaining slack and put Andy on belay.

'On belay! You can climb!' I shouted at the top of my voice. 'And don't rush,' I added after a moment of hesitation, but the mountain again played its acoustic tricks on us. Andy could not hear me, but I could hear him quite clearly, alternatively cooing and hurling swear words at the nuts and hexes I had meticulously wedged in the rock.

'No need to rush!' I shouted again, but to no avail. He soon appeared next to me, his face all red and sweaty, breathing heavily. Even before clipping into the anchor, he hurried me to get on with organising the gear.

'C'mon, chop-chop. It's getting dark,' he announced, all systems go.

For a moment I didn't move, not sure how to break the news to him. I wanted my voice to sound steady and cheerful when I announced that we were not going anywhere else.

'What? What do you mean, not going?'

'Well,' I said in an unnaturally high-pitched tone, 'I can't really see the path above us. We might not be in the right place.'

'Let's just go to the top. Then it's just the tourist trail down.' He was looking at me as if I were mad. I explained that the trail was more of a *via ferrata* than a path, and that there was absolutely no way we could navigate it with our gear-filled backpacks in the dead of the night. And that I would never, ever head out on the trails without a head torch, extra clothing and spare food and water. I could not explain what had got to me when at the base of our route I didn't object to stashing our backpacks under a rock, leaving all of our supplies and emergency gear behind. It was as if as soon as I tied to a climbing rope, I hurled all of my knowledge of the mountains aside.

'Let's call the rescue team,' he proposed, but it was my turn to look at him as if he had lost his senses. Hungry and tired, I felt the blood rush to my cheeks as I momentarily got angry.

'Are you mad? I wouldn't ever be able to show my face in these parts again! You saw the looks they gave us at the hut, they think we're gumbies!'

'We *are* gumbies. And we can't stay here. We have to call the rescue.'

'No way!' I protested again, but another realisation was dawning on me. At the shelter, we had written our names and route in the climbing log regularly checked by the rescuers. If a party was not back long after their estimated return time, a search was likely to be deployed.

'Actually,' I admitted, 'we have to call them and say we've decided to bivvy. Otherwise they'll come after us.'

'Let them. I'm not sleeping here.'

'Oh yes you are.' Andy looked at me, still not believing his ears, so I continued: 'We got ourselves into this, we'll get ourselves out. It's not even bad, just one night. We'll be fine. We'll call them and say we're staying cos,' I had to think of a reason, 'it's so pretty here.'

I took out my phone and hit the pre-saved number. After a moment, I heard a low voice with a strong highland accent and explained our situation, saying we'd be back in the morning.

'You got benighted? On this route?' he pressed, and I could swear there was amusement in his tone.

'No, we … I mean, yes. We did.'

'Have you got clothing? Food?'

'Yes, sure, we've got everything.' I tried sounding convincing but perhaps failed, because he repeated his question and I had to repeat my answer.

'Good,' he said. 'It's gonna be a cold night and I ain't gonna be impressed if you call us again at two in the morning.'

'Of course we wouldn't. We'll be great.' I thanked him for his time and hung up.

'Zof?' said Andy after a moment of silence.

'Hmh?'

'We don't have any clothing or food. We don't have any water.'

'I know. Type two fun,' I giggled hysterically and moved in closer for a cuddle.

We built a solid anchor, tied in and proceeded to find the most comfortable sitting position on our coiled ropes. Unsurprisingly, none felt luxurious and we soon started shivering, changing from one awkward position to another. I squatted with my back to Andy, pressing my shivering body into his chest.

Clear mountain nights are the coldest.

'I think we should not sleep,' he said. 'If you fall asleep and get hypothermic, you might not wake up again. We have to stay up.'

'Really?'

'Really.'

'Okay then … What songs do you know?'

* * *

As the darkness fell all around us, so did the temperature. It was far from freezing, but September nights in the Tatras cannot be called warm. I was shaking violently but couldn't stop myself from falling asleep, so after we'd gone through all of our singing repertoire, including every single Catholic and Anglican tune we could muster, I asked Andy to pinch my hand every time I dozed off. He was faring much better against the sleep deprivation and was adamant that I shouldn't sleep either.

When I'd finished translating all of my Polish jokes into English, the conversation ran dry. I started to rummage through my pockets to find something to do and found a forgotten chapstick. I smeared some on my lips. It smelled so good. Suddenly, I realised how hungry and dehydrated I was.

'Do you want some chapstick?' I asked.

'Why?'

'To eat. It's strawberry,' I added and bit half of the chapstick off. It wasn't that bad, so I passed the rest to Andy.

'Are you kidding me?'

'No, c'mon, fats give you energy,' I mumbled through my glued lips, trying to do away with the chapstick and laughing so hard that I nearly cried. More than anything, it was funny and helped to push forward the impossibly slow hands of the clock.

'You're mad,' he said through a mouth full of strawberry goop. We were now shaking not with the cold but with laughter, so we ate a tub of climbing hand salve that I found in my other pocket too.

'Something to tell the grandchildren,' I mused, still laughing and trying very hard to stop the gag reflex from the waxy hand salve. 'Two idiots stuck overnight on a mellow route, eating skincare.'

* * *

The sky got brighter and we got excited for dawn, but only a silver moon came up from behind the mountains, lending the amphitheatre of rocky ridges an aura of eerie beauty. Down below us, the Black Lake was glistening in the moonlight. The cold was getting unbearable and our spirits were getting low, so we made a plan for the morning and kept repeating it until almost memorising it by heart.

Get up. Warm up the muscles. Organise the rack. Fold one rope in half. Lead pitches of at most three points. Don't let the other get out of eyesight. Keep watching each other's hands.

Dawn finally came and we exercised the plan like robots. In our state of exhaustion, there was no space for more mistakes. It turned out that the terrain above was very easy, but we kept going with the belays and, after about two hours of steady effort, we finally stood on the ridge. It was eight o'clock and the sun came up from behind the mountains just as we reached the top, immediately warming us up. After the less than comfortable night, the perfectly blue sky and the view around us felt like a spiritual revelation. With the cold and hunger forgotten, suddenly we were ecstatic, enchanted with the view, drunk with the clear air and so very alive.

Approximately a kilometre to the west, on another peak, we saw two tiny figures quickly disappearing behind the ridge, abseiling for a route not accessible from the bottom. At least they had their timing right.

In the early morning sun, the mountains were more beautiful than I had ever seen them. We hugged and we laughed. It was perfect.

'Fuck,' I said pulling away from Andy.

'What now?'

'Our train to Warsaw. It departs at half three today.'

'Oh,' Andy sighed, but he smiled at me and his eyes were bright. 'Let's be quick about it!'

CHAPTER 10

ON STOLEN LAND

*'Being a Native Indigenous person,
you come from oppressed people.'*
Lonnie Kauk (born 1982), Native American
professional climber, son of Ron Kauk

From Maine's Eagle Bluff cliffs to the Santee boulders on the outskirts of San Diego in California, America has close to a thousand rock-climbing areas. Most of them are relatively small and known only to the locals, while others attract visitors from across the state, or even further afield. A few are world-class destinations, magnets for climbers from all over the globe who gather whenever the season is right. Red River Gorge, Joshua Tree, the Gunks, Buttermilks, Moab – these are the names known to almost every climber on the planet; among them is perhaps the most revered climbing destination in the world, the Yosemite Valley, with its iconic formations of El Capitan and Half Dome. In recent years, even the mainstream has come to associate them with climbing, but the Valley has been a climbers' mecca for nearly a century. It has the greatest big walls on the planet, single-pitch climbing for all levels and arguably the most famous boulder problem on Earth, *Midnight Lightning*.

* * *

As with Europe in the second half of the nineteenth century, bourgeois intellectuals from the biggest cities around the US became interested in mountain exploration. With a focus on hiking and natural studies, in 1876 two Harvard academics founded the Appalachian Mountain Club (AMC) – the first outdoor organisation in the United States. Similar clubs soon emerged on the east coast but, perhaps because of the still-vivid memories of the Civil War, most Americans were not inclined to seek out more adventure. By the time the Harvard Mountaineering Club was formed in 1924, two of the highest peaks of the country had already been summited, but most climbers still lacked the skills to tackle hard rock. Only those who travelled to Europe were acquainted with the latest mountain techniques, and one of them was Robert Underhill, a Harvard mathematician. Having fallen in love with the Swiss Alps, Underhill frequently visited the old continent and put up numerous first ascents. He was often accompanied by his wife, the mountaineer, feminist and pioneer of man-less mountaineering, Miriam O'Brien.

In the summer of 1930, after two continuous years in the Alps, Underhill returned to the States. Equipped with the latest knowledge on climbing gear and techniques, he promptly travelled to the Tetons and established the hardest climbs in the country. He then headed for British Columbia where, by chance, he reconnected with a fellow Harvardian, Francis Farquhar. The latter now lived in California where he was a member of the Sierra Club, an outdoor organisation founded in 1892 by naturalist John Muir. Fascinated with Underhill's alpine revelations, Farquhar requested that Underhill share his newfangled ideas with the Sierra Club and invited him to California.

The Sierra Club's founder, Scottish-born John Muir, had died some fifteen years prior to Underhill and Farquhar's meeting in Canada. Today, he is often regarded as the father of American national parks and even 'the patron saint of twentieth-century American environmental activity'.[1] He is especially revered by rock climbers, as his early exploits include scaling Mount Ritter, Mount Whitney and, in 1869, Cathedral Peak in Yosemite Valley, perhaps the first technical rock climb in the United States. Muir quickly became a legend and his famous quote – 'the mountains are calling and I must go' – inspired generation after generation of outdoor enthusiasts, but before that another story, less told, had to take place. It is one which played out in various forms over and over again throughout North America.

* * *

Yosemite Valley is located in the western part of Sierra Nevada, a mountain range stretching through the present-day states of Nevada and California. When in 1848 the first lump of gold was accidentally discovered in the foothills of the Sierra, the entire population of California amounted to roughly 157,000 people. Six and a half thousand were of Spanish or Mexican origin, and fewer than 800 were non-native Americans. The remaining population was composed of the Karok, Maidu, Cahuilleno, Mojave, Yokuts, Pomo, Miwok, Paiute, Modoc and other indigenous tribes.

Within less than a decade, the California Gold Rush brought to Sierra Nevada roughly 300,000 migrants from all over the world. The settlers introduced laws which displaced the native tribes and forced them into reservations. Organised rides were a punishment for those who disobeyed and, in 1851, an armed militia attacked the Miwok and Yokuts people. They destroyed villages and food stores, killing or imprisoning whomever they found. Chasing their victims, they entered into Ahwahnee – or, as it is known today, the Yosemite Valley. They found there the peaceful people of Ahwahneechee, as well as refugees from various other tribes. The few survivors were removed to the Fresno River Reservation.[2]

During the first two years of the California Gold Rush alone, around 100,000 Native Americans perished – murdered, starved or killed by diseases brought by the settlers. By 1873, there were only 30,000 left. The Ahwahneechee began returning to Yosemite as soon as their persecutors retreated. Finally, they were allowed to stay, but never again on their own terms.

Following the raid, accounts of Yosemite's stunning scenery soon attracted more white visitors and settlers. In 1855, English journalist and entrepreneur James Hutchings hired two native guides to see the valley for himself, later writing:

> 'Descending towards the Yo-Semite Valley, we came upon a high point clear of trees from whence we had our first view of the singular and romantic valley; and as the scene opened in full view before us, we were almost speechless with wondering admiration at its wild and sublime grandeur.'[3]

For $400, he purchased a dilapidated, crude inn at the heart of the Valley and proceeded to further publicise Yosemite's beauty. In 1861, his new employee was a thirty-one-year-old Scot, John Muir. He was as passionate about the Valley as his employer, but more charismatic. The visitors quickly recognised him as the expert, causing friction with Hutchings. John Muir quit his job and within two months found a new calling: an article about Yosemite's glaciers began his career as a naturalist.

Meanwhile, out of the estimated 10,000 Ahwahneechee who had lived in the Valley before, fewer than a thousand remained. The biggest village, rebuilt after the destruction wrought by the raid, counted 300 heads. But even for those lucky enough to stay, the living conditions were increasingly difficult – dispossessed of their traditional ways of life, the only way they could survive was to find employment in the service of the settlers. At best, they were seen as a tourist attraction, showing off their traditional crafts and selling their wares.

John Muir and other early naturalists, although concerned about the preservation of Yosemite's natural beauty, were not interested in the welfare of its original inhabitants. In 1890, largely thanks to Muir's vigorous campaigning, Yosemite was made into a national park, ensuring that it could not be destroyed by agriculture, farming or tourism. By law, the Ahwahnee no longer belonged to the Ahwahneechee. The national park was created out of 'pristine' and 'uninhabited wilderness', and history went on to systemically erase the violent dispossession of those who had once called it home.

John Muir founded the Sierra Club – 'to explore, enjoy, and render accessible the mountain regions of the Pacific Coast' – only two years later.

Much of the High Sierra was still unexplored by the whites, and the Club members devoted themselves to mapping the mountains and christening every geological feature they saw. When Francis Farquhar witnessed the new techniques brought from the Alps by Robert Underhill, he immediately commissioned him to write an extensive piece for the *Sierra Club Bulletin*. 'On the Use and Management of the Rope in Rock Work' (1931) for the first time exposed Americans to the gear tactics used by alpine climbers for decades. Underhill was also invited to California to teach in person. The Sierra Club climbers quickly formed a rock-climbing section and practised their new belay skills. Still, the ropes could not be trusted to arrest anything but a second climber's slip, and leader falls were still unthinkable.

In autumn 1933, three climbers – Jules Eichorn, Bestor Robinson and Dick Leonard – mustered the courage to attempt the Higher Cathedral Spire, one of the two impressive pinnacles standing opposite El Capitan. To protect it, they took a bunch of ten-inch-long nails which they intended to use instead of pitons, still unknown in the US. Despite their best efforts, after a few hours they had to retreat. Immediately after, they placed a mail order to receive some proper gear from Munich. They returned to the Higher Spire in spring 1934, this time with real pitons, and soon stood on top, using both free and aid climbing to reach the summit. The ethics taught to them by Underhill rejected any direct aid, but the sheer difficulty of climbing on the Higher Spire forced compromises.

By the end of the decade, only twenty-two more routes were

established in the Valley, testament to how challenging early Yosemite climbing was. Meanwhile, parallel to climbing, a more serious drama was unfolding.

From 1916, the Park Service took it upon itself to 'preserve, revive and maintain [the] interest of Indians in their own games and industries' and a fetishised ideal of an 'authentic Indian' was to be sold to white tourists during the Indian Field Days.[4] The Park Service would closely manage the Ahwahneechee way of life and use it for financial gain. In addition, the Field Days were an occasion for the officials to 'civilise' the tribe, include them in the capitalist economy and educate them to eventually become American citizens.

The rare times when officials seemed genuinely concerned about the decline of the native culture can perhaps be explained by the fact that it was seen as yet another commodity craved by the white settlers. The programme from the 1923 Yosemite Field Days announced that 'the interest centred on the problems of the fast-disappearing Indian race, should rank Yosemite's efforts to preserve their customs as one of national importance'. Around the same time, marketing strategies were employed to attract consumers to the event, turning it into a major fair and generating significant revenues for the Park Service. Tens of thousands of tourists per year poured into Yosemite to experience their fantasy of wilderness and the 'authentic Indian'.

The Ahwahneechee village, destroyed in the 1851 raid and rebuilt with traditional *u-mu-cha* dwellings, provided a backdrop for the Field Days. In front of its pointy wooden domes, native women wove baskets sold to the increasing numbers of visitors. However, the village had long been considered 'an eyesore' and 'a nuisance' by the Park Service, which even considered ordering hide teepees that could better fit with tourists' expectations. A new development plan proposed in the late 1920s provided an excuse to raze the village to the ground – without consulting its inhabitants. In addition, the authorities made sure to 'impress upon them in a proper way, that their residence [in the valley was] a privilege, and not a vested right;

[and] that this privilege [was] dependent upon proper deportment'.

A new settlement was constructed to reflect the white people's image of what they deemed the right balance between native authenticity and civilisation. Twelve cabins, all under forty metres square, housed up to eight family members each. This was all that in 1934 remained of the Ahwahneechee people.[5]

* * *

In December 1941, the Japanese Army attacked Pearl Harbor and the US was dragged into the chaos of World War II. Some one thousand Sierra Club members served in the war, many of them in the 10th Mountain Division which clashed against the Italian *Alpini*. The invention of the nylon rope, first used for parachute cords and glider tow lines during the war, was to revolutionise climbing in the second half of the century.

In 1945, the war came to an end and climbers returned to the cliffs of Yosemite. Among them was John Salathé, an eccentric ex-blacksmith from Switzerland whose sudden illness and a midlife crisis led him to find God and a calling for rock climbing. Salathé beat his ill health by converting to vegetarianism, occasionally talking with angels and spending most of his time plotting big-wall ascents. His vision was the thread which connected the pre-war Valley climbing to the watershed ascents of the late 1950s and 1960s.

Perhaps the biggest technical contribution by Salathé was his realisation that the European piton was ill-suited to Yosemite granite. Legend says that the smith fashioned his own handmade rendition of the piton from an old Model A Ford axle, resulting in a product that was tougher than its predecessor and, most importantly, reusable. Salathé could now take a number of pitons on a route, and hammer them in and out to use again on a higher pitch. Given the gargantuan size of Yosemite walls, the development was crucial. The only downside was that the hard steel pins left round scars in the rock cracks, but this would not concern climbers for another thirty years.

Equipped with the new gear, Salathé turned his attention to the Lost Arrow Spire. The slender, free-standing pillar detached from the Valley rim had attracted climbers even before the war, but they had quickly given up. Salathé was not only better equipped but more determined. Alone, he abseiled down the Valley's rim to the Notch of the Spire to examine its walls and search for cracks that would take his pitons but failing to find a climbable route, he prusiked up – a laboursome but effective technique involving fixing two sliding knots on to the hanging rope. With his famously dogged persistence, after an hour and a half, Salathé was back at the Valley's rim.

For his second attempt he enlisted a partner. They made considerable progress, but a mere nine metres from the top were turned back by the smooth tip of the spire where no pitons could be placed. Yet again, Salathé retreated, but news of his high point made the rounds among climbers. Two decided to make an attempt of their own, albeit with a different technique. Interested predominantly in standing atop the Spire and not so much in how they'd get there, they lassoed the summit from the wall of the Valley, and then prusiked up their rope.

They became the first people to reach the Lost Arrow Spire's summit, but many Yosemite climbers saw the ascent as a rope trick which was only another 'admission of the Arrow's unclimbability'. Salathé, true to his spiritual self, believed that the ascent was made with 'the help of the devil'.[6] Determined to find a route, he now planned to ascend not from the Notch but from far below, following an ominous chimney. Combining the two parts of the Spire would make for nearly 430 metres of vertical gain through technical terrain: a route requiring a multi-day effort. Salathé and his partner, Ax Nelson, had to carefully consider the logistics.

But another party wanted to snatch the first ascent away from the duo and the pressure was on. Salathé and Nelson prepared a surprisingly small rack – eighteen pitons and twelve carabiners – but this was complemented by an unusually large number of expansion bolts and all the tools required to place them. They also had thirty-six metres of nylon rope for leading, as well as additional, cheaper manila ropes for hauling their bags, along with slings and prusiks necessary for loops and other gear manoeuvres.

As a means of saving weight, Salathé and Nelson packed only a handful of nuts and raisins for each day, and six litres of water, making for a very sparse menu for the three planned days of climbing, and more of a starvation diet for the five days actually spent on the Spire. At the time, living on vertical rock was still a completely alien concept. Portaledges and modern sleeping bags didn't exist, and overnight the climbers simply curled up wherever they could. If they were lucky, they could stretch out on a ledge. If they were not, the night would be spent hanging in slings.

Although expansion bolts could be used to aid climb virtually anything, the process of hand-drilling them was extremely tiring and time-consuming. During this period, it was commonly accepted that lassoing rock was not a serious climbing technique, but placing a minimal number of bolts for aid (unlike pitons, bolts don't require finding a crack to drive them into) was perfectly acceptable – yet another example of the arbitrariness of climbing's ethics. Placing a few near the top of the Spire, Salathé was able to overcome the smooth slab and complete a valid first ascent.

The route, simply named The *Lost Arrow Chimney*, was made famous by a *Sierra Club Bulletin* article penned by Nelson. He not only recounted the details of the climb but also gave some philosophical consideration as to the climbers' motives – a first-of-its-kind piece in American outdoor literature, following a first-of-its-kind climb. The type of piton developed by Salathé is still known today as the lost arrow piton.

The next – and last – great climb for John Salathé was Sentinel Rock, a five-day effort with partner Allen Steck, again made more arduous by the insufficient amount of water that the climbers took with them. Incredibly, in 2000 at the age of seventy-four, Steck repeated the climb for the fiftieth anniversary of their first ascent.

Three years after the Sentinel, Salathé suffered a mental breakdown. After a stint in Europe as a member of a religious cult, he returned to the US where for two decades he lived in his car, wandering around the Sierra, living off his modest Swiss pension and any food that he could forage. At this stage he rarely talked about climbing, but during rare moments of clarity, younger climbers sometimes managed to get him to tell his stories. On one such occasion they revealed to him that the Sentinel had been done in three hours, but the old man only shook his head and chuckled to himself. 'Oh, now that the pitons are in,' he answered, 'maybe in three days.'[7]

* * *

When Royal Robbins arrived in Yosemite in 1952, he was a relatively unknown seventeen-year-old and Salathé was still king of the Valley. A year earlier, having dropped out of school to spend more time in the mountains, Robbins had climbed the hardest free route in the country. The line was located at his local crag, two hours west of Los Angeles, where Robbins also realised that the Welzenbach grading system – Roman numbers from I to VI – was no longer adequate given that the fifth grade covered a huge range of free-climbing difficulties. He decided to subdivide it into decimal points ranging from 5.1 to 5.9, and the scale travelled with him to the Valley where it became known as the Yosemite Decimal System (YDS) still in use today.[8]

Despite his lack of formal education, Robbins was an intense, intellectual young man with a 'perfect bearing and a measured speech pattern which set him apart from the […] crowd'.[9] Most importantly, he was ambitious, 'wanting to do something better than what's been done', and five years after his arrival in the Valley, Robbins did exactly that. His ascent of the Northwest Face of Half Dome, the scooped-out, imposing formation rising 610 metres from the meadow below it, was a breakthrough moment in the history of Yosemite climbing.

Had Robbins not snatched it, there was a rival trailing at his heels who'd do it soon after. His name was Warren Harding. Both in appearance and in his principles, he was the polar opposite of Robbins, describing himself as capable only of 'what required brute stupidity'. More than a decade older than Robbins, he arrived in the Valley in his ostentatious purple Jaguar with a string of women on his arm, drinking bottles of cheap red wine one after another. Both crude to the core and a visionary with zero regard for what others – including climbers, and Robbins in particular – thought was acceptable, Harding stood out among the middle-class intellectuals who formed the Yosemite community. He was known to be remarkably immune to exposure, fatigue and pretence – but not to ambition.

In 1957, Harding harboured the plan to climb Half Dome himself but, arriving in the Valley too late, learned that Robbins was already on the wall. To chase him was out of the question and, after five days of questing into the unknown, Robbins' team pulled over the summit. The route included the use of custom-made pitons – both extra wide and extra thin – as well as huge horizontal pendulums allowing the climbers to move over blank sections of rock to connect one crack system to another (a technique which before the advent of nylon ropes would have been entirely unthinkable). Harding awaited the party on the summit, congratulated them and promptly began plotting his next move.

Robbins was not the only one intent on pushing the standards, but the number of viable walls in the valley had seemingly been exhausted. Many loomed far out of the realm of climbing possibility, gargantuan tourist attractions, completely inaccessible and as 'distant as the moon'.[10] The biggest and proudest among them, El Capitan, was plainly impossible to climb, even in the eyes of Robbins, but Harding did not ask his opinion.

He decided to attack the 914-metre cliff using siege tactics. Go up, hammer in pitons and drill in bolts, retreat to the ground to rest and replenish the supplies, then ascend the fixed ropes to push the previous high point higher and higher, until the summit was finally within reach. The first milestone came with the initial push – nobody had ever spent seven days straight on a wall before, and certainly nobody had used discarded stove legs as extra-extra-large pitons.

Coming down to rest, Harding and his team were confronted by the Park rangers. Their escapade was attracting so many tourists that traffic jams had begun to form on the Valley floor. The climbers were told to take a break until after the Labor Day weekend. The second delay was even more serious: one of Harding's partners, Mark Powell, shattered his ankle. Harding was now short of partners. He extended an invitation to Robbins, but the chief 'Valley Christian', as Harding began to call those in his opinion too preoccupied with ethics, was against the siege tactics and declined.

Finally finding company, Harding went up again and turned the climb into a gastronomic orgy. His mother supplied the team with homemade meals which they hauled up the fixed ropes, including a whole Thanksgiving turkey. However, winter soon arrived and the manila ropes began to rot in the rain and snow. Nobody had expected that the siege would span all four seasons, and all the cords had to be exchanged for more durable nylon to be used in spring.

The following year Harding made good progress, but the summer holiday meant another ban on their project and later, with Thanksgiving of 1958 looming around the corner, he was feeling desperate. Most of his partners bailed, so he 'continued with whatever "qualified" climbers [he] could "con" into this rather unpromising venture'.[11] Toiling on the wall was not only incredibly tiring but simply boring, with even the exposure fading away to the rhythms of the hammer and drill. The routine would be punctuated with the occasional terror, such as the *King Swing*: the biggest rope swing traverse ever done, penduluming above 305 metres of vertical granite to then wedge fingers into the next crack system.

The final push began in early November, with Harding accompanied by George Whitmore and Wayne Merry. Twice, they needed to send one of them down to resupply gear, prusik all the way back up and haul it with them. They were now climbing so high above the Valley

The author topping out at dawn in the Tatra Mountains. © Andy Day.

Top left Pierre Allain jumping in Fontainebleau. © *Paul Allain.*
Top right UIAA founding meeting, 1932. © *Dr Walery Goetel/Polish Academy of Sciences.*
Above Ron Kauk on *Headcrash*. © *Thomas Ballenberger.*

Wolfgang Güllich on *Action Directe*. © Thomas Ballenberger.

Top left Johnny Dawes climbing at Burbage in the Peak District. © *Zofia Reych.*
Top right Alice Hafer bouldering in Bulgaria. © *Zofia Reych.*
Above Favia Dubyk, full-time doctor and elite-level boulderer. © *Favia Dubyk.*

Trad climbing on Jersey. © *Eleanor Lister.*

Kiromal Katibin, Villiers World Cup final in speed climbing, 2021. © Lena Drapella.

Ashima Shiraishi, Chamonix World Cup final in lead climbing, 2021. © *Lena Drapella*.

The author bouldering in Switzerland. © *Andy Day.*

floor that they might as well have been in a different dimension, its eerie strangeness captured well by climber and author Steve Roper:

> 'The upper third of the Nose is one of the most soul-satisfying places in Yosemite. Planes of marble-smooth granite shoot upward toward infinity. The various dihedral walls, dead vertical at this stage, converge in broad, angular facets, and climbing through this magical place is like living inside a cut diamond.'[12]

After twelve days on the wall, Harding worked through the night by the glow of his headlamp, drilling in bolt after bolt, until finally, at six o'clock in the morning, he made it to the summit slabs of El Capitan.

It was a moment of epiphany for all American rock climbers. The ultimate notion of the impossible was shattered. Horizons exploded. A huge amount of publicity followed, resulting in an influx of young people from all over California, and soon after, when the interstate highway system connected the whole country, from every state. Meanwhile, the delighted Harding basked in the limelight while the Valley Christians scoffed at the media attention.

With the myth of El Capitan's unclimbability firmly dispelled, there was only one thing that Royal Robbins could do to regain the upper hand, and that was to climb El Capitan 'right': no fixed ropes, no going up and down to replenish supplies, no reliance on anybody or anything that the climbers couldn't take with them in a single push from the bottom to the top of the enormous cliff.

* * *

Harding's original siege spanned nearly two years, during which he spent a total of forty-seven days on the wall. At that stage, he and most of his partners still held down regular jobs and climbed mostly at the weekend. As a result, the El Capitan assault lasted so long that most Yosemite climbers stopped holding their breath, engrossed in their own projects. It was around that time that some of them realised that to climb their hardest, weekends were not enough. The epicentre of the Yosemite climbing world, Camp 4, was previously deserted on weekdays, but it would soon find its first seasonal occupants. The first to 'move in' was Mark Powell, who had accompanied Harding on his early El Capitan push. Working over winter allowed Powell to save up for a whole season of hobo existence in the Valley. Without a car, life insurance or anything other than a tattered tent and a sleeping bag, climbers realised they could sustain themselves on as little as $1 a day and climb for months on end.

The atmosphere in Camp 4 was decidedly anti-establishment, and dirtbagging became not only a way of life but a political manifesto. At a time when rock climbing was not a recognised discipline, nobody imagined that it would ever professionalise. There was no career and no future to be had within the sport. Living without a fixed address, dumpster-diving for food and fully devoting oneself to climbing was a way of contesting everything that mainstream America embraced in the decade following the war: materialism and conformity.

* * *

At the vanguard of the post-war cultural rebellion was a small literary movement soon to be known as the Beat Generation and described as pushing back against 'Mom, Dad, Politics, Marriage, the Savings Bank, Organized Religion, Literary Elegance, Law, the Ivy League Suit and Higher Education, to say nothing of the Automatic Dishwasher, the Cellophane-wrapped Soda Cracker, the Split-Level House and the clean, or peace-provoking H-bomb'.[13]

The same year that Harding stood on the summit of El Capitan, Jack Kerouac published his *Dharma Bums*, a novel about a group of youngsters – modelled after Kerouac's own circle of friends, soon to become literary giants – seeking transcendence through drugs, alcohol, parties, orgiastic Buddhist rituals and forays into the wilderness. Kerouac's vision of a 'rucksack revolution' with 'millions of young Americans [...] going up to mountains' inspired a generation and, while most opted for the more obvious alternative of drugs and parties, some chose nature. (Usually not foregoing drugs and parties but simply changing the location from a bar to a campsite.)

Legend has it that Kerouac's next novel, *On the Road*, was written over three weeks of drugs- and coffee-fuelled manic creativity. Both books were instrumental in the creation of the countercultural pilgrimage, a Buddhism-inspired practice of itinerant wandering aimed at an intellectual and spiritual liberation. Before the 1960s and 1970s saw an unknown number of young Americans taking to the 'hippie trail' – the twentieth-century version of the grand tour, this time rebellious rather than conformist – scores travelled west, to California and Yosemite.

Travel – touristic, religious or otherwise – became more accessible than ever. The transient dirtbag existence in particular, living off cans of damaged cat food or stolen restaurant leftovers, seemed to offer an equal shot at whatever it aimed to achieve: enlightenment, full-time climbing, or both. But while the Beats were often acutely correct in their critique of the consumerist, post-war society, they were equally blind to some of its faults. When Kerouac's protagonist Sal takes a job as a seasonal cotton picker, he fails to recognise the difference between his situation and that of his fellow workers. His presence on the cotton field is voluntary, with plenty of other options available, while for the rest – Black and Latino migrant workers – it is a matter of survival.

The Beats romanticised the racial struggle, affirming it as a necessary prerequisite to the resultant art. The BIPOC (Black, Indigenous and People of Color) fetishisation of the era was steeped in white privilege, equally pervasive on the pages of Kerouac's novels as it was on the shady grounds of Camp 4. If dirtbagging was the young climbers' way to distance and differentiate themselves from the consumerist, white man's society, it was equally a result of belonging to that society in the first place. It is no coincidence that most of the volitional hobos of Yosemite ended up becoming academics, writers or entrepreneurs.

Meanwhile, the Ahwahneechee struggled to hold on to their homes and identity. One hundred years after the tragic raid, hardly any of the Camp 4 residents cared to look just one mile from their campsite, towards the small wooden cabins. Built by the authorities to represent the white man's view on 'harmony with nature', they were occupied by the Ahwahneechee who were relocated from their own village. Incredibly, the Park Service began to charge them rent, and only allowed those whose family members were employed in the Valley to reside there. In 1953, the situation worsened further when only full-time employees were allowed to stay – a callous rule given that most available positions were seasonal, giving the Park Service full autonomy to evict people at their will. Julia Parker, grandmother to Ahwahneechee climber Lonnie Kauk, recalled the 1950s in a recent interview for *Alpinist* magazine:

> 'We all had to sort of fight for our work. In the Valley they didn't want the Indian women working in offices, so they always put us in the laundry and said, "You can be a good maid." They tried to keep the Indian people down.'[14]

Soon, eviction notices started being handed out by the Park Service to the remaining inhabitants of the village. They were forcibly moved once again, this time to general Park employee housing. By 1969, the village community was entirely torn apart and dispersed. In an act of final destruction, the abandoned lodges were set on fire as an exercise for local firefighters.

CHAPTER 11

HARD GRIT

*'The working class, come kiss my ass,
I've joined the Alpine Club at last!'*
sung to the tune of 'The Red Flag'

It was the summer of 1951 when Joe Brown and Don Whillans arrived in the Llanberis Pass in Snowdonia to make their second attempt on the right wall of Dinas Cromlech. At the centre of the imposing cliff, shaped like a gigantic book opened at ninety degrees, is *Cenotaph Corner*, at that point still unclimbed, although Brown had already made an attempt; to its right, *Ivy Sepulchre*, E1 5b, led for the first time only a few years earlier.

Brown and Whillans had already made a foray on to the crack running alongside the right edge of Cromlech's right wall, overhanging for over sixty metres. Brown led up twenty metres to a belay stance at a holly tree miraculously growing out of the sheer rock. He brought Whillans up and the two eyed the next pitch, which seemed to be the crux. With the vastness of the Llanberis Pass opening up all around them, merely hanging in slings on the incredibly exposed route was a huge psychological challenge. Going further would require nerves of steel but, as they worked up the courage to do so, torrential rain made the decision for them.

After a few days of mulling over the exposure and difficulty, they returned with a better forecast and fewer doubts. Brown climbed again to the holly tree where Whillans took over to lead the second, crux pitch. Shards of rock broke from the wall under his weight and the only consolation was that the crack he was following provided ample opportunity to place protection. For the third and final pitch, they swapped the lead again. Brown continued up the crack before heading right towards the arête of Cromlech's right wall. Suddenly, he was in a precarious position, no longer in view of his belayer. After nine more metres of hard but 'continuously amazing' climbing, big holds led to a grassy ledge. Relieved, he shouted down to Whillans who, in return, let out a shriek of delight. The route was theirs. 'Never before or since,' noted Brown more than fifteen years later, 'have I known him to show emotion in this way.'[1]

They went back home to Manchester on Whillans' motorbike. Riding pillion, Brown spotted a bus destined for somewhere dramatic. Cemetery Gates. The name fitted perfectly with *Cenotaph Corner* and *Ivy Sepulchre* on either side of the new line. They graded it E1 5b – by far not the hardest in the country, that being *Demon Rib*, E3 5c, established two years previously at Black Rocks in Derbyshire.[2] But the *Rib* was a single pitch of eighteen metres; in comparison, the three exposed pitches of *Cemetery Gates* came as a psychological breakthrough. The route represented a new standard in British rock climbing and the two lads, Brown and Whillans, became its new, unlikely heroes.

* * *

At the turn of the century, British climbing was still dominated by the Oxbridge graduate type. Some of them, like Walter Parry Haskett Smith, took up an interest in home crags, but most still looked towards the Alps. In 1913, a lawyer by the name of John Laycock published *Some Shorter Climbs*, detailing routes done on gritstone, but the Great War soon put an end to the development.

Despite the war and the onslaught on the continent, the living conditions of the British working class were steadily improving. While in the early days of the Industrial Revolution there were no restrictions to work hours and no health and safety regulations, the second half of the nineteenth century brought about a class consciousness which empowered working people to demand change. Trade unions were decriminalised, working hours were cut and child labour was increasingly under scrutiny. Soon, even among the members of the poorest class, there were those who could concern themselves with more than just day-to-day survival. The development of public transport allowed them to seek solace outside of city bounds: Sunday visits to the moors of northern England and the glens of Scotland offered a soothing souvenir of what was lost in the process of industrialisation.

1900 saw the creation of 'the first Sunday workers' rambling club in the North of England', the Clarion Ramblers, named after a prominent socialist paper. The club put an emphasis on both the physical and mental benefits of time spent outdoors, and similar organisations sprang up across the country, but the ramblers soon happened upon an obstacle. Access to uncultivated land had been steadily curtailed by landowners, and the moorlands, previously freely enjoyed by the middle classes, were being fenced off to protect the upper-class hunting grounds from unwanted intrusion. The working men's societies picked up the fight to defend the traditional rights of way, culminating in the Mass Trespass of Kinder Scout, an organised protest on the highest moorland plateau in England. Despite persecution, tireless campaigning finally led to upholding the right to roam and to the creation of the first national park in 1951.

The wind of change had already been perceptible with the election of the first Labour government in 1924, but soon the financial crisis left many workers in the industrial cities without jobs or anything to do. Despite endemic poverty, there was no stopping the proletarian outdoor movement. Many working-class and student organisations began to provide budget accommodation in countryside hostels and bothies, offering shelter to those who couldn't afford traditional, expensive lodgings. From the 1930s, workers were able to leave the city not only during holidays but also at the weekends, although most could only escape after knocking off at midday on Saturday.

On the continent, some of the greatest alpinists of the early twentieth century hailed from the working class, but the British climbing establishment, centred around the Alpine Club, viewed their achievements with a jaundiced eye, suspecting them of merely hauling from one piton to another. The AC members were still consumed by the conversation about guideless versus unguided climbing, tangled in the web of conventions and tradition, while the working-class newcomers, free of such concerns, not only caught up with them but spearheaded rock climbing's development.

It wasn't until after World War II that the proletarian climbing revolution came into full swing. Working hours continued to fall, wages rose and healthcare was accessible to more than half of the population. Nutrition was significantly improved and the previously malnourished workers suddenly had excess energy to burn outside of factories and construction sites. Cars and motorbikes were about to further revolutionise everyday travel. The time had come for climbers from the lower classes to leave their mark on the sport. The social and technological changes laid out a path for a revolution. All it needed was the individuals who could embody it.

*	*	*

During the Industrial Revolution, the Manchester suburb of Ardwick 'epitomised the appalling social conditions and brutal struggle for existence forced upon wide layers of the working class'.[3] In 1930, the back-to-back terraced houses were still there, and the nearby train line provided a soundscape for the slum where Joe Brown was born as the seventh child in his family. He was still in a cot when his father died from complications following a work accident. To make ends meet, his mother took in laundry.

Brown attended school but, like many future climbers, didn't enjoy the organised games and sports that other children played. He joined the Scouts and was promptly kicked out for his unseemly attitude to church. Still, by his twelfth birthday, he had learned that his biggest interest was exploring the countryside. Studying in the classroom didn't take his fancy, so he wasn't sad when both of the schools he attended were destroyed in the Blitz. He left formal education as soon as possible and, at fifteen, became a plumber's apprentice, and later a general builder.

The influential handbook by Colin Kirkus – one of the few pre-war, working-class pioneers – was Joe's introduction to the idea of roped climbing. He promptly appropriated a discarded sash cord, thin and bleached from hanging laundry, and headed for the gritstone edges of Kinder Scout. Despite religiously studying Kirkus' advice, he failed to understand the principles of belaying and a sympathetic climber had to correct him. Looking at the white cord, he asked if it was one of the new, nylon ropes. Brown had no idea what the stranger meant.

Despite humble beginnings, by the end of the decade the still teenage Brown was not only the best climber in his circle of friends, but also unwittingly nearing the very limits of what was considered possible. It was 1948 when he was ready to make his first attempt at *Cenotaph Corner*.

Running belays were increasingly in use in the UK – hammering in a peg or wedging a chockstone into a recess in rock allowed for clipping the rope through, providing a point of protection for the leader. Pebbles of the right size were often carried under a hat, and carabiners were clipped into loops of copper wire stashed in a pocket.

Unburdened by the Alpine Club's disdain for pitons, on his first attempt on the *Corner* Brown decided to place pegs every six metres or so. Halfway up the route, he put his mason's hammer between his teeth to free up his hands. Forgetfully opening his mouth, he sent the tool plummeting straight down the vertical route. The hammer struck his belayer squarely on the head.

Brown devised an emergency system to lower himself down and assess the severity of the situation. Miraculously, despite blood dripping down his face, his belayer was not only alive but sound, demanding that Brown go back up to 'do this bloody thing'. And so Brown did, but six metres from the end of the route, he looked up to see that the difficulties didn't relent for another three metres or so. Unfortunately, he was out of pegs. In a time when ropes still couldn't hold big falls, there was no other option but to waste his belayer's sacrifice and bail for the day. *Cenotaph Corner* had to wait another four years.

The hiatus was in part necessitated by Brown's military service, in part by the high cost of trips to Wales. Instead, Brown honed his skills on the gritstone outcrops closer to home, amassing an impressive list of routes and an increasing notoriety within the working men's climbing community.

On a sunny Sunday afternoon at the Roaches, a gritstone crag in the Staffordshire Peak District, he was engaged with a hard, new route. Under a bulging buttress, a small crowd of onlookers gathered, aware that they were witnessing a first ascent. Among them was a short but stocky teenager by the name of Don Whillans. He asked around who the climber was, and got a lot of sideways glances for not recognising Brown's slender figure.

Whillans had travelled to the Peak District the day before, straight after his half-day of Saturday work. Like Brown, he was escaping city life and had organically graduated from rambling to climbing without much external guidance. Unlike Brown, he was from a better economic background, his mother a machinist and father a clerk in an upmarket grocery store, but he hailed from Salford, which at the time was one of the worst slums in Western Europe.[4]

In 1951, Whillans was an unknown seventeen-year-old lad, different from others perhaps due to his physical prowess, an ability to make sound decisions on rock and a degree of cockiness which, paired with heavy fists, earned him a reputation as a fierce fighter. Presently, he was watching Brown reach an anchor and shout to his belayer to follow but, to the crowd's dismay, the second failed to overcome the crux and had to be lowered. With little hesitation, Whillans – three years younger than Brown and without much track record to prove that he could follow somebody of Brown's ability – shouted up to ask if he could have a go and promptly tied into the vacant rope. In no time he reached Brown at the belay, astonishing the latter and marking the beginning of one of the most – if not the most – legendary partnerships in British rock climbing.

'I looked at his hands,' wrote Whillans, recollecting that first encounter, 'and noticed the wide palms and thick fingers covered with hard skin and deep cracks. That's what comes from mucking about with cement and plaster. He was definitely not a bank clerk.'

This first route they climbed together was named *Matinee*, HVS 5c, and, although the standards have changed dramatically, seven decades later it remains a popular testpiece for gritstone initiates who wield much more advanced gear than Whillans and Brown, making it not only easier but, most of all, much safer. The contemporary topo description, in keeping with the slightly esoteric character of British climbing, details the classic as follows:

> 'The lower crack is almost always damp and usually smelly. Ignore this fact and jam up it to a (possible) stance on the giant flake. The continuation is awkward, especially the fist-grinding belly-flop into the wider finishing section.'[5]

Matinee is not the only route in the Peak District to warrant being described as character-building. The capricious English weather certainly doesn't help gritstone's reputation as one of the 'unkindest of rocks, brutally steep, abrasive, studded all over with razor crystals'.[6]

> 'The climbs are short and steep; characteristically they deal out inordinately large quantities of pain and fear. Torn hands, scraped

knees, strained arms and a dry throat are all in a gritstoner's day: the cracks in particular are armed with vicious teeth. [...] Rounded holds, rough bulging cracks, and an overbearing angle; you just have to get used to them.'

And:

'There is a cultist – and it might also be said a northern chauvinist [...] – aspect to gritstone climbing. People love it with a religious fervour, or leave it strictly alone. It's not a rock for dabblers; it demands effort and commitment from its devotees.'[7]

These points can hardly be argued with; called by its worshippers 'God's own rock', gritstone has a merciless tendency to wear climbers' fingers raw. In the cult coffee-table book *Hard Rock,* describing the best of British routes, Jim Perrin goes as far as saying that 'the keynote of gritstone climbing is aggression'.[8] On the contrary, gritstone masters, like Brown, Whillans and many after them have an uncanny ability to float up this dark rock with seemingly not much effort but grace, flowing with its curvy angles, working with – not against – its rough texture and bulges. These are often the climbers who are not enduring but enjoying everything that comes with gritstone climbing, including even the most fickle of English weather.

* * *

Centred around Brown and Whillans, the working-class climbers formed Rock and Ice, a club which soon gained notoriety for its members' achievements. Unlike established, middle-class climbing organisations, Rock and Ice did not concern itself much with socialising or elegant dinners but focused on the practicalities of making climbing happen. The members budgeted their trips together, shared rides and searched for free or cheap accommodation in barns, bothies and hostels.

Their weekly wages averaged around £7 a week, amounting roughly to the buying power of £250 in 2020. As it was not enough to venture far from home, most climbed close to Manchester. They felt a sharp contrast between themselves and the Oxbridge types whom they sometimes encountered on the outcrops and ridiculed mercilessly, shouting in exaggerated accents: 'Raighto, I've got a bloody belay now, Cecil. Doo come hup!' But there was one clear similarity between the two groups: the desire to progress from outcrops to the mountains – although according to Whillans, most of his working-class friends didn't see how they could ever afford it. He and Brown didn't perceive such limitations. They were not only more determined but also distinguished by their ability, and opportunities soon came their way. Both went on to climb in the Alps, and later in the Himalaya, with Whillans forming another formidable partnership, this time with Britain's favourite mountaineer, Chris Bonington.

Brown and Whillans were the first working-class climbers to catch the attention not only of the wider climbing community but also the national press. Both stood only five foot four and the *Sunday Express* hailed them as 'Manchester's climbing pygmies', a description only slightly more ridiculous than that of 'the vertical beatniks' as per a 2005 *Guardian* article.[9] Brown, with his laughing eyes and a wide smile full of big teeth, quickly became the media's darling, earning yet another nickname: The Human Fly.

When in 1955 he stood on the summit of Kangchenjunga, Brown gained the respect of the climbing establishment, leaving Whillans – the blunter and more rough around the edges of the duo – behind. Their partnership was over. In 1960, Brown led one of his most impressive first ascents on rock to date: *Vector*, E2 5c. Perhaps to prove a point, Whillans quickly repeated it, as did a pack of new climbers coming into the mix. They were hot on Brown's heels, but he was not one to climb for the laurels, or to beat others – he just wanted to do it.

In 1967, he reclimbed *Vector* for a TV broadcast. One of his contemporaries remembered the film:

> 'Standing on minute footholds, Joe puffed a cigarette and carried on a conversation with the commentator below through a tiny microphone hung round his neck [...]. Completely relaxed, he rested in a position where most other climbers would barely have been able to stay on the rock [...]. Why should he smoke a cigarette? Force of habit? Perhaps, but I think not. Despite his modesty [...] Joe is only human. He knows his worth and place in British climbing history [...]. Smoking a cigarette in a position where others can barely stay in contact is part of the role.'[10]

Shortly after that, while Brown was exploring the newly discovered sea cliffs of Gogarth, soon to become one of the best British climbing venues, Whillans spent most of his time in the pub. He was still invited on a few expeditions – most notably in 1970 when he summited Annapurna – but his reputation as a difficult man and his declining fitness meant he was rapidly becoming a *persona non grata*. (To his credit, it has to be said that many of his companions owed their lives to his steady head in the mountains.) His involvement in the climbing community was mostly limited to hanging out at the crag with his mates of old, and giving lectures to audiences who loved him precisely for being the B-team hero, with his huge belly, broad Lancashire accent and a penchant for getting into trouble with the law.

His legendary status was solidified by his premature death. Most enduring climbing heroes die young pursuing their craft and something similar can be said of Whillans: he died in his sleep, of an extensive heart attack caused by a lifetime of alcohol and cigarettes.

He was a man of many faces, and privately Joe Brown remembered him as the best climbing partner he'd ever had but also 'an absolute bastard'.[11] On the ground, their friendship might have often been strained, but their partnership on rock was nothing short of perfection.

Unlike Whillans, Brown remained fit into his late years. After pioneering many of the hardest ascents around the country, he passed on the torch to the next generation, which benefitted not only from the technological advances in gear, but from the biggest innovation that British climbing has ever seen: physical training. Nonetheless, Brown continued to enjoy the rock until old age, opened a chain of outdoor shops and passed away in 2020, aged eighty-nine, a father of two and grandfather to four, in his Llanberis house.

* * *

One windy Saturday, on a weekend trip to the Peak District, I decided to measure up to the *File*, perhaps the most straightforward of Whillans' legacy crack routes on grit. They require a climber to jam, a technique which involves wedging a limb into a crack to almost passively hang from it – painful and awkward if done by the uninitiated but oddly graceful and effortless when executed by a master.

It had been raining for days and nearly every square inch of gritstone was soaked, so, unaccustomed to climbing in bad conditions, my partner Liz and I chose the exposed outcrop of Higgar Tor, where we hoped to find dry holds. As I tied into the rope to lead the nine-metre-tall VS 4c, the crag was lashed by a bitterly cold wind. It was my first foray into crack climbing but the grade was, at least in theory, far easier than any boulder I could climb indoors.

My confidence began to wane as I double-checked the gear on my harness – luxuries that Whillans hadn't even dreamed of when he opened the route.[12] In the 1950s, he still climbed with the rope tied around his waist, risking heavy bruising – or worse – in the event of a fall.

I chalked up, tightened my helmet and waited for my belayer's sacramental words.

'Climb when ready.'

'Climbing,' I responded gravely and wedged my hands into the consistent, gently overhanging crack, placing the sticky soles of my shoes on the left of it, on ledges which appeared slopey and treacherous but could actually provide very secure footing even for an average outdoor climber.

'C'mon, Zof, you're doing great!' Liz encouraged me over the howling wind as I searched the harness for the right piece of gear. I chose a big, light-blue 'walnut' and wedged it deep into the crack. It took an excruciatingly long time to find the right position for it, with my right hand all the while wedged above, getting minced by the rough rock as I worked the walnut in. A merciless gust of wind hit the outcrop, squeezing tears out of my eyes and making my teeth chatter despite being all sweaty under the many layers of clothing. My calves were sore, my whole body contorted into a harrowing, cramp-inducing position. My inexpertly placed feet were still no higher than two metres off the deck but, cold and stiff, I was terrified of the fall on to the uneven ground below.

Finally, the walnut sat well and I clipped the rope through its quickdraw. I looked up to see the cruel crack hanging over me, more exposed to the wind with every extra metre of height. Now not only my calves but my whole body was trembling with effort and fear.

'Take,' I pleaded, and Liz immediately pulled the rope through her belay device so I could rest in my harness, safely clipped to the walnut but distrusting its capacity to hold me despite my best efforts to make it secure. Gently, I pulled my palm out of the crack and clasped both my hands between my thighs. 'I can't do it, Liz, I just can't. Lower me.'

Uncoordinatedly, I sat on the ground and tried pulling my climbing shoes off. Liz offered to untie my figure of eight, as the pain in my fingers was rapidly growing much worse than in my toes. I pulled my wellies over my hands and keeled over.

The first thing I learned that day was never to go to Higgar Tor on cold, windy days. The second was why ice climbers refer to hot aches as the 'screaming barfies'.

CHAPTER 12
STEEL CITY, 2015

'I climb just as hard as anyone. I just do it on easier routes.'
Unknown

I graduated in autumn 2014 and suddenly there was nothing more to life than a boring PR job and the occasional visit to Mile End Climbing Wall. On top of that, an unregistered and uninsured car drove into me at a junction, catapulting me into the air, wrecking my bicycle and that sense of indestructibility which is absolutely necessary for riding in London. It was high time for me to leave, and my work in a PR agency could easily be done remotely. To my surprise, the bosses agreed.

I packed my bags, gave up my room and was all set to move to Sheffield, 'the UK's leading destination for people seeking outdoor adventure' as per the city's website. Not owning a car, the only option was to wait for Andy to drive me and my tattered luggage up north, and deposit me on a friend's couch while I looked for something of my own.

Waiting for Andy to get time off work, I spent a few days at his place. He shared a house with Alice, an American colleague from the climbing wall who often offended his delicate English sensibilities by not uttering a word *for the whole morning*.

In Andy's dusty room, wonky shelves leant precariously on either side of the bed, filled with photographic prints, negatives, notes and books. One night, I scoured the little library while he edited photos. My attention was caught by a book with a vintage image of a teenage boy on the cover. It could have been taken in the 1970s, and the boy's dark, intense eyes glowed brightly in a pretty face. It was hard to guess his emotions and the odd gaze transfixed me. A bunch of ropes and gear wrapped around the boy's body was a telltale sign of a climbing book and, before I knew it, I had read it from cover to cover.

It was an honest, somehow both bare-bones and poetic account of a life of passion for rock. Despite incredible climbing achievements and the book's title, *Full of Myself*, the author didn't manage – or perhaps didn't try – to obscure his struggles with life. I felt a strange affinity with the dark-eyed boy, one which I learned to name a few years later: autism spectrum disorder.

Set in the UK, the story only heightened my appetite for British rock. Finally, we set off for Sheffield where we spent a couple of days climbing. Then Andy drove back to London, promising to visit soon. I hated to see him go.

By then a few friends had already moved north and Sadie was the one who let me crash on her floor while I searched for somewhere to live. A former National Team member for competition climbing and a high-school art teacher, she impresséd me in every possible way.

Drifting off to sleep on her lounge floor, I dreamed of the incomprehensible rock of the Peak District, and of my fingers being tough enough to actually stand up to it. (Of course, Sadie excelled on gritstone.) I couldn't wait to be chewed up and spat out by 'God's own rock'; to become a hardy British cragsman, toughened by the weather, fearless, downing a pint at the pub after a day full of adventures. I felt like I was standing on the cusp of something new and great for myself, and that sensation barely allowed me to sleep.

It was late autumn and the weather was terrible, with rain blowing horizontally in the mad wind. I had a room viewing arranged for the evening, and the landlord mercifully offered to pick me up. The road in front of Sadie's house was one of those impossibly steep Sheffield alleys, and sitting in the little car among darkness and rain, I half expected us to slide backwards. Everything up north seemed to be about defying gravity.

The landlord introduced himself as Joe. He was in his fifties and had a very 'climbey' air about him – I immediately thought he might have been one of those guys whom I wanted to become. I asked him questions about the house and the guys who lived there already. I'd have only one flatmate and Joe said that he was into clay pottery. The description seemed somewhat odd and contrived, as if he wanted to hide something from me, so I asked if the guy was a climber (yes), so I asked Joe for his name.

'We might have friends in common on Facebook, or something like that,' I explained, but Joe said it was unlikely. I pressed some more.

'His name is Johnny Dawes.'

The name rang a bell and for a second my brain searched for the right box. Then a photo of a teenage boy with a dark, intense gaze floated to the surface.

'Johnny Dawes, the writer?' I exclaimed excitedly and Joe gave me a sideways look. At that point I knew nothing about both the near-cult and spiteful gossip surrounding Johnny Dawes the climber, only the boy from the book cover and the man from its pages. Riding through Sheffield in the tiny car, rain pounding on the windscreen, I wondered if Johnny Dawes the writer would be as I imagined.

Joe parked the car on one of the Steel City's run-down streets and we walked through a metal gate with a selection of rusty pitons serving as a closing counterweight. As is customary in these parts, the entrance was at the back and the narrow passage that led there was lined with climbing holds. I fell in love with the place even before we entered a dark, smelly kitchen. Somehow it managed to be both stuffy and cold in there, but it was exactly what I had wished for: the house where I'd become the climber that I wanted to be, far from London's urgency, pretence and noise.

We walked past the kitchen into the front room with a small gas fire and a dilapidated sofa in red plush. Stretched out on it was a middle-aged man with a bag of crisps on his belly, a PlayStation controller in his hands and a screen in front of him. He was racing Formula 1 cars.

Johnny sprang to his feet, crumbs flying everywhere, and we were introduced. He was intense, a little hyper, slightly overweight but quick-moving. We shook hands and Joe showed me upstairs to the room I could rent. It was much bigger than the one I had in London and there was a nice double bed with an almost new mattress, but the walk-in wardrobe stank and was full of mouse droppings. I didn't care.

We returned downstairs and Joe and Johnny seemed a bit embarrassed, perhaps about the state of the house, or more likely about being two ageing men in front of a woman who could easily be their daughter. They couldn't know I was smitten with the stinky house and with both of them, youthful despite their age, bright-eyed and so *climbey*. They started chatting away as if I wasn't there at all.

'How's the foot?' asked Joe, a physiotherapist, as it turned out. Johnny started balancing barefoot on one leg in a wobbly yoga-like position, supposedly showing that it had been getting better.

'Have you injured it?' I asked, trying to make conversation instead of just standing awkwardly.

'Fell off at Stanage. An open fracture,' Johnny said, waving it off as if it were a common occurrence. I imagined him soloing, then falling without a rope to the wet grass under Stanage Edge. I was still processing that image as he kept balancing and leaping on the visibly swollen leg.

Not to seem like a keener, I went upstairs again to have another look. The room was as run-down as a few minutes before, and the mouse shit was still there. When I came down, Johnny was back on his sofa and Joe was sitting in one of the ancient armchairs in front of the gas fire, watching him race.

'Ehm, I'd like to take it, I guess,' I mumbled and, before I knew it, Johnny passed me a set of keys.

* * *

'Johnny Dawes? Are you *kidding* me?' Sadie's eyebrows were high up and her mouth was half open. I nodded.

'That's incredible,' said her boyfriend, as we sat that night to dinner in Sadie's apartment. They both found the news of my new flatmate inordinately amusing – my first glimpse into Johnny's reputation within the British climbing community. Everybody had something to say and everybody had an opinion, from devotional admiration to vindictive gossip. After reading his book, I could imagine him as a divisive character – not through any fault of his own but because the world usually has trouble accepting those who dare to be different, or simply don't have the ability to conform.

Having lived in Sheffield for a few years, Sadie also had a story to share about Johnny, and it involved the annual Christmas rave at the Climbing Works climbing wall. Apparently, even if he didn't climb as hard as he used to, Johnny still knew how to party.

'Have you seen the movie?' asked Sadie.

'What movie?' Both she and her boyfriend looked at me as if I were a total philistine.

'Oh, man! I've got the DVD. Check it out after we've eaten.'

* * *

It was a fine March morning when Liz parked her car in front of our house and let herself in. I quickly stuffed the last bits of gear into my backpack as she used the bathroom. Liz had a real job in London and I had no idea how she managed to climb as much as she did while holding on to it. In winter, she was known to drive to Scotland on a Friday after work, do two days of ice climbing and drive back ten hours through the night to make it to the office on a Monday morning. Mercifully, it was spring. We were heading to Wales.

'Are you coming or not?' I shouted upstairs towards the attic room. Johnny's muffled answer was unintelligible.

'WHAT??'

'I'll see you LATER!'

'Seems Johnny's not coming,' I said in the kitchen as Liz and I grabbed a few bits from the fridge and headed towards the car. I put my backpack in the boot and my huge down sleeping bag next to it. One very long night of shivering in the Climbers' Club hut a couple of months earlier was more than enough.

'WAIT!' The front room window opened and Johnny's head peeked out. Less than a minute later he hurried past the disused climbing holds in the outside passage, slammed the metal gate open (the pitons did their job and it closed shut behind him) and crawled on to the back seat.

'Let's go! Ha-haaaa!' His eyes were shining a little madly. Liz and I both looked at him, then shrugged our shoulders and she started the car. The three hours between Sheffield and the west coast passed quickly, taking in the British countryside. Johnny told us his driving stories, how you could take this turn or that, and what cars he had driven in the past. Whatever he was passionate about would light him up from the inside, and even cars – a subject matter I cared very little for – would seem interesting.

We got to Gogarth reasonably early, but by the time Liz and I had organised our gear (with Johnny looking at us as if we were circus freaks) and found the right abseil spot, the tide was in. He was psyched to be out, but couldn't care less about what routes we'd climb. It was only my second time at the cliff so we abseiled in for the mellow *Imitator*, VS 4c. Going down a sea cliff of forty-five metres, with nothing but water as far as the eye can see on one side of you, and nothing but the vertical dark rock on the other, is like entering a different realm. Reality falls behind and time changes its meaning, with the rhythm of life dictated not by mundane mealtimes or work, but solely by the length of each pitch, a surprisingly complicated equation calculated with the difficulty of the route, the proficiency of the climber and the weather conditions.

It was windy, with not a cloud in sight, and the dark turquoise sea surged gently below us, only a slight pattern of white foam cresting the ever-changing waves. Babbling and goofing, we built a belay and Liz set off to lead the first pitch. After a whole week in the office, hours in the car and a couple of months off outdoor climbing, she placed her gear excruciatingly slowly, making me regret not bringing hiking shoes for the belay. As I stood on a narrow ledge, my climbing boots felt like a torture device – a result of the common mistake of taking a tight indoor pair for a trad outing.

Meanwhile, Johnny unclipped from the belay and soloed sideways along the cliff, comfortable as if he were back on his plush sofa, chatting so long as we were within earshot. For a moment, I envied him the freedom, but my head spun with vertigo as soon as I imagined not being tied to a rope. Thank God for the rope.

'You're doing great, Liz!' I shouted upwards over the roar of the waves. 'Take all the time you need!'

'I'm bloody slow!' she shouted back, grunting, and I quietly agreed, making sure she couldn't hear me. Johnny gave me a wide, amused grin from his superior position of freedom.

'Off belay!' Liz finally finished her pitch. 'Climb when ready!'

I dismantled our stance and followed her lead, taking my sweet time dislodging all of Liz's gear with the untrained strokes of my nut key. Halfway up, an alloy offset did not want to come out at all. I tapped at it from the bottom and the top, and pulled from every angle for a good ten minutes. 'And this … is why … bouldering … is better,' I muttered to myself as the offending piece finally dislodged and I nearly dropped it in the sea. A wide-winged seagull glided past, her squawk full of mockery.

When we topped out, it was already too late to test our luck and abseil in for another route, so we walked back to the car over the grassy plain above the cliff. The sun was casting long shadows in the golden air, and Johnny lagged behind us, going through all the contacts in his phone. He then caught up with us and announced that we were off to a party.

The Heights in Llanberis is a traditional pub and inn, a neat stone house with white windows and a porch sheltering the entrance. Surrounded by a low stone wall, it is elegantly framed by tall pine trees in the front and Snowdon in the background. Arriving well after the sun had gone down, I couldn't see much apart from a chain of multicoloured light bulbs on the building. The beat pumping from the inside made the car windows tremble and smokers came in and out of the front door. Johnny jumped out of the car and headed for the entrance with a spring in his step like I'd never seen in him before. Feeling a little intimidated, Liz and I followed.

A thick, colourful crowd tightly filled the pub, with every other person looking like a climber, and the rest like hippie artists. Johnny shook hands with a never-ending stream of friends and acquaintances, hugged and patted innumerous backs. He and Liz weaved their way to the bar and I gestured to the nearest table, where I hoped for deliverance. I sat down, trying to make myself as unnoticeable as possible, but a grinning type on the other side of the table waved at me and asked how it was going.

'Good, thanks.'

'So, whaddya doin' in Llanberis?' He was hell-bent on including me in the conversation going on at the table, but a few months of living in relative isolation from anybody but Johnny, and a day spent among the serenity of Gogarth, filled me with enough disregard for societal norms not to follow along. I took a deep breath and, trying to be as polite as possible, informed him I didn't like talking to strangers.

'No probs!' he shouted over the music and, without changing his friendly expression, passed me one of the pints that were lined up in the middle of the table. I gave him a tight smile and saluted with the glass. To my great surprise, nobody batted an eyelid. I was in heaven. I relaxed on to my chair and slurped the cold ale, watching, chilling, letting the beat fill me and beginning to move with it.

Liz appeared carrying a pint of Guinness for me and I guessed the polite thing to do was to set it in the middle of the table.

'I'm going to dance!' she shouted. 'You alright?'

'Never better! I'll join you later!'

I finished my ale, nodded at the people around the table and headed for the bar to get a gin and tonic. By the time I was clutching the cold glass, there were no seats left, so I squeezed through the crowd of colourful down jackets to the exit. The night was clear and the air outside was nipping cold, filled with the smell of tobacco, weed and stale beer. I sat on the stairs, sipping the G&T and rocking to the muffled tunes from the inside. There was a little circle of smokers right next to me and a kind soul offered me a drag of their spliff. With my drink running dry, I headed back inside towards the dance floor, where I found Johnny and Liz and everybody else.

I don't know how long we danced for but my heart was racing, my sweaty face burned and my head was clear again. I thought about climbing the next day and screamed into Liz's ear that it was time to go. She gestured towards Johnny, he replied with a gesture and she shouted back to me: 'Two more songs!'

Two more was fine. We danced again but I wasn't fully there any more, a part of me thinking of my berth at the Climbers' Club cottage and another part thinking of the cliffs of tomorrow. I didn't want to waste the day to sleepiness, but when I motioned to the guys to get going, they wanted two more again. Then one more. It felt like forever.

Finally, Liz was done. It was well past one and I was getting groggy. Johnny shouted to wait for him outside and that he'd be there in a moment.

We slipped out of the pumping, sweaty inside into the cold, still night. I breathed in the crisp air and looked towards the sky with all the stars out. 'Wow.'

'I know ... '

'Are you okay to drive, Liz?'

She said that she had had less than two pints and that she had sweated it all out, and that it was all fine. I looked forward to the few minutes of driving towards Llanberis Pass where the Climbers' Club cottage perched right opposite Dinas Cromlech. Liz offered to search for Johnny and disappeared inside. After a moment, he came out. He'd just met a friend and needed five more minutes.

'Fine. Just find Liz, she went in to search for you.'

They were both gone for another quarter of an hour. Then Liz came out and said she hadn't found Johnny. I tried calling him. Nothing. It was my turn to go in, but after ten minutes of wiggling through the crowd I gave up. The lights and the beat, intoxicating an hour ago, were now giving me a wretched headache. I went out again and told Liz that Johnny was nowhere to be found. Way more mellow than me, even Liz was getting annoyed by now. Leaning on the bonnet of her car, we were also starting to shiver, but decided not to get in just in case Johnny couldn't see us.

Finally, he stumbled out of the pub and we shouted from across the car park to get his attention.

'I wanna stay another half an hour,' he replied, swaying, grinning, sweating.

'No way, let's go,' I said in a tone that usually crumbles all resistance.

'I'm not going,' he said flatly, clearly impervious to my powers of persuasion. We were a good twenty metres from him, so everybody in front of the pub could hear us.

'What the hell, we've waited for you for over an hour. It's nearly three o'clock in the morning!' I was feeling a surge of anger that usually overcomes me when something stands between me and a good night's sleep. I could see Johnny was trying to figure something out and after a tense break he announced he was going to stay.

'Where the fuck you gonna sleep?'

He didn't know. Had he said it two hours ago, I'd be long wrapped in my sleeping bag.

'Are you kidding me? Get in the car and let's go.' I looked to Liz for support but it seemed that she was going to stay neutral.

'Get in, Johnny!' I repeated, this time shouting, but that proved too much.

'Do you think I'm a fucking child?!'

'I think exactly that! Get in the bloody car!'

'FUCK YOU!' He was fuming, a look of total madness on his face. Over the few months we had shared a house, he had never treated me that way and for a brief moment I was shocked. The moment was gone in a heartbeat.

'Fuck *you*, Johnny!'

We repeated the eloquent exchange at least three times before Liz packed me into the front seat, slammed the door behind me and we were off towards the Pass.

'Where is he gonna sleep?' I broke the moment of silence.

'He'll be fine. Don't worry.'

I knew she was right but still couldn't settle.

'Well, I worry about finding him. I'm not spending half of my day tomorrow searching for the idiot. We're gonna go climbing and it's his business to find us.'

'He will. We'll climb. Don't worry,' said Liz, ever the Buddha. I huffed and puffed for another minute or so, but finally reclined the seat and gave in to the rocking of the car.

We woke up at the Climbers' Club hut to the screaming of children and the barking of dogs. It was well past eight and the hut was busy with some finishing their breakfast and others already heading out to the crags. Those with small children were taking a more leisurely approach, taking another cup of coffee in the parlour or on the outside bench under the morning sun. Two huge Irish wolfhounds lounged on the carpet in front of the fireplace, oblivious to everything that was going on.

I clutched my own coffee and admired the shelves filled with old guidebooks, and the ancient climbing gear which adorned the parlour. Liz reminded me to leave my fee ('£10 per night for non-members;

must be accompanied by a member') in the float box, and register my stay in the guest book with yellowed pages. Apart from that, only by virtue of being Liz's friend, I was treated as if I had belonged in the hut my whole life.

After breakfast, we once again drove to Llanberis and headed for the slate quarries. From the end of the eighteenth century, slate – a dark grey rock, sleek and easily blasted into sheets – was in high demand and, split into tiles, it would end up on roofs across the UK and the rest of Europe. Sourcing it was a difficult and dangerous job, but it became the lynchpin of Welsh industry. The Dinorwig quarry in Llanberis was the second biggest in the world, at its peak employing 3,000 men, but the wages were low and the quarrymen worked long hours, often through rain and snow, their hands cramping on ice-covered tools. They protected themselves with ropes, but many lost their lives to rockfall.

By the 1960s, the once-booming industry was in sharp decline and there were only 350 men employed in Dinorwig. Dwindling demand finally dried up completely in August 1969 and the Llanberis quarry was closed without warning. The quarrymen's way of life was over. What endured was the otherworldly scenery: multi-levelled cliffs, amphitheatres and tunnels blasted in the rock by gunpowder, exposing the gut of the mountain. Slate debris, with some pieces bigger than cars, mounted precariously into steep slopes, with rusting industrial machinery scattered about. Pools of dark, still water were added to the landscape when an unsuccessful hydroelectricity development flooded some of the quarry holes. The resulting landscape is striking and weird, both an industrial cemetery and a fantasy lost world.

Only two years after the workers and machinery of Dinorwig stopped forever, Manchester climber Joe Brown went in with a keen eye for the smooth, nearly black rock. The result was his *Opening Gambit*, the first slate route ever, now described in guidebooks as 'geologically lively', meaning that bits of it tend to fall off, frequently changing both the line and the grade. A decade after Brown's first venture, in 1981, the first of the enduring slate classics was born with Stevie Hastings' *Comes the Dervish*, E3 5c, a beautiful splitter crack shooting vertically for forty metres. Very different from the few quarry routes done before, it added a high level of technical difficulty to the adventurous nature of climbing on slate. The eyes of ambitious climbers turned to the smooth rock, which, apart from its unique style, has one great advantage over any other rock: in Wales, which gets 270 rainy days per year, sleek-like-glass slate dries faster than anything else.

Liz, being much more experienced than me, chose my route for the day: the well-protected crack of *Bela Lugosi is Dead*, E1 5b, in the Rainbow Slab sector, but first we wandered around playing climbing tourism: scouting the lines that we might do one day and those which we'd never dare to try. I had seen the *Dervish* on our previous trip (the first category), so this time we went to Twll Mawr to look at some of Johnny's routes (the second). In 1987 he put up *Coeur de Lion*, leading through a seemingly blank wall which he graded E6 7a. It had to wait for the first repeat for twenty-eight years. James McHaffie and Pete Robins changed the grade to E8 and speculated that perhaps Johnny's grade was just a mean joke. I gaped at the route with Liz, utterly amazed that it was actually climbable. And to the right of it was the famous *Quarryman*, another one of Johnny's, with the iconic full-body stemming pitch which at one point has the climber put both hands on the left wall and both feet on the right, the body stretched out horizontally.

'Feel like giving it a go?' Liz taunted, and we turned back towards our sector, leaving the grand amphitheatre of Twll Mawr behind.

Throughout the day, I wondered how likely it was that we'd be waiting for Johnny until late again, and how likely Liz was to strand him in Wales. A part of me thought it would serve him right, but we ended up picking him up in front of Pete's Eats – no drama this time – where he was recovering from the night before.[1] Johnny got in the front, fastened his seat belt and immediately started chatting to Liz but ignored me completely. We played the silent treatment game until we were back in the Peak and finally got over ourselves as Liz was racing through the curves of the Snake Pass again.

She parked in front of our pitoned gate and stepped in for a coffee to fuel the second stretch of her drive to London. I looked in the fridge and realised it was empty. The previous week Johnny had made a great green curry with okra, and all of our veggies went in. He had brought the recipe back from a 1993 expedition to the Himalaya. The team didn't make it to their intended summit and Johnny took a 200-metre fall, but they all survived, and he came home with the curry recipe, and so the history of British climbing came to have a bearing on my menu.

I joined Liz at our kitchen table and cracked open a beer. Johnny opened our small freezer and examined it critically.

'Any luck?' I asked hopefully.

'Fish fingers.' He pulled the half-full box out. 'Find us some baked beans, will you?'

* * *

In the end, I never got to understand the Peak District's gritstone. I got on a tiny bit better in Wales, but grit did not seem to agree with me and it wasn't for the lack of trying. One time I had to downclimb from the top of *Mutiny Crack* because the wind was so strong that every time I peeked my head over the edge of the crag, I felt like it would rip me off the rock. My bouldering pad blew away from underneath me, and just as I was about to give in to panic, a random climber appeared from nowhere and pinned it down for me.

I climbed mostly by myself, taking the 272 bus to Fox House Inn and walking into Burbage or Millstone. I was usually done long after the last bus home and hitchhiked on the A625, almost always immediately getting picked up by some climbers. Occasionally, I would manage to convince Johnny to drive us out in his ancient Toyota Starlet.

One of my projects was a six-metre arête called *Technical Master*, a John Allen masterpiece first climbed in 1954. At 6b+, three decades later it presented no challenge for Johnny. In *Stone Monkey*, the movie that Sadie showed me on my second night in Sheffield, Johnny cruises it in trainers and with no bouldering pad, moving from one hold to another in his signature, fluid style.

Fast forward another thirty years, having spent four afternoons completely defeated by the climb, I was beginning to grasp Johnny's talent. Standing under the block together, I was feeling a little sad for my clearly less talented self, and mumbled that I should have done it already.

'Bullshit,' he reprimanded. 'Just climb!'

How useful, I thought. I nodded, but my demeanour must have been rather beat. Suddenly, Johnny kicked me on my shin and then on my backside.

'The fuck you doing?!'

'Get some fire in there!' he demanded, waving his arms about him and smiling maniacally. 'C'mon!'

I looked at him as if he were out of his mind. 'It ain't gonna work, Johnny.' I shook my head again and he was clearly disappointed.

'I only wanted to help … '

And he did help. His eloquent explanations on how to weigh footholds and how to use momentum will stay with me for the rest of my climbing life, but it was mostly his child-like passion for the rock, coming through even long after he gave up on pushing the limits, that showed me the most important thing about rock climbing. You absolutely need to love it.

I finally topped out *Technical Master* on a beautiful, sunny day when Millstone was busy with climbers of all levels. Many of my friends were there, along with Johnny, and many of his friends too. I calmed my heartbeat after the final mantle of the boulder and stood on the little platform, triumphant. Visiting from London, Andy's flatmate Alice snapped a picture.

I ran back down on the path which led around the crag and joined everybody at the meadow for celebratory hugs. Johnny walked around, loudly and mockingly announcing to all and sundry: 'Zof is a technical master!'

CHAPTER 13

THE POETRY OF MOUNTAINEERING

'This is a pastime epigrammatized by Yvon Chouinard with his customary wit as instant suffering.'
John Gill (born 1937), American professor of mathematics, founder of bouldering

The Needles Highway in South Dakota's Black Hills National Forest is a fourteen-mile-long scenic drive veering through pine and spruce forests, between soaring rock spires and through narrow tunnels cut into the granite. On one of the *virages*, next to a small car park, stands the Thimble – an eleven-metre monolith whose most severe, blank and gently overhanging face is clearly visible from the road.

If, on one fine spring day in 1961, a car stopped in the lay-by and a tourist got out to look up, they might have seen a tall man standing on nothing and holding on to nothing, yet advancing slowly up the Thimble's overhang. This was not his first attempt at it, but on previous visits, he either carefully downclimbed before reaching the point of no return, or jumped down, practising his skill at avoiding the potentially lethal handrail standing at the Thimble's base.

Having taken a good look at the holds leading to the summit, he had put himself through a preparatory training regimen. At home at the Glasgow Air Force Base in Montana, over four hundred miles north of the Needles, he took to squeezing metal bolts and nuts between his fingers, familiarising himself with the size of the pebbled holds on the Thimble – for of course there were some minute holds on the seemingly smooth rock. At the time, the man could do seven one-arm pull-ups (three if he used only his fingertips on a door jamb), and trained frequently on a gymnastic rope. Not only did his strength and physical prowess exceed the demands of the Thimble, but they far exceeded anything that his contemporaries thought possible. But to make it to the top of the climb, he also needed confidence, excellent footwork, a degree of power endurance and, most of all, a willingness to commit to a potentially deadly challenge.

Upon returning to the Needles in spring 1961, he was still unsure whether he'd go for the summit, not realising how much progress he'd made both in his mindset and muscle. At a height where it was no longer possible to turn back, he calmly decided to push on – or rather, it was decided for him as his body continued to climb higher, as if on autopilot. He later remembered his very state of mind:

> 'You not only get psyched up but you almost become hypnotized or mesmerized to the point where your mind goes blank, and you climb by well-cultivated instincts.'[1]

Despite his unusual strength, the route was so technically demanding and insecure that he still saw it as 'fortunate' that he had made it. Sitting alone on the summit, he experienced 'a peculiar absence of feeling'. Never again would he commit to a similar risk.

His name was John Gill and his route on the Thimble was to be recognised as the most difficult ascent in the US, a 5.12 at the time when the hardest climbs in America lingered around 5.10. The line would bring a wave of interest towards the activity he had been engaged in for a decade and which previously hadn't garnered any attention: climbing on small rocks and without a rope.

Often called the father of bouldering, Gill almost single-handedly invented the discipline but, somewhat ironically, in his view the Thimble ascent did not belong to that category but was a fully fledged climb.[2] The difference was twofold: first off, the Thimble's height and the gravity of potential outcomes were too serious; secondly, in bouldering, Gill didn't necessarily care about finding a summit. If a move caught his fancy, he'd do it half a metre off the ground, sometimes traversing horizontally, exploring his physical capabilities and the kinesthetic joy of movement without any intention of topping out. This approach didn't sit well with the climbing establishment – the members of the Alpine Club, stuck in their old ways, believed that climbs had to lead to the top and that mere pebbles were not worthy of anybody's interest.

But the Thimble's ascent was different. Perhaps, compared to the big walls of Yosemite, it wasn't really that tall at all, but it certainly wasn't small either. In addition, it did lead to a summit, and that was enough for the climbing world to take notice. Even Royal Robbins fancied his chances and had to eat humble pie, leaving a note of appreciation for Gill in the summit register, having ascended the Thimble via an easier route on its back.

Although Gill never sought recognition, he was suddenly in the limelight and with him his love for short, gymnastic ascents on natural rock.

*　*　*

Most of those who become climbing legends admit to experiencing some innate and nearly universal pull of the vertical – one that must find an outlet even in the absence of rocks. While his father was studying for a PhD in mathematics, the twelve-year-old John Gill, generally considered an unathletic child, climbed around the walls of the University of Texas. Throughout his later life, he'd develop climbs, both on rock and concrete, in locations dictated by his own academic career in mathematics.

In 1953, a high-school friend invited him on an outing for her archaeological project: they'd search a steep cliff in Fort Mountain for Native American treasure. Although they found no gems, they discovered 'the primordial appeal of climbing on steep rock, stimulated by exposure'.[3] From that day onwards, Gill sought out rocks wherever he could, travelling as much as possible and exploring the craft of climbing in hiking boots and with a rope tied around his waist.

Soon after, he entered the mathematics course at the University of Georgia, where he had to take three physical education units. One of them was gymnastics, but Gill's six-foot-two frame wasn't particularly well suited to tumbling. Instead, he showed a talent for apparatus other than the floor: climbing rope, still rings and flying rings. He was unusually powerful and, spending all his free time in the gym, quickly learned to execute moves verging on elite level. What interested him the most was an idea which nobody had had before: the possibility of applying gymnastic strength and movement patterns to rock climbing. His first experiments were carried out on the campus buildings, where he introduced another transplant from the world of gymnastics: chalk, a white magnesium carbonate powder used to decrease hand-sweating.

Thanks to the hours spent in the gym, within a few years Gill became one of the most skilled climbers in the country, completing boulder problems fifteen years ahead of their time. In later history, climbers with gymnastic backgrounds would repeatedly show their superiority; the best examples being Jacky Godoffe, Lynn Hill and Margo Hayes. Despite his skills, Gill operated on the very fringes of the climbing community, unrecognised by the establishment and without any ambitions to change that.[4]

Although for a time dismissed as 'only' a boulderer, Gill not only practised other forms of climbing with considerable success but also wasn't the first one to boulder. He was, however, the first to *conceptualise* bouldering as something that was done for its own sake, an autonomous discipline, with its own set of rules and ethics. And even if contemporary bouldering doesn't exactly follow Gill's original ideals, it is thanks to him that the sport found its own dedicated practitioners.

After retiring from university (while still keeping up his climbing, which he did until well into his seventies), Gill plunged himself into historical research on the origins of bouldering, resulting in an extensive website – today an antiquated specimen of Web2.0 – full of archival photos gathered from guidebooks, memoirs and other materials held by libraries of both climbing and gymnastic clubs around the world.[5] Coming across the page in 2017, I was surprised to learn that in an unrecognised way, bouldering had existed for as long as mountaineering, with Oscar Eckenstein and Aleister Crowley experimenting on the Welsh rhyolite blocks as early as the nineteenth century. Even if they were only amusing themselves on bad-weather days, the techniques they learned on small rocks set them apart from their contemporaries. In addition, the writings left by both make it clear that they really enjoyed their small-rocks exploits.

* * *

In the same vein and at a similar time, Parisian alpinists began visiting the quiet, shady Forest of Fontainebleau, sixty kilometres south of the French capital.

Centuries before the first pair of nailed boots arrived at its sandstone rocks, the *Forêt* served as a royal hunting ground surrounding a lavish chateau, a long-time residence of the French rulers. The first time the sandstone gained widespread attention was due to the Parisian demand for paving stones, mined on an industrial scale throughout the nineteenth century. Today, the disused quarries provide additional variety in Fontainebleau bouldering, offering incut, smooth-edged crimps which bring to mind Swiss granite.

At the same time as the miners were painstakingly extracting stone for the fashionable districts of Paris, French Romantic painters began venturing south of the capital and, in their search for the picturesque, discovered the *Forêt*. Soon they began staying long term in the village of Barbizon, which quickly became a chic destination for Parisian artists and elites. Hotels and galleries sprang up to accommodate the needs of the wealthy visiting not only from the nearby capital, but from all over Europe. Railway access further popularised the destination and it became a luxurious Parisian address in itself, one of the *Belle Epoque* hubs of culture and leisure. Inevitably, among its fashionable patrons were the well-to-do, well-connected mountaineers of the Club Alpin Français (CAF).

In 1878, four years after the Club was formed, a congress of international climbing organisations was held in Paris: a two-day affair which included an excursion to the *Forêt*, an alfresco breakfast and walks, and ended with a grand banquet at the chateau. While it seems that on that occasion none of the distinguished guests scrambled on any of the Fontainebleau rocks, at least some members of the CAF undoubtedly entertained the idea during their weekend outings.

The first evidence of climbing harks back to 1900 and another trip, this time to celebrate the twenty-fifth anniversary of the Club. Local and international guests visited such sites as Restant du Long Rocher and Dame Jouanne – both still popular 120 years later – with the trip's field notes making it clear that they were already established climbing locations:

> '*Enormous, sheer rocks among the woods of Larchant are the usual practice area of the Paris section [of the CAF]. Some of them measure from twelve to fifteen metres in height, and to ascend them is a small* tour de force *which necessitates the use of a rope. These were of great interest to our [visiting] colleagues; however, most of them contented themselves with photographic proof.*'[6]

A decade later, an informal group calling themselves *Clan des Rochassiers* emerged within the CAF, open to dedicated climbers wanting to practise in Fontainebleau. Like today, there was no public transport around the Forest. In the days preceding the popularisation of the motor car, climbers from Paris marched on foot from the train station in Bois-le-Roi or Fontainebleau-Avon towards their intended locations, sometimes for more than a couple of hours at a time. This didn't bother them at all, for their weekend excursions were to prepare them for the Alps – with heavy backpacks and in nailed boots they'd climb multiple boulders in a row, amassing vertical gain, honing their rock technique and training endurance. On the tallest of the rocks they practised rappelling and other rope manoeuvres, and to this day many a rusty piton lingers in the sandstone cracks.

The first boulder problem was officially recorded by name and date in 1908 when Jacques Wehrlin, the leader of the Rochassiers, ascended a flaring off-width crack at the site known today as Cuvier Est. Today, *La Fissure Wehrlin* is rather overshadowed by its more recent and flashy neighbour, *Duroxmanie*, but it remains a monument to the history of outdoor leisure – one for which no tickets are sold and which still can be climbed the same as it was over a century ago.[7]

In 1914, alpinist Jacques de Lépiney became the first to climb the narrow crack line of *La Prestat*, which, unlike Wehrlin's problem, is still a popular test of nerves for the contemporary boulderer.[8] Thanks to his Fontainebleau practice, de Lépiney moved to the forefront of exploration in the Mont Blanc range. He was also the first Frenchman to swap nailed boots for soft, rope-soled espadrilles which allowed for significant progression in technical difficulty. Archival black and white photos show him leaping from one Fontainebleau rock to another; in his soft-soled shoes and shirtless, he seems more akin to twenty-first-century parkour athletes than anything that could be seen in the early years of the previous century.[9]

For a long time, the history of Fontainebleau bouldering was inextricably tied to the history of French alpinism. Even Pierre Allain (1904–2000), whose name is almost synonymous with bouldering, was first and foremost an alpinist, although it seems that his heart was almost as evenly set on the snowy peaks of Chamonix as it was on the pines and heather of Fontainebleau. His legacy is not only a host of testpiece problems, including perhaps the most famous, *L'Angle Allain*, but also the development of the first rubber-soled climbing shoe – a direct ancestor of the asymmetric, sticky climbing shoes of today. Once more the standards were pushed forward thanks to a technical development.

* * *

In 1940, long columns of Wehrmacht soldiers entered Paris. France was divided into two zones, with the capital and nearby Fontainebleau falling under Nazi occupation. Climbers from Paris were suddenly cut off from their beloved Alps, which fell outside of the Nazi-controlled area, and the Forest of Fontainebleau became the only refuge for mountaineers longing for rock. Even when in 1942 camping became strictly prohibited, many ignored the severe warnings and spent as much time in Bleau as was possible, finding refuge from the everyday reality of resistance and collaboration, curfews and rationing.

It was at this time that the term *bleausard* – one still in use today – was coined and popularised. Today it simply describes a dedicated local boulderer, but at the time of its creation the community was much smaller and more close-knit. In addition, most of the Forest activity had to be undertaken covertly, binding climbers with a secrecy that intensified friendships and experiences. They distributed among themselves a typewritten bulletin containing fresh climbing news and a good dose of rowdy humour, much-needed during the bleak years of occupation.

After the liberation, climbing resumed a more normal course. Although the collective consciousness was scarred by its atrocities, the war could be credited with one thing: a technological leap that found its way into everyday life. Buses and private cars changed the social mix of those who visited Bleau, partly putting an end to the camaraderie and the unique atmosphere of old, but beginning the slow process of democratisation. The relative proximity of the Alps, once again opened to all, meant that many of those who learned to climb in Fontainebleau still ventured to the mountains. One of the prominent *bleausard*-alpinists representing the post-war generation was Robert Paragot. In 1953, the same year that John Gill was introduced to climbing in the US, Paragot climbed *La Joker*, the world's first 7a (V6 in the American Hueco scale which didn't yet exist), likely containing the hardest climbing moves ever done by a human.[10]

Without fingers of steel, strong core and shoulders, as well as a great deal of balance on minute footholds, getting to the top of the *Joker* is utterly hopeless. Even worse, at its top the climber is met with the most classic of Fontainebleau manoeuvres: a slopey mantle without much to hold on to but friction. Those initiated in the style will push down on the rounded holds and lift themselves up seemingly without effort. Fresh arrivals from the climbing gym, however honed their muscles might be, can hope for nothing better than to belly-flop their way up, the inglorious beached-whale technique saving them from a fall on to the soft padding below.

When Paragot did his first ascent, there was likely a half-burnt cigarette at his lip, and, if the weather was hot, he climbed in nothing but a pair of high-waisted briefs. He also had no bouldering pad – only a little door mat, or perhaps a towel to wipe off the soles of his rudimentary rubber boots.

* * *

In the course of the late twentieth century, the density of boulders, the quality of rock and the variety of styles made Fontainebleau the world's most celebrated bouldering destination – a mecca regularly visited by scores of climbers from all over the planet, from fresh gym-babies to the most seasoned pros. A few generations of *bleausards* spread across a century had a tremendous influence on the sport's development, which, in a way, makes the contributions of one American professor of mathematics even more impressive.

Unlike the *bleausards* who stood on the shoulders of the generations that came before them, John Gill operated in a void, bringing together his interest in gymnastics and natural rock and creating something where previously there was nothing. It took nearly two decades, but by 1969, his achievements and views on bouldering were recognised enough that the American Alpine Club commissioned Gill to write an article explaining his craft. In 'The Art of Bouldering' he laid out how climbing small rocks can be a sport in itself, while also describing and justifying his dynamic movement techniques which previously would have been seen as a reckless display of bad form.

In a time before nylon ropes and safe harnesses, climbers always strived to maintain three points of connection with the rock to account for breaking holds or unforeseen slips. The potential consequences of falling were far too serious. By climbing closer to the ground, Gill removed the risk of imminent death and opened the possibility for more daring movements and a much lower success rate.

Gill's other breakthrough was the idea of transplanting physical training straight from gymnastic apparatus on to the rock. While the *bleausards* trained for the Alps in Fontainebleau, and the Brits trained in the pub, Gill advocated a punishing exercise regime and developed physical strength previously unheard of in climbing:

> *'Basic upper-torso exercises include the front lever, the one-arm chin, the slow muscle-up and the one-arm mantle-press. Some desirable additional exercises are the cross-mount on the still rings and the one-arm front lever. The weakest physical links between the climber and the rock, the fingers, must be strengthened as much as possible with perhaps greater emphasis on pure strength and power than on endurance. The dedicated boulderer will cultivate squeeze-grip chins on beams of varying widths, one-arm finger-tip chins on door sills and one-arm, one-finger chins on a bar.'*[11]

While these, according to Gill, add 'a certain polish or finesse to one's climbing', luckily they're also 'not absolutely essential'. Even in 2021 only the most accomplished professional boulderers can boast of such 'finesse'. How Gill, a full-time scientist and professor, managed to achieve such strength remains a mystery – and the famous photo of him performing his one-arm front lever in the 1960s remains an inspiration to his followers.

Bouldering is a sport in which almost anybody can find something for themselves: it can be a sociable way of keeping up a degree of physical fitness, or a form of training for larger climbing objectives. And for some, like for John Gill, it is a complete microcosm of movement and emotion not requiring an end beyond itself. To paraphrase Pat Ament, fellow climber and Gill's biographer, it is shorter and more intense than any other form of climbing while having all of its best elements in the most concise of expressions – 'the poetry of mountaineering'.[12]

CHAPTER 14

CLIMBING FREE

'It goes, boys!'
Lynn Hill (born 1961), a climbing legend

In the summer of 1983, Lynn Hill was twenty-two and feeling that her life was at a crossroads. She had just lost a close friend to suicide and her relationship with boyfriend John Long was no longer working. A string of random jobs was leading her nowhere, and an accidental track-running career was sapping her energy. She needed to refocus, finish college and, most of all, find a way to do more rock climbing. When the telephone rang and a New York journalist offered her a free ticket to attend a press interview on the east coast, she jumped at the opportunity. The Shawangunks, the US's oldest rock-climbing destination, was only two hours north of Manhattan.

It took two days in the Gunks for Hill to fall in love. Within a month, she was back in California to pack all her belongings. After driving her van across the country, she enrolled at the university in New Paltz, six miles from cliffs that offered some of the best climbing in America.

In a matter of one season, Hill adapted her granite skills to the brownish conglomerate of the Gunks and began pioneering new routes with the local elite. They always climbed ground up, placing modern removable protection of nuts and spring-loaded cams in the tiny cracks of the rock.¹ Yo-yo style was *de rigueur*, meaning that after the leader fell, they would be lowered to the ground, leaving their runners in for the benefit of the next person up. The latter would quickly ascend to the previous high point, having observed the beta and not facing any dangers as long as the rope was above them, before venturing into the unknown. Boldness was the name of the game and mental fortitude was respected as much as, if not more than, physical ability.

In 1984, Hill made herself known freeing a longstanding Gunks project, *Yellow Crack Direct*. Later, her belayer told the *New York Times* that the ascent was one of the boldest leads he had ever witnessed, but it was Hill's next route – *Vandals* – that was a real breakthrough.²

The line features a large, horizontal roof which was soon to be graded 5.13a – at the time, the hardest pitch in the Gunks and one of the very hardest in the world. Working it in the yo-yo style, Hill was repeatedly rejected by a strenuous, shouldery move in the steepest section of the climb. Suddenly, she had an idea that, in her own words, verged on heresy. Instead of having her belayer immediately lower her to the ground after a fall, Hill decided to save her shoulder from a potential overuse injury and inspect the rock. This tactic was derogatively referred to as hang-dogging and widely regarded as cowardice but, faced with unprecedented difficulties, Hill at once felt ready to bend the rules.

> 'In one moment I had, to some degree, thrown out years of climbing philosophy [...]. The subtle advantage of hanging on the rope to figure out the crux moves gave me the added information that helped me learn and eventually succeed on the route. The old style of climbing suddenly seemed rigid, limited, and contrived.'³

Only five years earlier, Tony Yaniro was chastised for doing a similar thing on his ascent of *Grand Illusion*, the first 5.13b/c in the world, a beautiful, sail-like overhang with a narrow finger crack splitting its dihedral in the middle. Having taken a look at the holds, he made replicas at home and trained the movement sequence. Finally completing the first ascent, not only did he feel ashamed of these tactics, but he also didn't receive the community's recognition. Up until then, the mountaineering tradition of old was still strong and the only ascents seen as valid were those done without any prior knowledge of the terrain. By 1986, the rift in ethics had grown so wide that a special debate of the American Alpine Club had to be called to resolve the issue.

* * *

The back and forth between those wanting to get to a summit by any means and those who care more for how it's done is as old as the history of climbing itself: guided versus unguided ascents in the early days of mountaineering; the nearly religious zeal of Paul Preuss against pretty much everybody else; the infamous lassoing of the Lost Arrow Spire put right by John Salathé; Harding's siege against Robbins' sportsmanship. To make things more complicated, the two camps have never been clear-cut, with the definition of fair aid or free climbing changing depending on who you ask.

From early on, it was obvious that technological change would often become the catalyst for climbing progress. It began perhaps with Oscar Eckenstein's inventions, followed decades later by the introduction of the nylon rope. The arrival of the soft-soled climbing shoe revolutionised footwork without much controversy, but the expansion bolt, first used in a climbing context in the Dolomites, resulted in far more tension. Like the piton in the times of Preuss, the bolt became a bone of contention that would linger for decades.

Initially, climbing was driven by the spirit of geographical exploration – attaining a summit that no one had stood on before – and using artificial aid was a widely accepted style of climbing. But as virgin peaks and feasible rock faces were in shorter and shorter supply, a new avenue of exploration had to be found. Instead of relying on their gear for aid, climbers were beginning to turn to the natural features of the rock as a means of propelling themselves upwards. Instead of being pulled at, pitons and other means of attaching the ropes to the route were increasingly used only for protection in the event of a fall. The new game became known as free climbing, but the definition of what that actually meant was for a long time muddled. In some areas, combined tactics (standing on the shoulders of a partner to overcome a blank section of rock) were an accepted strategy, while in others, resting on gear between passages of free climbing was also part of the convention.

Slowly, climbing was breaking up into specialised subcategories. Cragging – typically easily accessible, single-pitch climbing – was already an established if not entirely respected discipline, and many climbers made it neither to the mountains nor even to multi-pitch walls. At the same time, some dedicated themselves purely to the art of 'nailing', or aid climbing, and revelled in weeks spent in the vertical realm, sleeping on the newly invented portaledges, making glacial progress up featureless walls.

Meanwhile, the newest game was repeating already established climbs while minimising the use of aid, or even making first ascents of new walls entirely aidless – this was what the young generation considered free climbing, their next frontier of exploration, this time not so much geographical but seeking the limits of the human body: how small were the holds that they could grasp with their fingers? How steep a wall could they cling to and for how long could they keep going? The perceived impossible was once again to be completely redefined.[4]

Confined to the limits of their comparatively humble outcrops, climbers in the British Isles never developed a reliance on the piton in the same way as the rest of Europe. While the scale of the Alps and the Dolomites warranted driving in pitons, from very early on the British realised the merits of removable protection. By the 1970s, free climbing was the dominant tradition in Britain, but it was much less known on the continent.[5] At a similar time in Yosemite, the relatively small area of the Valley floor became the focal point for scores of climbers dedicated to testing themselves on the incomparably vast walls. It became a melting pot of climbing ideas from all over the world, inevitably putting it at the forefront of climbing's development.

In 1963, Yvon Chouinard (later of entrepreneurial fame as the founder of Patagonia) was only twenty-five years of age but, having established many first ascents, was among the Yosemite elite. The *American Alpine Journal* – the mouthpiece of the old establishment – ignored their exploits for as long as it was possible, but one forward-thinking editor chased Chouinard down and convinced him to contribute an article. It thoroughly detailed the style, ethics and techniques used by Yosemite climbers:

> 'In the Alps climbing is not called artificial until a stirrup is used. Free climbing in California means that artificial aid of any sort is not used, whether it be a sling around a knob of rock, a piton for a handhold, foothold or to rest on. After a piton is placed for safety, it may not be used for aid in climbing without changing the classification of the climb.'[6]

On the opposite end of the spectrum was Warren Harding, whose defiant attitude as a rebel among rebels led to the controversial ascent of the *Wall of Early Morning Light* in 1971. To complete the blankest section of El Cap (together with Dean Caldwell, no relation to Tommy), Harding drilled an unusual amount of expansion bolts into the rock, attracting widespread contempt. Unlike pitons, bolts didn't require a crack to be hammered into the wall but could be drilled into compact rock practically anywhere.

Despite the community's outrage, Harding and Caldwell's escapade garnered much attention from the mainstream media, in large part due to the spontaneous publicity efforts by the ground support team ready to provide journalists with the most outrageous titbits. As photographers with tele-lenses appeared on the Valley floor, the Park

Service was increasingly twitchy about the amount of time the two climbers were spending on the sheer wall. Finally, a helicopter rescue was sent out to get them down, but Harding and Caldwell never contemplated asking for help. A message sent in a metal can thrown down the cliff made things clear ('A RESCUE IS UNWARRANTED, UNWANTED AND WILL NOT BE ACCEPTED') and only added to the hype surrounding the climb.

When the climbers finally pulled over the edge of El Cap, they were greeted by a crowd of scoop-hungry journalists. In the aftermath of the ascent, both Harding and Caldwell appeared on a host of daytime TV programmes, with the general public as much fascinated by their vertical ordeal as unable to comprehend the complexity of issues surrounding the climb. For most inhabitants of Camp 4, it was seen as 'yet another nail in the coffin of the once-idyllic Valley scene'.[7] The media circus, the chasing of publicity and money, and the excessive drilling into the sacred El Cap granite were all culprits in equal parts.

Robbins, ever the Valley Christian, set off to repeat the climb while chopping off all of Harding's bolts. 'We felt deeply that the sport of climbing has to have limits, and that these limits had been breached,' he wrote five years later in an article reviewing Harding's book, *Downward Bound*. Only after decades had passed did he admit that his ego had been hurt by the media attention directed at Harding. Nonetheless, he abandoned chopping off the bolts on the *Wall of Early Morning Light* and in the end repeated the route, admitting brilliance in the way Harding had led it. Despite this admission, the Valley outcry about the bolting was so clear that nobody else dared to repeat Harding's feat of scarring a major Yosemite wall with an expansion bolt.

But the Valley was changing. In the 1930s, 250,000 people visited annually, and by 1970 that number had increased tenfold. As a new generation was about to arrive, another one was wistfully observing the shift which came about as a result of organised campsites, commercial climbing schools and even a bank appearing on the Valley floor.

Garbage was scattered not only on the meadow but also on the climbing routes, proving that even climbers who liked to believe themselves better than mere tourists were not above littering. The technical standards were rising exponentially, with climbers from all over the world queuing for routes once considered cutting edge.

Outside of the insular microcosm of climbing, the Yosemite Valley Ahwahneechee continued the struggle for the preservation of their identity. And beyond the Valley's bounds was the raging civil rights movement and the outcry against the Vietnam War. The climbing newcomers were seen as part of the flower-power cohort, but there wasn't much beyond their long hair that likened them to the hippie movement. While the latter was mostly preoccupied with peace, love and rock 'n' roll, the climbers cared for not much beyond the actual rock.

Like most youth of that time, they were happy to experiment with drugs, but when it came to free love, the majority of climbing accounts agree that it was not easy to come by. There were simply not enough women willing to spend their time at Camp 4, and the usual explanation was that it was too squalid. Nobody paused to think that perhaps it was also the limitations imposed on women by society that prevented them from enjoying the hobo existence at Camp 4 – clear proof that gender equality would benefit everybody, perhaps saving the frustrated male climbers from 'drenching [their] sleeping bags in semen'.[8]

One positive change was the shift from the piton to the removable protection invented by the British. During a visit to the UK, Royal Robbins learned the craft of placing nuts from Brown and Whillans, saving Yosemite rock from permanent damage caused by driving steel pegs into its cracks.

Jim 'The Bird' Bridwell was the link between the old and the new. The lanky teenager with huge ears ventured into Yosemite searching for bird nests, but he stayed for climbing. With Frank Sacherer, one of free climbing's prophets, Bridwell completed many free ascents, absorbing the new ethics from the irritable physicist. At the same time he was learning aid climbing directly from Robbins and Harding. When the older generation faded away, it was Bridwell's time to make his mark. To realise his vision, he gathered around him a group of newcomers; under his wild tutelage they were soon to become legends.

'These new guys coming in and claiming they were better than us,' recalled Steve Roper. 'Jim Bridwell [...] had a boombox at his camp whereas we, old-timers, thought that was not appropriate. You were supposed to be communing with nature, like John Muir or goddamn someone, instead of a fucking boombox.' Chouinard, on the other hand, was less critical. 'I was pretty stoked. They were pushing the limits and also really pissing off the entrenched status quo.'

The new crew, led by The Bird, called themselves the Stonemasters and, as Lynn Hill admitted years later, the name was not only indicative of their ability on the rock. They came in greater numbers than the previous generation, and they were even more scruffy. Incidentally, in the eyes of the law enforcement, they were very hard to distinguish from the hippies who in 1971 ignited a riot on the Valley floor.

It was the era of Jimi Hendrix, experiments with consciousness-altering substances and an itinerant, hobo lifestyle which contested the quintessentially American materialism. The Stonemasters' exploits – both on and off the rock – would become a well-known part of contemporary climbing mythology – perhaps mostly because many of its heroes are still active on the scene, some still climbing, others mostly as patriarchs. American climbing's greatest bard, John Long, authored numerous books and provided the idea for the Hollywood blockbuster *Cliffhanger*. Incredibly, the unbelievable events of the movie plot were based on an even more unbelievable story that actually took place in Yosemite and involved a plane crash and 6,000 pounds of Mexican marijuana. The illegal cargo was promptly collected by frenzied climbers and fabulous fortunes were made and lost.

In the end, it wasn't the Stonemasters' lifestyle but their ascents that made them into legends of climbing. In the mid-1970s, nearly everything that was climbable in Yosemite had already been climbed, so the youngsters invented a new game: speed. What took Harding two seasons and Robbins a week, Bridwell wanted to achieve in a day: an ascent of El Capitan in less than twenty-four hours.

It had been attempted by a number of teams but, in Bridwell's eyes, they had failed for their lack of commitment. In 1975, he was the first one who dared to venture on to El Cap without a heavy haul bag full of the gear and supplies necessary for an overnight bivouac. Leaving all but essentials on the ground, he and protégés John Long and Billy Westbay went all out, becoming the first climbers not only to ascend El Cap in a day, but also to make it down before the pub closed.

Another frontier that continuously provided a challenge was eliminating old points of aid and freeing harder and harder routes. Initially, it was believed that scale was free climbing's limitation, but that notion was also shattered in 1975 when John Bachar, Ron Kauk and John Long freed the East Face of Washington Column, now known as *Astroman* and still a classic testpiece. It was the first big wall to be climbed without aid and it was made possible only by unprecedented levels of physical fitness.

An unlikely combination, the Stonemasters were not only hippie bums but also highly conditioned athletes. Among the shabby tents and sleeping bags of Camp 4, the Valley floor was littered with free weights, pull-up bars, balancing devices and hangboards. Running was a popular pastime and most of the climbers also honed their skills on Yosemite boulders. In 1978, Ron Kauk realised what became perhaps the most famous problem in the world, *Midnight Lightning*.

Within just a few years, most of the iconic walls of Yosemite were freed and finally, only one remained. The crown jewel had seen a siege ascent, a ground-up ascent and a one-day ascent. In 1979, the West Face far on the left side of El Capitan became the first route of the cliff to be free climbed. But its most prominent and proud feature,

The Nose, turned away the best climbers in the world for the next fourteen years.

* * *

Lynn Hill was thirteen when her parents' RV slowly rolled into Yosemite Valley and brought them into full view of El Capitan. However active and outdoorsy they were, none of them knew anything about rock climbing, and a visit to the Valley was just another stop on their family holiday. On school days, they encouraged their children's athletic ambitions, and little Lynn was first part of a swimming team, and then did gymnastics at the local YMCA. She quit at twelve, unimpressed with the scoring system which valued feminine poses and smiles as much as, if not higher than, athletic skill. It was around that time that Lynn realised that not only in sports but also at school and at home, girls and boys were treated differently.

The same year that Jim Bridwell's team did El Cap in a day, Hill was introduced to climbing by her sister's boyfriend. He took them to the local crag where Hill, donning a swami belt for a harness and a pair of borrowed shoes that were far too big, had her first taste of the rock. Within only a few outings she began showing talent, but the first disillusionment came as soon as she became relatively accomplished: men often turned hostile as soon as she outperformed them. Expecting climbing to be an egalitarian utopia, Hill was more hurt by these incidents than by the gender gap within mainstream society, but, instead of backing out, she forged her own path.

In 1979, she was eighteen years old and getting ready to complete her first voyage up the steep walls of El Capitan. Hill was already a fixture of the Stonemasters crew, her small fingers, flexibility and body awareness making up for her five-foot frame. After paying her dues over a few seasons on the big walls of Yosemite, she travelled around the country free climbing on smaller crags.

In 1986, she was a part of the American Alpine Club's 'Great Debate (Or, Is 5.14 Worth It?)' that took place as part of the annual meeting to discuss the shift in ethics which saw more and more climbers pre-inspecting a route before committing to an ascent. On certain types of rock, expansion bolts had become an acceptable part of the game, but whether they could be placed on a top rope, or only ground up, was also hotly disputed.

In the end, despite some traditionalists completely dismissing the new approach, no consensus was reached, but the momentum of change could not be stopped. New types of climbing and new ethical standards were soon to coexist with the older ones, and Europe was at the forefront of the development. To encourage a trade in skills and opinions, the AAC organised an exchange with France, and Hill was put on a flight for Charles de Gaulle Airport.

She fell in love again, this time with France. Having purchased a dilapidated stone farm, Hill spent years on the old continent, where she excelled on the rock and dominated the newly established competition circuit. Suddenly, she was in a unique position of being one of the most physically capable athletes in the world while also having a solid background in traditional big-wall climbing. She needed a challenge that would combine all of her expertise.

In Yosemite, various teams had been trying to solve 'the last great problem in American climbing': an all free ascent of *The Nose*.[9] One of the climbers to spend multiple seasons on it was Brooke Sandahl. Although the overhang of the Great Roof defeated him, his contribution meant that only two out of thirty-three pitches remained for *The Nose* to go free. One of them involved finger jamming in a narrow, horizontal crack at the base of the Great Roof. Lynn Hill's small fingers would have been an undeniable advantage.

In 1993, she made history by leading that section of the climb, but was stopped by the second-hardest pitch known as *Changing Corners*. Running out of food and strength, after numerous unsuccessful attempts, she had to call it quits. She escaped the wall using aid-climbing techniques.

After a week of rest, this time partnering with Brooke Sandahl,

Hill returned to El Cap. They hiked the back trail up, set up their ropes and rappelled down over the summit overhang to *Changing Corners* to work out the moves on a top rope.

> 'We spent three days working on this pitch, and by the end I had pieced together a sequence of moves that went together like a crazy dance. I had invented a wild tango of smears with my feet, tenuous stems, back steps and cross steps, lay backs and arm bars, and pinches and palming maneuvers.'[10]

After another week of rest, in September 1993, Hill finally completed the first free ascent of the entire route. It took four days. Pulling over the edge of El Capitan, she uttered her famous exclamation of 'It goes, boys!' Years later, writing in her autobiography, she described the *Changing Corners* pitch:

> 'Even after having done it, I would say the most accurate grade would be to call it "once, or maybe twice, in a lifetime". I rated it 5.13b/c, but it could have just as easily been rated 5.14b. Scott Burke, who spent 261 days over a three-year period in an effort to free climb this route in 1998, was quoted as follows in Climbing: "There are no holds," he said, claiming difficulties of 5.14b. If his grade holds, *The Nose* sports the hardest free climb of its size in the world.'[11]

Today, the general consensus is that the pitch is a solid 5.14a/b or, in European money, 8b/c – unbolted and suspended nearly 3,000 feet over the Valley floor. Yet for Hill that still wasn't enough. After an intense period of training, she returned to El Capitan a year later and completed a second free ascent of all thirty-three pitches of *The Nose* – this time in under twenty-four hours.

Her performance remained unmatched for twelve years until Tommy Caldwell managed to free the route, halving her time. Since then, despite the unprecedented increase in climbing's popularity, and advances in training and gear, only six other climbers have completed *The Nose*. As of the beginning of 2022, no climber has achieved it in under a day.

CHAPTER 15

TO BOLT OR NOT TO BE

'The best climbers in any generation will want to climb harder than anyone has managed before. If necessary, they'll change the rules to achieve that.'

Ron Fawcett (born 1955), English rock climber

It was a sunny August day in 1983 when the seventeen-year-old Ben Moon arrived at Pen Trwyn, a limestone cliff overlooking the bay at the seaside resort of Llandudno in North Wales. Unusually pale even by British standards, wearing tight black clothing and with a mass of long, dirty hair, he had just given up his rented apartment in London to head for the latest climbing hotspot. He was mild-mannered, skinny and looked no older than fourteen, and upon arriving at the cliff, immediately began tying in to lead a serious E5 route. The regular Pen Trwyn residents, most of whom dossed out under the overhanging rock roof known as Parisella's Cave, looked on, stretching luxuriously on seats pulled from the back of one of their cars. Among them were some of the best climbers in the country, including Jerry Moffatt – perhaps at that time the best in the world. With such an audience, the pasty-skinned newcomer was hell-bent on making a good impression. With backing out not an option, he soon started skipping bolts, too pumped to place his quickdraws. Then, feeling that a fall was imminent, he pulled the rope up to clip at least one runner, but in that very moment his other hand lost its grip on the rock. To the glee of the onlookers, Moon took a massive upside-down whipper.

That same evening, he rolled out his sleeping bag under Parisella's roof and moved into the cave. Sleeping in 'the dustbowl of sheep shit', he finally felt that he *belonged* and it was as much about the place as it was about the people: the pack of semi-nomadic youth, moving from one crag to another, searching for the next great line, shoplifting without remorse and stretching their unemployment benefits to last a whole climbing season.[1]

* * *

The Thatcher era was a curious time in British history when unemployment rates crept to almost twelve per cent – the highest since the Great Depression. Getting a job would only seem like taking it away from somebody else, so scores of people signed on to the dole without any second thoughts; among them the young climbing misfits whose full-time cragging lifestyle was effectively funded by the government. The meagre handout was supplemented by petty theft; meals of rice sprinkled with curry powder were commonplace, and sleeping rough was the norm, but it was the first time in history that a small cohort of young men could go climbing without any financial or societal restrictions. Committed in full, they achieved more than ever before.

Scrawny Moon served his apprenticeship over the course of two years during which his level quickly rose to match the elite. Having done all of the existing routes on Pen Trwyn – cutting edge at the time – he took a trip to France and climbed one of the most recent testpieces, the *Chimpanzodrome*.[2] Returning to the UK in 1984, he began looking for new possibilities on the Llandudno cliff. An improbable and largely unexplored overhang of the Lower Pen Trwyn provided what he was after and, following a brief inspection, Moon grabbed a cordless drill – an invention which would make the impending sport-climbing revolution possible – and placed a point of fixed protection: a steel bolt. Then he placed five more. After five days of practising the moves of the twenty-metre climb, he made the first ascent, naming his line *Statement of Youth*.

It was as if somebody had dropped a bomb into the still waters of British rock climbing.

Before *Statement*, the old limestone aid routes were already popular with the new wave of free climbers. Here and there, they had replaced a rusty piton with a much safer expansion bolt, but nobody had dared to pre-bolt an entire new line on top rope. For Moon, this was exactly the style he had learned in France, where sport climbing was far more established than in the UK – and, as a teenager, he had little attachment to rules laid down by climbers of the same generation as his parents.

For traditionalists, risk was an inherent part of the game and *Statement* constituted the emasculation of climbing. It was 'no longer rock climbing but quite another beast tamed to suit the trainer and about as fearsome as a bull with no balls … the notion of ethics, as we quaintly called our unwritten rules, [was] also gone, leaving an ungoverned shambles'.[3] Testicles – or lack thereof – feature quite heavily in the discourse of the era.

The grade of E7, proposed for the new route, was also hotly disputed, as the 'E' in the British adjectival system stands for 'extreme' and relates to risk. With six bolts spread across the twenty metres of the climb, *Statement* could not be considered bold (although since its inception two or three more runners have been added, testament to the changing perceptions of risk-taking), but for Moon the 'extreme' could also indicate the effort, both physical and psychological, that went into operating at the cutting edge. Meanwhile, the traditionalists were not ready to acknowledge the challenges and pressure associated with projecting a pre-bolted line. Trying over and over, gradually edging towards a breakthrough but not knowing for sure if it was physically possible, was simply not something they had experienced or sought out.

In the end, a sort of compromise allowed for trad climbing to stay as it was and for sport climbing to evolve as an independent offshoot. The adjectival grades began to be used only for climbs without fixed gear, while bolted lines soon adopted the French system, landing *Statement* a solid F8a.[4] Yet the controversy was not about to fade; trad ethics were too ingrained in the British climbing community and, for a time, the freshly drilled bolts shone in the Pen Trwyn rock like a steely insult.

* * *

Despite its controversial beginnings, the roots of sport climbing go far back in time to the first free climbers of Saxon Switzerland in Germany. One hundred and twenty years after the daring Sebastian Abratzky, another generation of youth was longing for freedom. It was the era directly following the West German student movement which in 1968 gave young people increased political awareness and fuelled the German civil protest culture of today. According to climbing photographer Thomas Ballenberger, who took many of the now iconic photos, the evolution of free climbing was just another 'expression of trying to set yourself free', regardless of whether it was from the hypocrisy of domestic politics and the tensions of the international political scene, or from the rigid climbing establishment steeped in incomprehensible traditions. And from free climbing blossomed the next offshoot of the sport: climbing on pre-bolted routes, known later as sport climbing.[5]

One of the moments essential to this progression happened in 1973, when Kurt Albert, a young climber from Nuremberg, took his first trip to the Elbe Valley. The seventeen-year-old was already a promising alpinist but, exposed to the unique climbing ethics of the area, he turned his interest to the rocks. He then introduced the new ideas to the limestone crags of the Franconian Jura which, much like steep British limestone, had been a popular training venue for aid climbers. Dubious about their approach – which essentially made a ladder, even if a very uncomfortable one, of any climb – Kurt Albert began to bypass the old aid points, relying only on the natural features for upwards progression. Soon, he decided to mark the unused aid points with a little red cross – an insolent challenge thrown at the old guard.[6]

By 1975, he had progressed to painting a red dot at the base of routes he had completed without using any aid at all. The practice became referred to as *rotpunkt*, but was soon to be known worldwide by the English term 'redpoint'.[7]

The Frankonian ethics crystallised to become a new standard, with the biggest difference from the American version of free climbing being that for an ascent to be valid, a climber had to make all the clips from the bottom to the top – no yo-yoing allowed. This provided an objective measure of their abilities without the benefit of the top rope hanging down from the height of the previous climber's high point.

The Frankenjura was a particularly fertile soil for the new approach because of its very relaxed attitude towards placing permanent runners. The steep, grey limestone, considered merely a training ground for the mountains, did not have the sacred status of British gritstone or Yosemite's granite. When alpinist Oskar Buhler came to the Frankenjura in the 1950s and considered many of the old pitons unsafe to climb on with his daughters, he simply replaced them. The rusty, three-decade-old scrap was swapped for his new invention: the shiny *buhlerhak* of stainless steel, securely cemented into a pre-drilled borehole.[8]

The widespread acceptance of the new, safe runners allowed climbers to minimise risk and focus on the pure difficulty of their ascents, ultimately leading to the biggest ever leap in grades. At the same time, the rapid development would not be possible without factors external to the climbing community: a network of fast motorways and the increased affordability of transport. On top of that, advances in colour print technology allowed the first commercial climbing magazines to spread information much faster than by word of mouth or through expensive, biannual climbing club publications. And the Western European standards of living were so high that even a penniless youth could afford to climb full-time if they were willing to rough it out.

Many lodged in housing provided by the state, and no other location was more infamous than 124 Hunter House Road in Sheffield, where Jerry Moffatt, Ben Moon and a number of other climbing personalities of the era all lived for a while with sometimes as many as thirty random housemates. For ease of coming and going, the back door was permanently taken off its hinges. Nobody worked and nobody bothered to clean, but everybody partied and many climbed hard. It wasn't long before the house became so unsanitary that it had to be evacuated by the authorities, as it was unsuitable for human habitation. Nonetheless, 124 Hunter House Road went into the canon of climbing community legends.

While climbers of the era prided themselves on how much they rejected materialism and societal status in order to pursue their passions, the relatively poor British economy was still robust enough to pay out the dole and, in effect, fund the climbing boom of the 1980s. Nearly all of the climbers of the time had families to fall back on should their lifestyle land them in genuine trouble, and sleeping rough and hitching are both much safer for white cisgender men than anybody else.

**

In the mid-1980s, the legendary, remote cliff of Clogwyn Du'r Arddu in Wales became the scene of the biggest showdown in British rock climbing. In that moment the discussion on climbing ethics spilled beyond the new direction of development and threatened the old tradition; it was a moment of reckoning which boiled down to one unclimbed line running across the great slab of the East Buttress on Cloggy. Since the days of Joe Brown, it had been known as Master's Wall – a prize unclaimed for over two decades.

A few years earlier, *Strawberries* (E6 6b), claimed by Ron Fawcett, was a route of similar status. Perhaps under the influence of his time in France, Fawcett decided to abseil-practise the moves on top rope before leading the line. This break with tradition intensified the competition among the top British climbers of the day. John Redhead, an artist and climber based in Wales, was the great loser on *Strawberries*, hot on the heels of Fawcett. Having come second simply because of his rival's disregard for the rules, Redhead decided that next time he'd be the one to bend them. And, with *Strawberries* done, the next big prize was *Master's Wall* on the East Buttress of Cloggy.

Surviving a horrific twenty-five-metre fall and a number of other close calls on the route, Redhead was the one to make the greatest progress, but even on his best attempts he still couldn't complete *Master's Wall* in full. 'As if to draw a line under his efforts,' recalled Jerry Moffatt, 'Redhead abseiled down the wall, drilled a hole in the rock and placed an expansion bolt runner.'[9] Artificially marking the top of the route, Redhead himself admitted to the not-so-admirable intentions behind this act:

> '[I] thought about it quite intensely. And I thought, I'm gonna place a bolt, fuck it, you know. It doesn't have to stay, nothing is permanent. [I] mentioned it to a few people, [and they said] you've got a right to do it, you're highest on the wall. An afterthought was that it was a bit of a daft thing to do really but that was my high point [...]. Arrogance of the day [...]. It was pissing against the tree. I placed a bolt. And I never went back. Never went back in sticky boots.'[10]

He called his contrived creation *Tormented Ejaculation*. It took three years and a pair of sticky rubber boots for the route to be completed in its entirety. The first pair in the country belonged to Jerry Moffatt, who modestly considered himself the best climber in the world (and, at that moment, successfully straddling the two worlds of trad and sport climbing, he could well have been right). Like most climbers of the day he also believed that bolts could only be used on 'some kinds of limestone' and 'had no place on Cloggy', even as the anchor of a route. He decided to better Redhead's effort by abseiling down and investigating the holds above the controversial bolt. Unsurprisingly, it was here where the crux of the entire line lay. Falling there would entail decking – and in climbing lingo this light-hearted word means falling to the ground. It was almost certain death.

After a rest day, Moffatt returned to *Master's Wall*, abseiled down to Redhead's bolt and chopped it off. Then he led the route in its entirety, protecting the crux with only two nuts, and veering slightly right to avoid the blankest section of the wall. It was, in Moffatt's words, 'the biggest thing on British rock'. The grade was E7 6b and the year was 1983 – the same year that Moon put up his *Statement* at Pen Trwyn.

The interest surrounding *Master's Wall* proves that while the sport-climbing revolution was well under way, traditional ethics were not waning.[11] The vehement opposition to bolting in heritage areas was the only way for trad to safeguard its identity in the face of change – and, as time has proven, it was successful.

But the story of the hardest trad climb in the UK doesn't end there. In veering right and avoiding the hardest moves around the removed bolt, Moffatt's route left room for an even harder ascent. The grand prize attracted a twenty-two-year-old Johnny Dawes. Working the route on a top rope, Dawes noticed that some of the nut placements became noticeably better and accused John Redhead of altering the rock. The latter denied the accusations and Dawes used cement to carefully fill in the allegedly manufactured placements. Grown over with lichen, they have since disappeared into the rock surface, leaving it as if untouched.

The unclimbed line was even more technically demanding and more dangerous than Moffatt's, involving extremely difficult moves over dubious protection. Consequently, not many climbers wanted to go for it and as Dawes admitted, his depressive state was a necessary enabler. With an abandon typical only of those who feel like they have nothing left to lose, and hungover to the point of vomiting on the walk-in, Dawes climbed the hardest trad climb in the UK, naming it *The Indian Face*, E9 6c. A quarter of a century later, it has only seen a total of eight repeats.

'Indian Face gives you something that isn't a fucking reflection, [...] it makes me feel more involved in being alive,' summed up Dawes, paying testimony to how dangerous climbing can provide a sense of validation to those who at times struggle to find it in everyday life.

* * *

Meanwhile in continental Europe, sport climbing was about to come of age with its own set of ethics and rules. While the largely removed risk factor and focus on pure athletic performance were definite points of difference, some of the new terminology and by-laws were soon to be accepted across all of climbing.

With the French, British, German and American climbers now forming a transnational community, competition was fiercer than ever and standards rose at an unprecedented rate. While in 1981 there were only thirty-nine seventh-grade routes in all of France, and perhaps only one or two eights worldwide, within just ten years the world saw its first 9a – Wolfgang Güllich's sensational *Action Directe*.

* * *

Located halfway between Frankfurt am Main and Strasbourg, Pfalz is a small climbing area where the red sandstone brings to mind the famous rock of the American Red River Gorge. In 1974, thirteen-year-old Wolfgang Güllich was introduced to the region during a family hike but instead of being content with the trails, he looked up to the rocks tackled by mountaineers in big boots, with pitons and hammers at their sides. The sight fascinated him so much that his mother had no choice but to sign him up for a climbing course. The somewhat withdrawn, almost fearful, teenager, with no interest in schoolwork or parties, was entirely consumed by his new climbing world. At the same time, this very world was confronted with new, almost sacrilegious ideas brought from the West, from the US and from closer by in the East – the Frankenjura.

Up until then, climbing in Pfalz was traditional, with free climbing considered impossible beyond grade six and aiding perfectly acceptable even on easier terrain. All routes had to be opened bottom up and with no pre-inspection on top rope. Beyond reusing existing pitons, no fixed gear was allowed, limiting new routes to rock faces where it was possible to hammer pegs on lead.

The generational conflict intensified when a group of youths, at first in great secrecy, began placing bolts on rappel. It was as much a clash of different climbing ethics as it was a clash between the new liberals and the old conservatives. When the latter chopped the new bolts, the young ones called them fascists. In revenge, they removed some of the old pitons and replaced them with bolts spread so far apart that it was not possible to go between them on aid.

Wolfgang Güllich quickly found himself gravitating towards the free-thinking, anti-middle-class climbers with bulging torsos and colourful leggings. For many, climbing in the new mode was a political statement, but Güllich's focus was solely on the rock. 1976 was probably the year when he did his last route in the old, traditional style, in big boots and standing in slings. By 1983, together with first mentor and then partner, Kurt Albert, Güllich was at the forefront of the European free-climbing movement. He eloquently laid out its rules in a magazine article: no yo-yoing allowed and the best, most valued way to climb a route was without any prior knowledge of it.

From early on, it was obvious that Güllich was physically gifted, able to build muscle and power faster than most of his peers. On top of this genetic predisposition, he was set apart by his fanatical attitude to training. In 1986, during one of his pilgrimages to the US, he first led – and then soloed – the horizontal roof of Ron Kauk's *Separate Reality*. Around the same time, he beat the best climbers of the era to ascents of the world's first 8b, 8b+ and then 8c, yet he remained an affable person without a taste for the limelight. When he met skint

Moffatt and Moon living in a cave in Verdon, he took them out for a meal, gave them a shiny, new rope to replace their tattered cord and invited them to the Frankenjura.

In 1987, to climb *Wall Street* (his first 8c) he employed unheard-of tactics: instead of climbing, then believed to be the best preparation for climbing, he stayed away from the rock for months, training in the gym with the help of a renowned professor of physical education. Then, after success on *Wall Street* and craving a different experience, together with Albert he headed for the Trango Towers in Pakistan. With almost zero alpine experience on Güllich's part, they completed the first ascent of one of the most impressive high-altitude routes, *Eternal Flame*. Upon their return home, the duo became media superstars.

Professional opportunities coincided with Güllich meeting his future wife, Anette. For the first time, his non-materialistic attitude had to be revised – he wanted to marry, build a house and settle, and for that he needed money. Reluctantly, he signed his first serious sponsorship deal with Adidas, only because of a friend working in the company's HQ.

Four years after his peak form for *Wall Street*, Güllich felt the urge to push himself again. He began another manic training cycle, using the first-in-the-world campus board put up at the local fitness gym: a plywood box with an overhanging face and small wooden rungs attached to it. Dangling on their edges by the tips of his fingers, he performed then-improbable pulls and snatches. Between training sessions, he searched the forests of the Frankenjura for the right objective – at this level, finding the right route became a challenge in itself.

The line he chose ran up a steep rock face never thought climbable, with the first move being a violent jump between two small finger pockets. To complete it, Güllich subjected his fingers to a systematic assault designed at rebuilding the joints and tissues so that they could support his considerable muscle mass. His radical approach to training gave him the idea for the route's name: *Action Directe*, after a French far-left terrorist group. Then, eleven days of effort on the rock was required for Güllich to complete the line, which was considerably harder than anything he had done before. Cautiously, he proposed a new grade of XI on the local Frankonian scale – or an unprecedented 9a.

Not long after this success, a call from Hollywood put an end to Güllich's worries over his unstable financial situation. Sylvester Stallone, impressed with one of Güllich's training videos, reached out to recruit him as a stunt double for his upcoming movie *Cliffhanger*, the basis of which was a story written by John Long and inspired by the infamous plane crash in Yosemite. Stallone's second double was Ron Kauk and both climbers were expected to put on more muscle before the shoot. When it was implied that they should take steroids to speed up the process, both nearly lost the job. It took an intervention from Stallone himself to get them off the hook, but from then on, Güllich maintained that bodybuilders had forgotten what honest, undoped training was.

Meanwhile, jealousy stirred within the Frankonian climbing community and many looked to dethrone Güllich, some even suggesting that he hadn't done *Action Directe* only by virtue of the fact that they themselves were not able to pull off the first move. Others speculated about the grade, and although Güllich didn't acknowledge many of the libels, his wife recalls that the hostility affected him much more than he was willing to admit. The controversy died down only when in 1992 Ben Moon visited the Frankenjura to attempt *Action Directe* and confirmed the route's unusual level of difficulty. Although he had to throw in the towel due to a finger injury, he praised Güllich's achievement, adding that he was not 'in a position to give an honest grade to this astonishing feat'. Still, Güllich was relieved.

Because of *Action*, Güllich went down in history as one of climbing's more celebrated heroes; however, more recent evaluations suggest that the accolade should go to Moon and his route *Hubble*, climbed one year earlier in the UK. Initially graded 8c+, now it is more often considered a 9a, while *Action Directe* perhaps hovers closer to a hard 8c+. The difficulty with discerning the grades comes from the completely different styles of the routes and from the fact that they were initially graded using two different systems.

* * *

As Güllich's career was advancing, so was his disillusionment with professional sports.

> 'Climbing is becoming a reflection of society, climbers' image of themselves as part of an alternative culture is changing to the ideology of the dominant concept of sport. Commerce and the media are affecting what happens.'[12]

Yet the co-option of climbing by the capitalist machine was nothing new. His sentiment stemmed from a utopian belief that climbing was somehow immune to being affected by the external world, while in fact it had been the push against industrialisation and commercialisation that created it in the first place. What in his life manifested itself as a certain loss of freedom symptomatic of changes in the climbing community was likely much more to do with what many experience entering adulthood in a capitalist society.

Meanwhile, his recognition in Germany grew to the point that one of Güllich's speaking engagements attracted an audience of 1,500. Juggling his obligations as a professional athlete with training and climbing was tiring, often making him nostalgic for simpler times. Yet he was only thirty-one, newly married and with a brilliant career path stretching ahead of him. In the summer of 1992, after a late-night interview in Munich, he was driving back home in the Frankenjura. Momentarily, he lost his focus and dozed off for a split second – enough for the car to shoot off the *autobahn* and into the concrete wall of a water retention basin.

Two days later, the medical team at the Ingolstadt hospital switched off his life support.

CHAPTER 16

SWITZERLAND, 2019

'Not everyone feels the need for a baptism of fire, or wants to take part in a direct deed that gives them an immediate feeling of life and death. Yet the jeopardy and the supposed romance are usually overstated, and in fact it's the subtle little things words can never get at that I cling to now. But there was nothing subtle about getting hurt, the flip side of the dream.'

John Long (born 1953), American rock climber, author and storyteller

The bone-chilling cold in my tent woke me up before dawn. I shifted, trying to find a comfortable position against the frozen ground, but my sleeping mat must have deflated. If I ignored it and I tucked myself deeper into my down cocoon, maybe I could go back to sleep.

The sun wouldn't rise in the valley before eleven o'clock and there was no point in trying to climb earlier than that. Chilled by the rock and the wind, our hands would become too numb to hold on to anything. So many times have I cursed the poorer blood circulation of the female body, making my fingers unusable when the conditions were just about perfect for most males.

Now I was cursing my deflated sleeping mat and the cold that was steadily seeping into my bones. I tried lulling myself back to sleep, imagining that I was in the Himalaya, camping at altitude before the summit attack. They say that the cold can freeze your eyelids shut and to open them, you have to tear the thin layer of frozen moisture apart. It can happen even well below the death zone, at over 8,000 metres, where the human body holds on to life just through willpower.

Camped out in a Swiss village at 1,300 metres above sea level, 1,000 metres from the nearest public toilet and 600 metres from the pizzeria, I certainly wouldn't make a good mountaineer, but the images of the top of the world floated in my drifting consciousness like a National Geographic movie. Then, a sharp ping from my mobile phone snapped me back to reality. Damning data-roaming and all modern technology, I stuck a reluctant hand out of the sleeping bag, then squinted at the screen. 'Are you okay, Alice?' read a text from Andy in a group chat between him, Alice Hafer and me.

I felt an instant jab of fear as my brain served me an image of Alice taking a fall off a desert tower somewhere in Utah, or, worse yet, multi-pitching in Yosemite. We hadn't spoken for a few weeks and, beyond knowing that she was back in the States, I had only a vague idea of what she'd been up to. I knew she had quit her part-time job and developed a taste for more adventurous climbs. This new passion intensified after meeting Brad Gobright.

A few years earlier, Gobright had been featured in a popular climbing movie, *Safety Third*. A broken back and a shattered ankle seemed a relatively low price for climbing hard routes without a rope, but most solo climbers seemed better than that at calculating risk. The movie depicted Brad as undeniably talented but equally reckless.

When they met in the desert just outside of Las Vegas, Alice must have been stoked out of her mind to climb with him. He turned out to be much more sensible and mature than his movie portrayal. He proved to be an experienced mentor and was her gateway to bigger, bolder routes. He also had an outrageous sense of humour and deep brown eyes, and all he cared for was rock. Not only did their climbing partnership work out perfectly but they also became fast friends.

Soon, I could hardly believe Alice's photos and updates on the routes they did. She was living the dream and it didn't even cross my mind that something could go wrong.

Feeling a build-up of anxiety, I clicked on Alice's Instagram account.

She had posted the night before, two selfies of her and Brad. In the first one, Alice with a mock-fear grimace, Brad with a silly duck face. In the second, Alice with a genuine smile and Brad adding a Japanese-style peace sign to his pout. In both, the backdrop of a rocky gorge steeply falling behind their belay. I scrolled to read the caption, and suddenly my stomach dropped.

For a moment my mind stayed completely empty and still, as if by not processing what I had just read I could deny the words their meaning. Then, a delicate eggshell-like barrier cracked for the reality to seep in. When the pressure became too great, it imploded.

Brad Gobright was dead.

'Fuck,' I said out loud, sitting up abruptly in my sleeping bag. Suddenly I wanted to be out in the cold air. I rushed to dress and unzipped the tent. The valley was still frozen, grey and blueish in the distance; sparkling with a dusting of frost up close. To the north, the snow-covered peak of Cima Bianca, with a few others grouped around it, seemed to close off the valley.[1] The sun was hiding behind them but, towering over the village on the other side, the vertical wall of Poncione d'Alnasca was already bathed in sunshine. Its base, adorned by dense trees, was dark green and perhaps grey, with a touch of bright red and yellow splattered here and there.

There was a winding road running through the village, and it crossed a fast-flowing stream. Workmen came nearly every morning to fix the tarmac destroyed by the harsh Alpine winter. Houses perched on either side of the road, some hundreds of years old, made of giant granite stones; some completely new, with builders rushing to finish the facades in time before the first snow. But every year there was less and less of it and it seemed as though this year they needn't hurry. It was already November, but the temperature at night barely dropped to five below zero, and in the brief hours of sunshine, between eleven and three in the afternoon, it rose all the way to ten. A temporary mercy courtesy of climate change.

I walked through the village on autopilot, unaware of my clattering teeth. My entire being was filled with thoughts of Alice and Brad.

I made it to the public toilet, where I sat down and got my iPhone out. The single cubicle smelled sharply of cleaning products and was heated to prevent the water from freezing over, making it the best place to read the news.

I exhaled with relief learning that the accident had happened not in the US but in Mexico, and Alice was not involved. While she stayed in the States, Brad and his partner Aidan were preparing to climb El Sendero Luminoso, a 450-metre multi-pitch 250 kilometres south of the Texan border. The route, a grey, vertical slab of limestone, rises straight up from the valley floor, running through the middle of the most prominent buttress and leading to the summit of El Toro. The climbing is technical, with tiny handholds and smears for feet. Rated 5.12, it was well within Brad's abilities.

They reached the top in just a few hours, Brad onsighting every pitch and Aidan following on top rope. To save the descent time, they decided to simul-rap, threading the rope through the anchor to go down at the same time on either end of it.

There was a gentle breeze, but the air felt pleasantly warm when they got down to the top of pitch nine and eyed their options. Again, they put the rope through the anchor and clipped their devices on both sides: Brad on the right, Aidan on the left. They looked down and noticed that below Brad, the rope had tangled in a tree miraculously sticking out of the sheer rock. They couldn't see its end, but it was surely long enough. Brad said to Aidan he'd untangle it on the go.

They started rappelling, but before long there was a sudden pop. The rope was still running through Aidan's device, but he found himself in freefall. Somewhere above him, he heard Brad scream. He screamed too as vegetation arrested his fall and branches slashed him across the body. Then there was a thud, the odd solidity of a ledge, and the agonising pain of a shattered ankle. From the corner of his eye he caught sight of Brad's bright blue T-shirt as he too hit the ledge, bounced off it and disappeared.

Aidan wrapped his arms tightly over the nearest rock, expecting Brad's weight to pull him down. If the anchor above them had blown, they were still connected with the same piece of rope.

But the anchor was solid and there were no stopper knots at the ends of their rope. Brad had untangled its length tangled in the tree, but there wasn't enough of it on his side to reach the next ledge safely. His device slid off the end of the rope and suddenly he was no longer attached to anything. Without counterweight, the rope through Aidan's device became useless, sliding freely through the anchor above it.

He fell, but the shelf caught him, causing minor injuries. Brad tumbled down over the edge and continued falling for another 180 metres.

I wiped a tear off my cheek and got up. My legs felt numb from the edge of the toilet seat. I had to write to Alice, but there was nothing to say, so I got dressed and went out of the building and into the cold air. The village looked grey and abandoned.

My friend's van was parked next to my tent. I pulled on the sliding door to let myself in, shutting it fast to block the cold air out. Wrapped up in a blanket, Amy looked at me from above her coffee cup.

'Morning,' she said with her usual Kiwi twang. 'Psyched?'

'Yeah.' My own voice sounded flat as I perched myself on the passenger seat. As in most converted vans, it was turned to face the back of the vehicle. I still hadn't written to Alice.

'Brad Gobright is dead,' I said in a matter-of-fact way.

'Crap. How?' Like me, Amy didn't know Brad in person, but she knew Alice and that they'd been climbing together a lot. I summarised the accident report and she asked how Alice was holding up.

'Dunno. I'm guessing badly.'

Amy made a low sound common among Kiwis but, even after a year of hanging out together, I still had no idea what it meant. 'There's some pancake mixture next to the stove for you,' she said, getting up. 'I'm gonna start warming up.'

I looked into a metal bowl filled with oats, eggs and mashed banana – a staple climbers' recipe. I wasn't hungry, but put the pan on anyway. Amy opened the van's back door, inevitably letting the freezing air in, and fumbled to attach her pull-up bar to it.

When the sun came up, we found ourselves walking up the trail. It wasn't a long hike, but with bouldering pads strapped to our backs it was dreary. I wasn't noticing the views, the roaring water and the huge granite blocks littering the riverbed, with the stream foaming around them. You're supposed to take it all in, but it usually escapes you. Instead, you think about the straps of the pad digging uncomfortably into your shoulders. About your core muscles, quads and butt getting wasted even before you get to the climb. You wish yourself there already. You think about the climb.

My brain was hung up on the straps and the muscle burn, both good enough to take my mind off grey limestone slabs and how they look when scrolling in front of your eyes at great speed.

Despite the chill, when we stood in front of *Black Pearl* my back was soaked with sweat. Amy managed not to comment on my mood and we placed our pads under the block, a little overhang shaped like a ship's hull. She started trying out the positions between the holds, suspending herself to test out how she felt that day.

The starting position is on tiny sharp edges, with the right heel hooked over a good hold and the back completely horizontal. Then, the first move is a right-hand throw to a better edge – the kind of move that requires you to forcefully will your body into motion. Bring your left hand to the right and shift the feet, careful not to lose the tension throughout the body. A split second of weakness and your feet will scoot off, mercilessly dragging your ass on to the pad.

With two hands matched on a crimp, push from your right foot, now in contact with the rock by the tip of the climbing shoe. Making sure the rubbery toe stays precisely on its prescribed spot the size of a penny, throw your right hand again and, if you make the distance, your fingers will curl into a deep slot. Another two hard footsteps, the body still parallel to the ground, bring you to the crux. With your left hand resting on a flat part of the rock, push through the left foot and extend the left side of the body, reaching far to the side.

A short climber must then let their feet lose contact with the rock, suspending the body momentarily by only the curled tips of the right hand. If the move is executed correctly, the left hand will wrap around a sharp arête – the edge of the fallen rock. You end up hanging off almost straight arms extended in a wide V-shape above your head. Keeping the legs tucked in so they stay clear of the pads, you avoid a dab which would make the whole effort invalid. Then lift the feet to your hands' level, hooking the right heel over your right hand. One more hard move brings the right hand to the same arête on which the left is resting. With a little bit of luck you can then make the five easier moves that bring you to the top of the *Pearl*.

'NOOO!' shouted Amy as her legs heavily brushed the pads on the move from the slot hold to the arête. 'Why? For fuck's sake, why?'

The question wasn't directed at me but at her own body, muscles unwilling to execute what the brain had envisaged, and at the universe for creating a mysterious twist of circumstances known as a high-gravity day.

I sipped sweet ginger tea from my flask, trying hard to care. My detachment wasn't helping and I was well aware of it. Amy needed me to share the effort, the fight with muscle fatigue and the burning fingertips, and I had driven for eight hours to reach Switzerland and slept in a tent in the dead of winter to do exactly that. I had wanted to climb the *Pearl*. The night before I had wanted it so much that I couldn't sleep, rehearsing the moves over and over again in my head until my consciousness slipped away.

But then, I didn't care. I had nothing to share with Amy and the climb. Partially in an attempt to annoy her less, and partially to warm my face in the sun, I turned my back to her and squinted at the sun which hung low over the snowy mountains. It reminded me of how I used to often do the same squint three years earlier. In another valley overlooked by snow-covered peaks I had worked a nine-to-five job and pretended that I had no intention of quitting. During my lunch breaks, I looked to the mountains.

* * *

Trying to forget that in under half an hour I'd have to be back in the office, I was sitting between Elena and Martina, basking in the late winter sun.[2] They were much better than me at not thinking about work, or at least much better at hiding these thoughts behind the facade of their innate Italian chill. Completely absorbed with sipping their beers, they sat motionless in their big sunglasses, making the most of the sun like an exotic lemur species.

'It's so hard to have a proper *aperitivo* in France,' Martina said with an air of superiority, pointing with her chin at a small dish of peanuts the waiter had brought a moment earlier.

'*Oh dio*, stop moaning,' laughed Elena, bringing the sweaty glass to her lips. The lunch break was too short for worrying about getting back to the office, or that France wasn't in fact Italy.

Then came the spring, melting all the snow in an instant and filling the streams with roaring water. Birds chirped cheerfully in the mornings and evenings, and we were as much chained to our office desks as we were in winter, with the brief relief of the lunch break when we'd escape to pretend we were in Chamonix to make the most of our lives and not for the unimpressive pay cheques.

One afternoon, when we should all have left work a good hour earlier, Elena's head stopped bobbing up and down over the rows of numbers on her printed spreadsheets. She looked up, sending a wave through her curls. A spark of excitement lit her face.

'Do you know the Vertical Kilometre?'

I shook my head.

'Bring something to run in. We'll go tomorrow after work,' she proclaimed and refused to tell me anything else, so I did as instructed and brought some leggings and a pair of trail shoes that I had bought a while ago and had never worn. Elena gave me her spare running backpack with a little tube for sipping water on the go. I couldn't tell if it made me feel more professional or inappropriate. I had no idea about running, while Elena had completed a few mountain ultramarathons more than eighty kilometres long.

'It's an incredible feeling,' she said. 'At first it's horrible, your whole body is aching, your muscles, they scream for you to stop. Sometimes you really hear them. You hear and see many things that are not there. That's when you stop feeling the blisters and all the chafes from the shoes and the backpack and everything else. You stop feeling it and you are with God.'

She paused for a moment to think about her races. 'No, you *are* God,' she corrected firmly, and a faint smile curved her lips upwards.

Driving back from work, I looked at her with a mixture of admiration and anxiety. The Vertical Kilometre begins at Place de l'Église in Chamonix, and is a course gaining 1,000 metres of elevation between its start in town and its finish on the imposing peak of Le Brévent towering over Chamonix. Only 3.8 kilometres in distance, the trail inclines on average at an unforgiving twenty-six per cent, making it steeper than a black diamond ski run. Just thinking about it, I could almost feel the sharp pain in my lungs and the burn in my legs.

We arrived at our starting point, tightened our shoelaces and the straps of our tiny backpacks containing nothing but water, phones, head torches and a rescue blanket. We started marching at a fast pace and soon the city cobblestones gave way to meadows. We crossed the grass, passing by a small herd of grazing sheep, and entered the trail proper: a narrow path of gravel zigzagging between the pillars of the Brévent cable car.

Elena set the pace, hopping lightly from one leg to another in a half jog, half march forced by the steepness of the terrain. I was focusing hard on every step and every breath to conserve energy and retain a chance of reaching the peak on two limbs rather than all four. Soon enough, lactic acid started building up in my puny calves, thighs and butt.

Endurance athletes call it the pain cave: when the brain zeroes in on nothing else but pushing through that awful sensation. Twenty minutes after our departure from the town, my climber's legs and I crawled into our own little cave, not noticing anything around but determined to keep going. One leg in front of another, again and again. A wheezy breath in, a wheezy breath out.

A foot sliding on loose stones and a hand landing on the ground snapped me back to reality. I looked up to scan the trail for Elena, but she was nowhere to be seen. I shouted her name once, then again.

'*Si, sono qui*, I'm here!' came the answer, unbelievably from somewhere below me. I looked down but still couldn't see her. Then I noticed a bunch of ferns shaking a few feet to the side of the path and Elena's curly hair level with their tops. When she stood up, the greenery was nearly up to her waist.

'Pissing?' I shouted through a throat tight with exertion.

'Not any more!'

'What then?'

'Wild strawberries!' came the triumphant answer as she squatted back down.

I pressed my hands on to my thighs, bent in half, still panting. I was utterly confused but almost ready to resume when Elena caught up with me.

'Come, you must taste them!' She pulled me off the trail and towards a little bush heavy with red fruit. I picked one and the flavour burst in my mouth, sweet and sour, with the intensity of at least ten fruits off a supermarket shelf.

We kept stopping every now and then to forage. Then the vegetation changed with altitude and we left the ferns and strawberries behind. Gnarly miniature pines accompanied us to the end of the Kilometre, up high and in the open, where the raging wind chilled exposed body parts and made us shiver despite the hot sweat running down our backs. We grabbed the metal cables fixed to assist with the steepest section of trail.

There was a little viewpoint at the finish where we snapped photos, hugged and registered the proud time of one hour and nine minutes.[3] Exhilarated, we vowed to do the Kilometre at least twice a month. Getting fitter could not hurt my climbing.

Night was falling fast so we dug out our head torches and rushed off the exposed terrain to hide from the wind. The sun, setting behind our backs, painted the snow on Aiguille du Midi and the rest of the range in dreamy shades of orange, peach and pink. They were still glowing as the darkness set and the lights of Chamonix came to life under our feet.

I was choosing my footing carefully while trying not to lose sight of the Midi, regally distinguished from the surrounding peaks. By that time I had been in Chamonix for a few months and had only lapped two unchallenging multi-pitches with Elena, both of them on Mont Oreb, by Alpine standards a very average-looking lump of granite summiting at the modest height of 2,634 metres, far below the line of perpetual snow. Undeniably, we had fun, but what I really wanted to do was to get on something like *L'Arête des Cosmiques*, a classic mixed route on the Midi. Relatively easy by technical climbing's standards, the Arête still requires a full bag of serious mountaineering skills, leading through extremely exposed terrain 2,500 metres above Chamonix, and more than 3,500 metres above sea level.

To do the routes surrounding the Midi, lazy mountaineers (or those not wanting to pay for lodgings) take the last cable car of the day, the same that carts scores of tourists up and down the peak. Once the top station empties of staff and visitors, they make their beds on the toilet floor, ready for an Alpine start the next morning. Elena had done it herself and if I were to stay in Chamonix, I too wanted to experience it in all of its glory. If it meant setting fire to my lungs on the Vertical Kilometre and toilet camping on the Midi, then so be it.

With my loud breath and the rattle of footsteps on gravel the only sounds I could hear, we'd been jogging lightly down the steep trail with Elena less than a metre in front of me.

'Will you take me climbing … up on … the Midi?' I uttered with mild difficulty, trying to sound as casual as possible.

'No,' came the short answer, startling me for a moment.

'But I do have some … mountain skills, like … I've been scrambling all my life … I know about objective hazards … and stuff … and … I will listen … to all you say.' I was already pleading way more eagerly than I intended.

Elena suddenly slowed her pace and I bumped into her back. We wobbled a little, coming close to tumbling down.

'You good?' She held my elbow and I nodded. 'Listen—' she started, but I didn't let her finish.

'We'd climb the *Cosmiques* together, we'd have so much fun and you'd teach me everything I don't know!'

'It's too dangerous.'

'But … '

'It's just that it's too dangerous.' We came to a halt and Elena pulled out a phone from the flat pouch on her shoulder. She tried taking a picture of the still glowing peaks, but the little lens couldn't cope with the stark contrast between the night and the snow still faintly alight with the setting sun. She shoved the phone away.

'What do you mean?' I demanded.

'My friend died last year. A freak accident. He did everything fine and got done by lightning. Fried on the spot,' she added for emphasis.

'Fuck. I'm sorry.'

'You can't control it. It's the mountains. I'm done with it.'

We were walking at a slow pace now, enough to stay warm and talk comfortably.

'But your dad is a mountaineer and it's what you've been doing your whole life. He's still doing it, and he's seventy-something!'

'Yup. And I'm done. It's not worth dying for.' There was a certain finality to Elena's voice and I could tell that fuelled by still fresh grief, she had full belief in what she was saying.

'But *you* wouldn't die!' I suppressed the notion that her friend had been probably thinking the same. 'You will climb again and you know it. And when you do, I'll be with you.'

'In the valleys, like on Oreb. And at Gogarth.' Ele smiled, referring to my promise to take her to the sea cliffs of North Wales. 'But not up there.' Her chin pointed towards the Midi.

'We'll see about that,' I said in a teasing voice, breaking into a run and setting off a little avalanche of loose stones with my feet.

* * *

Usually a quiet climber, Amy uttered a furious growl that made me rapidly turn back to her.

'Are you okay?' I asked despite myself, my mind still lingering on the steep trail down from the Brévent. Amy was panting hard, with her fists on her hips and eyes fixated on the arête of the *Pearl*.

'It's the jump. I can't get it from the move before. I can do it in isolation but not link it.'

'But didn't you just do it?' I vaguely remembered her sticking it while warming up.

'Yeah, in isolation, but not linked.'

'Fuck.' I tried to be sympathetic, while reaching again for the flask of tea. The sun had just set behind the mountains and shivers began to run down my spine.

'Are you going to try?' I could hear the accusation in her voice, despite her best attempts to hide it. I knew I was guilty of being a really shit session partner and besides, couldn't sit still for much longer in the rapidly cooling air.

'Sure, let me warm up.'

* * *

That evening in my tent I was thinking about Brad Gobright again. And about Elena Carpignano. And all the other people losing their lives in the mountains every year, every season. In Chamonix it's hardly news when yet another person dies, swept away by an avalanche or swallowed by a crevasse. In rock-climbing circles it's a bit more of a shocker. The rocks may claim fewer lives than the mountains but, with the exception of those close to him, nobody was surprised by the news of Brad's death – only by how it happened. It is always easy for strangers to say, 'he was asking for something to happen'. Friends never imagine friends falling, until something actually happens.

I had known Alice for years, but I had never felt closer to her than that night, despite at the same time acutely feeling the physical distance between us: her somewhere in Vegas; me wrapped in my sleeping bag in Brione. Now that we had both lost close friends, I wanted to hold her hand and make her feel that I was there for her. During the day, I had sent a bunch of awkward messages, all my words coming out clunky, inadequate and insufficient.

The friendship between Alice and myself took nearly a decade to form. To feel an instant connection with somebody and have the knowledge that, despite not spending much time together, you understand one another fully, is nearly a once-in-a-lifetime experience. Alice had that with Brad, and I had that with Elena.

* * *

I will never forget when I got that phone call from Chamonix, from Martina.

After less than a year in the office, I had finally quit my job and moved to Bulgaria to do some sport climbing, while staying in close touch with the girls. Martina got a dog. Elena got back into mountaineering. She enrolled on a guiding course, finally admitting to herself that there was no life for her away from the Alps. She was ready to make a living from climbing, saving for a deposit to get her own house and settle for good in Chamonix.

Memory is a curious thing and, when I really think about it, I can't say for sure if I first got a text message, or if the phone really just rang as I was sitting in my Bulgarian armchair, reading a book by the fire.

'Ele is dead,' said Martina's voice with her melodic Italian accent. 'They haven't found her because she's in a thousand pieces.'

I felt caught off guard by the turn of phrase, which struck me as gruesome. Then, in a split second, the meaning behind the words caught up with me. There were not many details of the accident yet, but Martina passed on what she knew. Elena, hit by an icefall while descending from Aiguille du Jardin, fell for over 480 metres.

Some weeks after receiving the news, I began imagining her turning into glittering diamond dust and diffusing herself into the mountain, but before that I had had other images in my mind. I had seen historic pictures from rescue missions. The human body doesn't hold up well ground up between rock and ice, and I needed time for these thoughts to stop bothering me. I remembered that some years ago I had watched a movie about Tibetan sky burials whereby human remains are left to be devoured by vultures. Processing that image for years, I finally shed my European preconceptions and was able to appreciate its liberatory qualities.

* * *

On the day of the Potrero Chico accident, the medical respondents were unable to reach Brad's body. The next day, a group of climbers assisted the rescue team in retrieving it for burial in the US. Some weeks later, friends scattered his ashes from the top of El Capitan in Yosemite. They hiked up the trail on the back of the cliff, carrying with them an urn, beers and doughnuts. Alice stayed in Vegas.

In Brione, in Amy's van, we raised a glass to lost friends. The next day we went climbing. My usual motivation was gone, but I thought

I was hiding that fact well. I tried talking to Alice, but the small matter of the Atlantic Ocean between us was making things harder.

Exactly one week later, still in Switzerland, I got a text from Martina.

* * *

I looked at my phone and read the message. It was about Martina's best friend, an off-piste skier.

'There was another accident,' I mumbled towards Amy, but she didn't lift her head from above the little kitchen surface. She was filling her coffee jug with grounds. I could tell there was something going on inside her.

'I don't want to know. Not now. Let's warm up and go climbing, okay?'

CHAPTER 17

THE AGE OF PLASTIC

'Some twenty-two centuries before, the Romans had filled the Colosseum with gladiators, lions, and ill-fated prisoners and slaves. It looked to me as if this crowd were gathered to see a circus maximus *of the vertical [...].'*
Lynn Hill about the 1986 Bardonecchia competition

While the end of the nineteenth century saw Western Europe in the grip of a mountaineering craze, Tsarist Russia was on the brink of a major crisis. The vast country was struggling to sustain its own development, feeble industrialisation efforts were largely unsuccessful and social pressures were building from within.

Before long, the Bolshevik Revolution of 1917 changed every area of life. The USSR was born three years later, and its propaganda machine was immediately operating at full speed. It promoted the image of the new Soviet man working selflessly for the benefit of the collective which, in return, would care for him. Under the ambitious plan of the Communist Party, the people would receive not only food and shelter but also access to leisure. Soviet mountaineering and mountaineers were created and depicted within this framework. They represented man's struggle against nature as well as promoting the spirit of collectivism and, during World War II, militarisation.[1]

After the Potsdam Conference of 1945, the Eastern and Western blocs settled into the volatile routine of the Cold War, which played out not only on the battlefields of Vietnam and Korea, but on every other possible front, including science, art and sports. The promotion of mountaineering among the masses allowed the Soviet state to produce talent that could impress on an international stage. In addition, within the confines of the strictly guarded borders, the supposed access to leisure was used to exemplify the many successes of the Communist Party.

The 'sportisation' of mountaineering meant that winners could not only be made on Himalayan summits, but also on podia around the country.[2] The first official competition was organised in the summer of 1947 in the West Caucasus village of Dombai, today a ski resort. The founder was Ivan Antonovich, a physical educator, alpinist and war veteran, preoccupied with the idea of raising Soviet climbing standards, and all the athletes were instructors from a nearby mountain hut. They competed to commemorate the thirtieth anniversary of the Soviet state, racing up huge alpine-style rock walls.

The event was a success and a year later it attracted the financial support of the national trade union federation. In 1949, the organisation staged trade union championships with representatives of all professions eligible to compete. The same year saw the organisation of the first judges' seminar, and by the mid-1950s a circuit of state-supported competitions was developed across many of the Soviet republics. In 1955, the same year that Ivan Antonovich published his book *Climbing Competitions*, the first national championships of the USSR were held in Crimea. In less than two decades, Russia was ready to invite foreign athletes to her arenas.

Two people who remember that period first hand are the grandparents of the 2010 World Youth Champion, Jenya Kazbekova. Vasily Ponomarenko and Valentina Kurshakova, both living in the Ukrainian city of Dnipro, shared their story with me over a video call in August 2021, with Jenya helping to translate.

* * *

It was 1964 when the fifteen-year-old Kurshakova saw her first rock cliff at the granite quarry not far outside of Dnipro, then called Dnipropetrovsk, a city famed for its rocket and missile industry. She soon lived and breathed climbing, winning the city championship within only a couple of years.

Vasily Ponomarenko was an engineer at the aerospace project where the workers' union provided climbing opportunities. Like most at the time, he was first introduced to climbing through mountaineering, and developed an interest in the distant Caucasus. To prepare himself for infrequent expeditions, he began training on the rocks of Crimea, 800 kilometres from Dnipro, and later at the granite quarries beloved by Kurshakova. This was where they first met and began climbing together.

'It was very special and romantic. Every university had a mountaineering section,' recalled Kurshakova, 'and sometimes 500 people would meet up in Crimea to climb and then sit around the fire and sing songs.' The trips were short and usually spanned only a weekend, but being good at sports was a way to enjoy a little more freedom under the stifling Soviet regime. Still, it wasn't possible to be a professional rock climber – everybody who climbed was a state employee or a student. I asked if they were pleased with the Communist Party's support for the sport, or if they would have preferred climbing to be independent from politics. Valentina Kurshakova laughed good-heartedly at my question: 'We didn't know anything else. We were just happy to climb and that it wasn't forbidden.'

In 1973, the second USSR Open Championships welcomed foreign climbers to Crimea, and this time the delegation included athletes from the US. Kurshakova recalled competing in a race against the only female visitor, an American. In the spirit of mountaineering, all Soviet athletes were dressed in long trousers and sleeves, so the arrival of the foreigner in booty shorts caused a little commotion. The hosts were also curious about their guests' climbing shoes – the Russians all wore simple rubber overshoes called *galoshe*, and it was the first time they had seen gymnastic chalk used for climbing.

With the scoring system focused on speed as opposed to the difficulty of the ascents – a format unfamiliar outside the USSR – Soviet athletes took the top spots. Although they were not as technically skilled in free climbing as their guests, it would be unfair to say that they couldn't hold their own. In fact, it was in the East that training for climbing developed the earliest. In Dnipropetrovsk, on weekdays after work or school, climbers ran and exercised in preparation for their Saturday trips to Crimea. During the warm season, they climbed at the local quarry, and when the temperature dropped below zero, they resorted to their indoor training wall. 'It was built inside of the Meteor sports stadium,' recalled Kurshakova, 'about ten metres high, made of wood. For holds, we had screwed on pieces of parquet flooring.' The year was 1974, making the Dnipropetrovsk wall one of the earliest in the world.

For Kurshakova and her husband, the first opportunity to go abroad came shortly after the dissolution of the Soviet Union. In 1992 they were both working as coaches and, with a pool of young talent, they decided to attend the first Youth World Championships in Basel.[3] But even with Ukraine an independent country and passports more readily handed out to its citizens, organising a delegation was not easy. Only after the community raised $300 to fund the undertaking was a bus of thirty-four athletes and fifteen coaches ready to depart. After crossing Poland, they were stopped and held for hours at the German border until the purpose of their travel could be confirmed. Then they stopped for a rest in Nuremberg where the local Red Cross provided them with food and a place to sleep. In Switzerland, they lodged in an old bomb shelter adapted as a hostel and, unable to afford Swiss groceries, they cooked all their food on little gas stoves brought from home. All of the supplies – pasta, groats and cans – travelled with them from home.

'You must imagine this. It is our first time abroad and we come to

Switzerland,' said Kurshakova, and I could understand the culture shock. Having grown up in the Eastern Bloc, I too still have memories of empty shelves in shops and hours-long queues for food rations.

> 'The kids didn't do particularly well. Natalya [Kurshakova's daughter] took fourth place. But what was best for them was that the competition was sponsored by Coca-Cola and the Snickers bar. You could get them everywhere, on every shelf and in every corner around the event. And in Russia there was no candy. Natalya ate so many Snickers that for years after that she couldn't even look at them.'

* * *

In 1980, the Secretary General of the USSR Mountaineering Federation visited France and declared his intention to organise an international climbing competition that would welcome French athletes. Two years later, the French sent a delegation of three of its best climbers – including perhaps the first climbing star of nationwide fame, Patrick Edlinger – to a speed-climbing competition on the cliffs of Crimea. Following the event, the French climbing community was plunged into a debate: the French Mountaineering Federation (FFM) conducted a poll which revealed that only thirteen per cent of respondents were in favour of competitive climbing, and over half were strongly against. It was still enough for a dissident organisation to be born – the French Climbing Federation (FME) – which made staging large competitive events one of its main goals. Its ostensible reason was to dissipate the myth of mountaineering as an unapproachable sport and to popularise it among young people.[4]

The sportisation of climbing – taming it in man-made arenas, binding it with rules and co-opting it into the agenda of the authorities and businesses – was inevitably met with pushback anywhere that was more liberal than Soviet Russia. Since the early days of mountaineering, climbers have seen their pastime as something more – if not better – than other sports, creating a narrative of 'a sport apart'.[5] Seeing it used as a tool by mainstream structures – neoliberalist economy and the state – was anathema to climbers who valued their independence.

In 1985, the best athletes in France signed an open letter known as the Manifesto of the Nineteen:

> '[…] climbing [rejects] certain social models and is in opposition to all sports that are timed, judged, official and over-institutionalised.
>
> Full-time climbing involves sacrifice and perhaps a kind of living on the margins. But it also implies adventure, discovery and a play in which everyone sets their own rules.
>
> We don't want coaches or selectors because climbing is first and foremost a personal search. If no one acts, competitions, designed by and organised for a minority, can quickly and too easily become the gold standard. Tomorrow, we may have competitions with participants with bibs, broadcast on television. But there will also be those who will continue to practise the real game of climbing: the keepers of a certain spirit and a certain ethic of climbing.'[6]

The signatories, 'keepers of a certain spirit and an ethic' practising 'the real game of climbing', did not leave room for doubt as to their opinion on competitions, yet most of them ended up giving in to the pressure that was building in the climbing industry; it was a small and very new field, but one on which they became dependent for their livelihood. When in 1985 the first large-scale competition was staged in Bardonecchia, Italy, a host of French athletes took part – including Jibé Tribout and Catherine Destivelle, both of whose names were on the open letter. The same year, after much debate, France organised its first large-scale competition in Vallon-Pont-d'Arc. The competing associations then merged into the French Federation of Mountaineering and Climbing (FFME), which subsequently gained state recognition.

The competition of 1985 was held on the cliffs of the beautiful Valle Stretta on the French–Italian border. So as not to give advantage to the local climbers, holds were chiselled and glued into the granite wall, a practice which shocked Jerry Moffatt. In the UK, altering the rock was unconscionable but, with the Alps at their fingertips, neither Italians nor French had such reservations. Moffatt, then injured and unable to compete, was invited as a guest to raise the profile of the event, which aimed to gather the *crème de la crème* of the climbing world. The usually quiet and serious Wolfgang Güllich was also there, but the prospect of competing in front of an audience proved too much. On the eve of the competition he got drunk and a monstrous hangover prevented him from performing even close to his full potential.

Moffatt recalled that the atmosphere was stiff and business-like, and it was obvious that climbers were there because of their sponsors' expectations. The male division was won by the then unknown Stefan Glowacz, soon to become one of the most successful climbers of his time. The female winner was Catherine Destivelle, who nonetheless described the event as a 'circus' and a 'horrible experience', and admitted that she only took part because of professional commitments.

The second Bardonecchia competition in 1986 was also attended by climbers from across the Atlantic. From then on, the alleged rivalry between Destivelle and Lynn Hill was the main narrative spun by organisers and the media to promote the events. Recalling Bardonecchia, Hill's first impression was in line with Moffatt's and Destivelle's comments. The chipped holds, crowds of spectators and rocks defaced with advertising banners were 'completely against the "pure" climbing ethics and generally solitary sport [that Hill] was used to'.

At the same time, Hill noticed with surprise that the level of climbing professionalisation was much lower in the US than in France, where stars such as Edlinger and Destivelle practically lived off their sport. Meanwhile, Hill had to make money guiding tourists and beginners, and the competition prizes were an interesting bait – but even that wasn't without its problems. Registering at Bardonecchia, Hill overheard that the main prize in the male division was a brand-new car. Enquiring if there was a car for the women, after a moment of debate, she was informed that female athletes would be given the same prize if they climbed without their tops on.

In the end, just like her friend and rival Catherine Destivelle, Lynn Hill gave up competitions after only a few seasons. Both athletes were put under tremendous pressure, and organisers frequently manipulated the rules in order to pitch them against one another. Writing about her experience on the developing circuit, Lynn Hill used phrases such as 'petty nationalism', 'monumental egos' and 'emotional toll'.

* * *

Across the Atlantic, the first large-scale competitions were openly tied to commercial interests. Bob Carmichael, a climber and filmmaker from Colorado, was the first to see that climbing could find its place within the booming fitness industry. He was the first to show climbing not as a weird fringe activity but as an athletic pursuit much like aerobics. He also realised that for climbing to have an appeal to a large-scale mainstream audience, the 'strictly participatory endeavour' had to 'become a spectator sport'.[7]

He partnered with Greg and Jeff Lowe, brothers owning a sporting goods company (Jeff was also a prominent alpinist). Their business had operations in Europe, providing them with an opportunity to witness the rise of the competition circuit, and Jeff went about transplanting the concept on to American soil.

In 1988, a $155,000 climbing wall was constructed on the side of Snowbird's Cliff Lodge hotel in Utah. A complicated rig allowing Carmichael to film the climbers was erected next to the wall, and a composer was hired to give the event a proper musical setting. To make the huge undertaking financially viable, the crucial challenge of selling it to TV was accomplished when CBS committed to broadcasting.

Much like Bardonecchia, Snowbird gathered the best climbers in the world and a crowd of spectators and journalists – and much like Bardonecchia, it wasn't without its problems. Fontainebleau climber Jacky Godoffe, invited to the second Snowbird edition, recalled that the routes were 'horrible' and there was a tangible feeling of a business-like venture in the atmosphere. The one thing that the athletes enjoyed was the use of Snowbird's luxuries, but despite the high-end touch, the event was a financial failure. Perhaps it was the legendary moment when Patrick Edlinger won the men's division – with a golden beam of sunshine illuminating his blond mane and his rival, Jibé Tribout, mumbling swear words in the audience – that gave Snowbird its lasting appeal which ended up legitimising competition climbing in the US.

Soon, Jeff Lowe was appointed by the American Alpine Club (AAC) to organise a circuit of official events. By 1990, he had prepared an ambitious project involving a huge climbing wall transported from one venue to another at enormous cost. It was the same year that the World Cup, which developed in Europe, was to pay its first visit to the US, and it was decided that one of Lowe's events would double as both an American and an international competition. He managed to secure sponsorship from The North Face and the venue was to be Berkeley's Greek Theatre, which boasted 8,500 seats.

Despite the ambitious plan and a budget of a quarter of a million dollars, the total attendance was barely more than 2,500 spectators and the media coverage was less than satisfactory. Lowe's venture had to announce bankruptcy and the remainder of the circuit was cancelled, while the AAC found itself liable for the bill racked up with the European federation.

After the flop, nearly twenty years had to pass before another official international competition was held in the US. This would have been the premature death of American competition climbing were it not for a grassroots movement that was sprouting all across the country – one which directly contributed to the climbing boom around the world.

* * *

In 1987, America's first commercial climbing gym opened its doors in Seattle. The owners glued pieces of rock to the two-inch plywood walls and for the first couple of years, barely scraped by. But, trickling into mainstream consciousness, rock climbing was steadily growing in popularity.

In 1989, David Letterman invited Lynn Hill, then ranked the world's number-one competitor, to the *Late Night* show. On live television, Hill scaled a small climbing wall constructed in the studio, letting her feet dangle in space for dramatic effect. The same year, Emeryville in California saw the opening of City Rock, the first commercial climbing gym catering not to seasoned climbers but beginners who would start their climbing careers on plywood. The owner was Peter Mayfiend, a Yosemite veteran and protégé of Jim Bridwell.

> 'Back then, [exercise] was all about pumping iron – and it was this really objectifying scene: people were working out to look good in bathing suits [...]. There was no pilates. There was no yoga. Wellness wasn't a word. So, in a way, City Rock was part of the early trend of functional fitness. Climbing at the gym wasn't objectifying. It was good for people.'[8]

More climbing gyms kept popping up across the country, often in suburban locations without an established climbing community. In 1993, the release of *Cliffhanger*, admittedly almost completely divorced from climbing reality, affirmed the status of the climber as a masculine action sports hero. In 1995, the inauguration of Extreme Games, soon rebranded as X Games, was ESPN's fairly successful attempt at monetising the trend.

Two years later, Scott Rennak purchased Climb Time, a struggling Cincinnati gym, and equipped it with a brand-new bouldering wall. To celebrate the reopening, he laid on a bouldering competition with music and drinks, and a relaxed party atmosphere with the added thrill of pulling hard on plastic. Encouraged by the positive response, Rennak reached out to other gyms in the region to organise an informal circuit christened the Midwest Bouldering Tour. Without ropes and ties to a stiff climbing tradition, the events were open to everybody who walked through the door. The first edition of the Tour racked up a profit of $1,700, promptly given away by Rennak to charitable causes.

The following year the circuit involved sixty events and separate route-setting workshops. Then, in 1999, a catastrophic storm hit Cincinnati and Climb Time had to close. Unfazed, Scott Rennak packed up his belongings and drove 1,200 miles west to Boulder, Colorado, where he pitched his idea of a bouldering comp circuit to the manager at the Boulder Rock Club. Thus was born the American Bouldering Series (ABS). Gyms were given a free hand in how they chose to run the competitions, and Rennak himself dealt with providing small prizes and modest sponsorship deals, making the events hassle-free for the hosts. It wasn't a profitable position: with no staff beyond himself and no office, for two years Rennak delivered pizzas to fund his ABS work, and later took business management classes at the local college. Where he definitely succeeded was in creating a country-wide movement and a community which was welcoming to beginners and saw young talent emerging as its new stars – ones very different from any kind of sports star known before.

The proliferation of indoor gyms soon gave rise to new professions: managers, indoor instructors, route setters, hold shapers and wall designers. Introduced to climbing through gyms, more and more people were interested in bouldering outdoors, and the niche strand of climbing, until then cultivated by very few practitioners, was about to blow up.

CHAPTER 18
THE RISE OF A ROCK STAR

'The medium is the message.'
Marshall McLuhan (1911–1980), Canadian philosopher
whose work is among the cornerstones of media theory

Much like neighbouring Ibiza, Mallorca tends to be associated with last-minute holidays, tacky resorts and drug-fuelled raves, but there is a lesser-known side to the island. A short drive from the tourist hotspots, sleepy haciendas and olive groves take the place of bar-lined promenades and glow sticks. The rugged, dramatic landscape is both peaceful and desolate. All around the coastline, compact limestone cliffs rise from the sea at a variety of steep angles; from coves sheltered by horizontal roofs of rock to exposed, technical slabs.

In the late 1970s, the cliffs attracted Miguel Riera, a Spanish climber who had first visited the island for its bouldering potential. He quickly realised that Mallorca's coastline offered a unique opportunity for climbing without a rope, sometimes eighteen metres above the sea. Riera called this *psicobloc*, which translates into English as 'psycho-bouldering'. It is scary, it is exhilarating and it is the most free you can feel on the rock without risking immediate death.

* * *

Born in Santa Cruz, California, Chris Sharma has a tanned complexion, sun-bleached hair and a well-known affinity for cannabis, all of which make him appear more like a surfer than a climber. Nonetheless, by the early 2000s, Sharma was recognised as one of the very best climbers in the world, putting up the hardest sport routes and boulders, as well as winning numerous competitions. He was unfazed when in 2001 his World Cup title was revoked after THC had been detected in his blood.

It was likely because of Sharma's coastal upbringing that *psicobloc* drew him to Mallorca where Miguel Riera introduced him to the most striking rock feature of the island's shoreline: a perfect limestone arch rising more than eighteen metres straight out of the sea. Riera wasn't sure if the formation – called Es Pontàs – was climbable at all. It seemed improbable but, after surveying the arch, Sharma knew that he had found his 'king line'. It had everything: the perfect rock quality and a dramatic location. It also looked more challenging than anything else he'd done. Eleven metres above the sea, the crux section began with a huge dyno: a two-metre, all-points-off jump. Over a few seasons, Sharma took more than a hundred attempts to stick this one move. Higher up, a physical, gymnastic sequence led to the arch's headwall.

The moment Sharma latched the dyno hold, his body swinging wildly over the blue sea, was caught on camera and instantly became one of the most iconic climbing film moments of all time. *King Lines* the movie was released in 2007 and the cinematic footage of Sharma climbing above the Mediterranean with no ropes brought him more mainstream attention than ever before. Soon after, a major American radio station crowned him the best climber in the world.[1]

* * *

The media and entertainment industries benefit directly from sport's potential to command human emotions. A striking example is the revenue accumulated by the International Olympic Committee, seventy-three per cent of which comes from the sale of broadcasting rights. NBCUniversal alone is responsible for forty per cent of the amount totalling $4.38 billion paid for the rights to the 2014–2020 events.[2] No business would pay this much for anything that doesn't promise a return; broadcasters profit from selling advertising time, which for the Rio 2016 Games alone brought in a record $250 million.[3] Exhilarated and emotionally invested, audiences gathered in front of their screens are particularly susceptible to advertising.

A symbiotic, four-way relationship between the private sector, the state, the media and sports is nothing new. The birth of modern sports coincided with the emergence of capitalist societies, and every major development in the world of sports can be linked to a media revolution.[4] The arrival of the steam press in the early nineteenth century – along with the railway and the telegraph – rapidly increased the speed of the news cycle. The public became hungry for the latest information, and while crime was one of the most exciting subjects, even Victorian times did not provide enough to fill the daily newspapers. The blanks were seamlessly topped up with sport.

As thousands of people moved from the countryside to the cities, sports participation replaced waning religious observance and provided life with the rhythm it lacked away from the seasonality of farming and fieldwork. It gave people a feeling of control over their nearly non-existent free time and kept them in good shape, necessary for remaining productive at work.

At least partially excluded from these relations are less structured disciplines which developed away from commercial interests, often participatory activities performed in nature, without judges or formal competition. With ties to exploration and being far more elitist than football, the only media coverage of mountaineering and early rock climbing was a result of the intellectual aspirations of middle-class participants. They had the time and means to produce art and write journal articles, and these activities were not a response to the public's demand, but were undertaken for the prestige and recognition within the peer group, the climbing club or at the salon.[5]

As most middle-class people relied on their professions for income, those who wanted to climb full-time had to find a way of making a living from it; Albert Smith's theatrical show of his ascent of Mont Blanc and later the photography of the Abraham brothers were early examples of the combination of a passion for climbing, storytelling and the need to generate an income.

For decades, the way that climbing news was produced and disseminated remained the same. The occasional mention in the mainstream media, such as during Warren Harding's siege of El Capitan, treated climbing more as a curiosity than a regular sport. Major changes didn't occur until the 1970s and 1980s, when two new media formats became available and affordable: the glossy magazine and the VHS tape. Following the example of skateboarders, a young generation of climbers made them their own. It could be argued that modern content marketing was born when skateboarding brands started featuring in and sponsoring skateboard media. A similar process occurred within climbing, with discrete advertising for gear appearing among magazine pages, on VHS covers and in the videos themselves.

With a few exceptions, climbing was rarely represented on film until the 1990s, when cameras became cheaper and more portable. Suddenly, climbers could film themselves, especially if they could convince a sponsor to chip in, or at least attempt to sell the end product to the mainstream media.

In the US in 1991, a series of films called *Masters of Stone* debuted with stories about Ron Kauk, Tony Yaniro, Dan Osman, John Bachar, and others. Made almost entirely by climber Eric Perlman, the series evolved into six hour-long documentaries, with the last instalment made in 2009. They followed the best American climbers, documenting the most impressive ascents and creating a new, rock 'n' roll style of climbing film. Some called them 'life changing'.[6]

Across the Atlantic, in 1996 the first feature-length documentary about bouldering starred Jerry Moffatt and Ben Moon. The film had the feel of a 1990s skateboarding movie, with nothing cinematic about it and the thirty-something protagonists playing like teenagers and spinning their wheels in the car parks of Fontainebleau. An avalanche of now-iconic productions followed, including the British *Hard Rock* and *Stone Love*, and the American *Rampage*. The latter was filmed by brothers Josh and Brett Lowell, both recent high school graduates, and followed the bouldering exploits of youngsters Chris Sharma and Obe Carrion. None was more than twenty years of age and most of the time they appeared completely stoned. With the brothers Lowell the future of climbing filmmaking, Chris and Obe were the future of climbing.

They were the first generation to start young and benefit from better training facilities and affordable travel in addition to the achievements of all those who came before them. Cutting out the time-consuming stage of learning how to be a mountaineer or a big-wall trad climber, they went straight to realising their full free-climbing potential both on the rock and on plastic. Some, like Beth Rodden or Tommy Caldwell, went full circle, taking their unprecedented skills from gyms and using them in more traditional, adventurous forms of climbing. With frequent coverage in magazines and videos, both increasingly available online, they were also the first generation of climbers who came of age while being followed by the media. Sponsors' support allowed those with the best results to climb full-time.

* * *

'For more than a decade, Chris Sharma has been the strongest climber in the world, but nineteen-year-old Adam Ondra is eager to take the torch. […] The king of climbing and the driven prodigy battle it out on what could be the hardest route ever.'[7]

The somewhat epic intro sets the tone of the 2012 documentary directed by Josh Lowell, which follows Sharma and Ondra as they work together on an unclimbed route. Bolted by Sharma a few years earlier, it had been left behind as an unfinished, perhaps impossible project. In the film, Sharma comes back to the cliff in Oliana, Spain – a limestone wall with the greatest concentration of elite-level climbs in the world – to share his envisaged line with Ondra.

Hailing from the Czech Republic, Adam Ondra burst on to the scene in 2006 when he climbed his first 9a route as a skinny thirteen-year-old. Over the following five years, he ripped through all of the hardest lines in the world, and by 2012 none of the existing climbs offered enough of a challenge. His search for the next level took him to Oliana, where Sharma introduced him to *La Dura Dura* or 'the hard-hard', as he'd been calling his project. Seeing Ondra's attempts, a mixture of genius and a fanatical level of drive possible only for a teenager, thirty-two-year-old Sharma decided to give the abandoned project a go. The friendly competition between the two best climbers in the world and their distinct personalities made for an unforgettable story.

Screened in cinemas and gyms all over the world, the *La Dura Dura* documentary electrified the climbing audience, not only because it captured the ultimate rivalry but also because of its unusual outcome: both Sharma and Ondra were bested by the route, which remained unclimbed. It seemed tantalisingly possible and unattainable at the same time – a combination which often produces an intense climbing obsession. In preparation for another round, the two climbers went back to training.

In February 2013, climbing magazines reported that Adam Ondra had made it to the top of the route, completing the hardest ascent in the world. Although the first ascensionist usually gets naming rights, he decided to stick with Sharma's name: *La Dura Dura*, the first 9b. It seemed like the ultimate moment of passing the torch from one generation to another, but while Sharma had taken on the role of mentor, he wasn't ready to quit. A month later, the climbing community was delighted to learn that he had completed the second ascent. Of course, both were recorded on film and *La Dura Complete: The Hardest Rock Climb In The World* was released on YouTube in 2014. To date, it has had over nine million views.

To paraphrase the title of yet another climbing documentary made four years later, it was the beginning of the age of Ondra: a time when climbing limits got redefined by young athletes. The same year he did *La Dura Dura*, Ondra completed an ascent of *Change* in Norway's Flatanger, the world's first 9b+. Five years later, he did it again, also in Flatanger, with *Silence*. Graded 9c (5.15d), it remains the hardest climb on the planet. Meanwhile, Daniel Woods, Emily Harrington, Nalle Hukkataival, Hazel Findlay and many more were all pushing boundaries in their specialist disciplines.

In 2009, coached by Obe Carrion, eight-year-old Ashima Shiraishi from Brooklyn climbed her first V10 boulder problem. Three years later she became the youngest person ever to sport climb 8c+ (5.14c) and then in 2016, aged fourteen, the first woman to boulder 8c (V16), only half a grade below the world's hardest ascents. And, although Shiraishi was certainly one of the brightest stars at the forefront of climbing's development, she wasn't the only one to drastically diminish the gap between women and the best men. Alex Puccio, Shauna Coxsey and Isabelle Faus all had 8b+ boulder ascents to their names. In 2017, American Margo Hayes became the first woman to sport climb 9a+ (5.15a), and in the same year Austrian Angela Eiter repeated Adam Ondra's *Planta de Shiva*, making it the first female 9b ascent. In 2021, Lor Sabourin became the first openly non-binary, trans climber to perform at the cutting edge, sending 5.14 trad, and a few months later, twenty-year-old Laura Rogora was the first female to sport climb 9b/+. The gap between the genders began to rapidly close at the same time as the climbing community opened up to the possibility of a more nuanced approach to gender in general.

* * *

In 2014, I was finishing a master's degree in anthropology with a research paper titled 'Climbing Women and Niche Media: Beyond Alternative Femininities'. It adopted a feminist framework to analyse women's perception of climbing media, focusing on cultural production by climbers and for climbers at a time when mainstream interest in the sport was still marginal.

As I look back at my own research, it is almost incomprehensible to realise how much climbing culture, the community and its media have changed over the last few years alone. Even more baffling is that my own line of inquiry was one that reinforced the division between genders, instead of moving away from it altogether – another testimony to how much the climbing community, and myself with it, have moved on.

Over the last two decades, not only has there been an unprecedented number of climbing breakthroughs, but climbing media has also followed them more closely than ever before. Nearly every development is now captured on camera and, with the arrival of social media and instant information sharing, much of it is disseminated in real time. Increasingly dependent on commercial sponsors, athletes are expected to use these tools to raise their profile and benefit the brands that support them. Some have transcended the boundary between the niche and the mainstream and signed contracts with global non-climbing companies, including energy drinks producers, airlines and high-street fashion brands. Ashima Shiraishi became an ambassador for All Nippon Airways, Alex Honnold starred in an Academy-Award-winning documentary and Chris Sharma will soon host a reality TV show. If climbing isn't yet firmly established within the entertainment industry, it will undoubtedly soon be a part of it.

At present, two currents seem to be clashing within the climbing culture: one continuing in the anti-establishment tone that climbing forged in the 1960s, and another heavily influenced by mainstream values. Their coexistence makes climbing a unique vehicle for uncommon ideas to reach a vast audience. A question remains of how much they will become distorted and diluted in the name of serving commercial interests, and how much climbing will become like any other well-established, modern sport, while losing its unique values and character.

CHAPTER 19

'AGENDA 2020'

'In brief, sport, born of truly popular games, i.e. games produced by the people, returns to the people, like "folk music", in the form of spectacles produced for the people.'
Pierre Bourdieu (1930–2002), French sociologist and public intellectual

Over the course of a century, the Olympics have changed almost beyond recognition. In 1908, twenty-two nations were represented by 1,971 men and thirty-seven women. One hundred and four years later, 5,992 men and 4,776 women represented 204 nations.[1] The 1908 budget was £81,000, amounting to just under £10 million in today's money; by contrast, the cost of the 2012 Games was estimated at just shy of £9 billion, making it more than a thousand times more expensive.[2]

From their very inception, the Olympics were inseparable from commercial interests. The amateurism envisaged by Pierre de Coubertin quickly gave way to the professionalisation of athletes, accelerating after World War II when the USSR orchestrated its own brand of state-supported 'amateurism'.[3] At the same time in the West, the most successful athletes were already making a good living from their public appearances and other activities only indirectly linked to their sporting careers.

Beyond totalitarian regimes using the event as a means of demonstrating power, practically every state realised the potential of the Games as a medium for its agenda. In 1972, the Munich Olympics demonstrated how West Germany had distanced itself from its fascist past; in 1988, South Korea wanted to highlight its economic and technological development; and Australia used the 2000 Games to increase its tourism.

Limited television coverage had been introduced at the 1936 Berlin Olympics, allowing the Nazi state to harness the power of broadcasting, but it wasn't until 1960 that bidding for TV rights became a cut-throat fight between commercial networks. The 1960 Rome Olympics sold the exclusive rights to CBS, becoming the first summer Games to be telecast in the US. Around the same time, Adidas and Puma engaged in what is referred to as 'the sneakers wars' – and the Olympics were their main battlefield in both 1964 and 1968.

In 1976, the Games brought huge losses for the host city of Montreal with a budget that overran by a whopping 720 per cent, becoming a cautionary tale for any nation considering hosting the event. Four years later, Los Angeles had a solution to the problem: money was raised by selling 'official sponsor rights' to brands representing a variety of product categories. By 1984, the Games' financing model went from nearly fully funded by the public sector to almost entirely financed by the private sector. Still, losses for the hosts can be enormous. It is hardly surprising that for the 2022 Winter Games the only competition to Beijing was the city of Almaty in Kazakhstan. All other bidders withdrew from the process. Due to the enormous costs (including environmental), as well as the disruption to everyday life, the summer Olympics have become less and less attractive for prospective hosts, with some observers suggesting that this might be the beginning of the biggest crisis ever faced by the Olympic movement.

In pulling out of the race to host the Games, city officials are responding to public opinion, enraged by practices associated with the organisation of the event. Already in 1968, Mexican students protested against government spending on the Olympics and hundreds were killed when soldiers opened fire. More recently, ahead of Beijing 2008, 1.5 million people were evicted to prepare the area for the construction of sporting venues, and the demolition affected historic buildings. By no means is this an isolated example – the displacement of underprivileged communities is a common occurrence during preparations for the Games.

Many venues created for the Games do not stand the test of time and, instead of improving local lives, become derelict. The internet is full of haunting images of abandoned Olympic buildings – some very recent – looking more like ruins left behind by fallen totalitarian regimes rather than souvenirs from the world's biggest sporting spectacle.

In addition, frequent corruption, bribery scandals and questionable sportsmanship all plague the Games. Regressive gender policies are the most recent addition to a long list of issues that all contribute to the Olympics' diminishing popularity.

For an event that hinges on television coverage, the growing importance of the internet also poses a major challenge, as young viewers have significantly different media-consumption habits. In 2016, *The New Republic* ran an article titled 'How the Olympics Lost Millennials':

> 'The median age of U.S. viewers for the 2008 Beijing Olympics was 47, rising to 48 for the 2012 London Games. The 2014 Winter Games in Sochi rang in at 55, compared to 48 for the 2002 Salt Lake City Games. These numbers only include TV viewership, which skews older in general, so they don't tell the whole story. Still, in London and Sochi, a large majority of viewers watched the games on TV (89 and 78 per cent, respectively). More recent numbers from Rio show that, in comparison to London, there has been a 30 per cent drop in TV viewers between the ages of 18 and 34.'[4]

As viewing habits change, the Olympics will no doubt adjust, and it is likely that social media, and soon perhaps even virtual reality, will transform the Games into something more closely resembling a reality show.

Even before the internet revolution reached full speed, in 1995 ESPN's X Games attempted to lure viewers by staging an event that featured skateboarding, BMX, downhill mountain biking and other youth-oriented adventure disciplines. The IOC realised that by sticking solely with traditional sports, it would lose the youth audience. Only three years later, snowboarding – an adventurous, outdoor discipline sharing many of climbing's characteristics – was in the programme of the Nagano Winter Olympics. Many practitioners were dubious about the benefits of associating with the Olympic movement, and their fears were confirmed when the IOC pushed them under the control of the International Ski Federation, disregarding the newly formed Snowboard Federation and effectively robbing the sport of its autonomy.

Despite the less than smooth beginnings, the importance of snowboarding for the Games has only increased, firmly establishing the discipline as a mainstream sport. (At the 2010 Olympics it accounted for a forty-eight-per-cent increase in eighteen- to twenty-four-year-old viewers.[5]) However, whether it actually benefitted from inclusion remains contested. In 2014, a prominent snowboarding magazine ran a feature entitled 'Boycott The Olympics: The IOC Needs Snowboarding More Than We Need Them'.[6] Two years later, after the Sochi Olympics, viewership reports confirmed that snowboarding was one of the most popular events and a valuable asset in the IOC's negotiations with sponsors.[7] Many top snowboarders bemoan that none of this prosperity trickles down to the sport itself.

Meanwhile, the IOC realised that actively tapping into the adventure niche would become critical to its future. In 2014, the organisation introduced the so-called 'Agenda 2020': 'a set of 40 detailed recommendations whose overarching goal [is] to safeguard the Olympic values and strengthen the role of sport in society'.[8] In practice, officials were openly admitting that the influence of the Games was dwindling. They had to win over younger audiences, be it through choosing more exciting sports or more relevant media. Action sports became their opportunity to reach the elusive Millennial and Generation Z market sectors.

Suddenly, the IOC turned its eyes to competition climbing.

* * *

The International Climbing and Mountaineering Federation (UIAA) was founded in 1932 in Chamonix when twenty associations met for a mountain congress. In keeping with the times, a Swiss count was chosen as the organisation's first president, and the UIAA was ready to begin its mission to lead the 'study and solution of all problems regarding mountaineering'.[9] It has since grown to become the world's most important mountaineering organisation, setting standards not only when it comes to alpine route grading, but also safety certifications for life-saving equipment, such as helmets and ropes.

In the 1980s, the UIAA became responsible for the new and rapidly evolving European competition scene. With the 1992 Olympic Games coming up in Albertville, France, the federation hoped that the country's strong mountaineering tradition would help advance the sport. However, climbing's governing structures weren't yet ready and, especially with the situation in the US still unclear, the UIAA wasn't able to convince the IOC. The organisations compromised, and climbing was scheduled to feature in a pre-Olympic event one week ahead of the opening ceremony.

The UIAA's limited experience of hosting competitions was not enough for them to work successfully with the IOC and showcase climbing's potential. The event was held on an artificial lead wall built at an ice rink arena where lycra-clad athletes had to focus more on surviving the cold than on getting to the top of their route. The climbs were set in a way which necessitated long rests and, with athletes suspended motionless for minutes at a time, it made for dull viewing. Instead of fast-tracking climbing towards Olympic inclusion, the event proved that competition climbing was not ready.

Undeterred, the UIAA petitioned the IOC to become climbing's official governing body and received recognition in 1995. Realising how different the competitions were from outdoor climbing, a new body was created within the UIAA in 1997. A decade later it was to become independent under the new name of the International Federation of Sport Climbing, or the IFSC. Lead climbing, bouldering and speed climbing fell under the IFSC's jurisdiction, while ice climbing, with its stronger ties to alpinism, remains under the control of the UIAA and separately strives for its inclusion in the Winter Olympic programme.

Meanwhile, the IFSC, established by forty-eight national federations, was recognised by the IOC in 2010. (Among the founding members was USA Climbing, the new national governing body which had taken over American competition climbing in 2004.) At this stage, the sport had matured and developed structures which could allow it to become a part of the Olympic programme, though it is interesting to ask why this became the goal in the first place.

Olympic inclusion by no means guarantees a surge of interest in a given discipline. Take for example the modern pentathlon, table tennis or short-track speed skating – all Olympic sports, none of which have garnered international mainstream interest. However, for those who have a shot at attending the Olympics, inclusion makes a world of difference. Athletes stand a chance of landing a commercial sponsorship deal or finding professional opportunities, such as punditry or speaking engagements. But beyond the podia of major disciplines like gymnastics or skiing, most Olympic athletes struggle to make a decent living. Worse than that, a 2020 study revealed that nearly sixty per cent of elite athletes across the globe do not feel financially stable.[10]

Apart from a few top performers, a small group of officials might also benefit. On the back of Olympic inclusion, the IFSC signed four TV deals for its 2021 and 2022 competitive season. 'We are confident that these partnerships will provide climbing fans around the world a more comprehensive offering of our events,' said Marco Scolaris, president of the IFSC.[11] However, given that up until now most international climbing competitions were available for free live streaming on YouTube, it is difficult to grasp his meaning.

The question of inclusion is more easily answered if looked at from the perspective of those who truly benefit from the Games: the private sector. For advertisers, adventure and lifestyle sports have a tremendous value due to their authenticity factor, a quality much studied by social scientists in the realms of surfing and skateboarding.[12] Associating with these kinds of disciplines, which, like climbing, evolved together with their own subcultures, allows brands to capitalise on consumers' emotions and the aspirational value of lifestyle sports participation. In short, disciplines which emerged in opposition to consumerism are now used to create consumerist attitudes.[13] Not everybody needs to be as strong as Chris Sharma, but most want to be as cool as him, wearing the same flip-flops and taking the same brand of rope to their local gym. When an alternative sport enters the mainstream, that influence is suddenly extended far beyond its original niche.[14] Finally, and most importantly, every sport which brings the attention of audiences to the Olympic broadcast becomes a mule for the advertisers of laundry powder, car insurance and toothpaste.

For a long time, researchers studying the entry of alternative disciplines into the mainstream understood this process as a one-sided story of co-option: a corporate sector's invasion into futilely resisting niche sports. However, this view obscures the role of the entrepreneurial climbers or surfers who facilitate and accelerate the relationship between the two. Despite their countercultural heritage, they see the benefits of the bargain.

* * *

Given that the most recent Olympic Games cost $15.4 billion – that's nearly $1 billion per day of the event – it is obvious that their gravitational power remains huge. Somehow, someone is willing to pay, and it happens for two reasons: firstly, because there's still a profit in it, and secondly, because most of the world is still buying into the lofty Olympic values as envisaged by Coubertin. Even with full knowledge of the controversies and problems associated with the Games, it is nearly impossible not to get excited about the event: it is something most of us grew up with, like a major religious holiday we observe even if the original meaning has long been lost.

The IFSC continued to push climbing towards Olympic inclusion but, despite the 2006 bouldering and speed-climbing demonstrations held as part of the Torino Winter Olympics, in 2013 the IOC voted against it. It wasn't until the introduction of 'Agenda 2020' that the atmosphere changed: in August 2016 the International Olympic Committee formally announced that climbing would feature in Tokyo. This inclusion was to be a one-off, subject to a review before the following event.

'The mutual respect is unique between climbers, judges and officials. In the super-final of an international event, competitors discuss sequences and help each other. In isolation I see climbers talk about routes they did recently and make plans for rock trips. This sport is really something special. We hope the IOC recognises that,' said Marco Scolaris, listing the reasons why the discipline should be a part of the 'Olympic family'. Unfortunately, it is more likely that by pushing competition climbing as the mainstream and most popular facet of the sport, it is going to become increasingly divorced from its origins. Athletes training to win medals at the Olympics may never touch rock, spending all of their time in the gym. And, as much as it is not inherently a bad thing, climbing will become less like the climbing we know.

This could not have been more true for the format which emerged from the talks between the IFSC and the IOC. The latter offered climbing only two gold medals – one for women and one for men

– despite the IFSC World Cup circuit for years having included three separate events: lead, bouldering and speed. In order not to exclude anyone, the officials decided to combine them into a kind of triathlon, with three disciplines all counting towards one result. The combination would include lead, the oldest competitive climbing discipline in Western Europe; speed, hugely popular in Eastern Europe; and bouldering, which had taken first the US and then the rest of the world by storm. Unfortunately, in an effort to please all, the IFSC pleased none.

'It's a bit like asking Usain Bolt to run a marathon and then do the hurdles,' Briton Shauna Coxsey, an Olympic hopeful, said in a press interview. Adam Ondra was also critical, expecting nothing more but 'quite a big mess' and questioning whether he'd want to compete at all.[15] Veteran climber and Bardonecchia's 1985 winner Stefan Glowacz was even blunter, calling the format 'simply ridiculous' and 'downright stupid'.[16] However, once the dust of the controversy had settled, the best athletes in the world began training to qualify for the Games. Many of them, like Coxsey and Ondra, had to learn a completely new discipline. Some, like speed climbing's specialists from Indonesia and Poland, had to learn two. Nonetheless, everybody wanted a ticket to Tokyo.

The 2019 World Championships held in August in Hachioji, Japan, became the first of seven qualification events. Two more were held, one in France and one in the US, before an inconspicuous media side-story rapidly took centre stage. It had started with a mysterious pneumonia attacking the inhabitants of the Chinese city of Wuhan in December 2019. By March 2020, the US was in a state of national emergency and the death toll in Italy alone exceeded that in China. The SARS-CoV-2, or the novel coronavirus pandemic, was in full swing.

As the infection and fatality rates kept going up, many around the world were forced into confinement, and all public events, including competitions, were cancelled. Soon it became obvious that the 2020

Summer Olympics in Tokyo would not be feasible. Despite the $12.35 billion already sunk into preparations, for the first time in modern Olympic history, on 24 March 2020 came the official announcement that the Games would be postponed, 'beyond 2020 but not later than summer 2021'.[17]

The individuals most affected by the decision were undoubtedly athletes completely thrown off their training programmes five months before the biggest event of their careers. A few unlucky ones, like Akiyo Noguchi, were forced to push back their retirement by a full year. Meanwhile, concerned with the possibility of ongoing risks to global safety, numerous health experts as well as seventy per cent of Japanese citizens continued to press for complete cancellation. As the pandemic continued to wreck the lives of those who got infected and those who tried to avoid it, nothing remained certain.

For most, the Games of the XXXII Olympiad were of little concern.

CHAPTER 20

BLEAUSARDE WITH AN E

'Over half a lifetime of climbing is stamped on my body, from crowded toes and undainty knuckles to overdeveloped back and elongating spine. It seems that what we think, what we feel and what we do changes us in ways both physical and less visible.'
Steph Davis (born 1973), climber noted for
her solo ascents, base jumper and writer

The wood of the chestnut flooring felt warm under my feet, heated by the late morning sun outside the window. I looked down at my toes and the parquet which extended across the two rooms behind my back. I had spent several weeks laying it and it was beautiful. But it ended ten inches in front of me, and six feet before the wall. I had run out of wood.

After a couple of hours on the phone and even longer on the computer, I was now absolutely sure that my chances of buying chestnut parquet flooring during lockdown were zero.

I focused my eyes on the border between the smooth wood and the rough OSB boards, trying to decide if the emotion I felt was panic, indifference or both.

As of that morning, the Forest of Fontainebleau was off-limits – the one place where we hid from reality, pretending that everything was fine. Now we were truly confined to the house, one resembling a building site much more than a home, with a one-kilometre perimeter for dog walks. Reality had caught up with us.

* * *

Since taking up climbing again in my mid-twenties, I had been obsessed with progress. I loved being out on the rocks but my *raison d'être* was to be better, and better, and better. When I wasn't succeeding, I cried and hated myself. I went wherever I could climb the most, I trained, I partially gave up a career – every single one of my decisions was influenced by the overarching ambition to catch up with the elite. Not realising that it wasn't a good reason to climb, I didn't have any goals other than hard grades.

Moving to Fontainebleau seemed like a logical step. Every day when the weather was dry, I was in the forest for at least a couple of hours, trying to climb, falling off and getting frustrated. The rest of the time I trained or worked remotely on random projects I didn't care about.

I found a small community of motivated climbers, but mostly headed out alone. Suddenly, I noticed something that had previously slipped my attention: the vast majority of Fontainebleau boulderers were white men. It wasn't uncommon that I'd find myself the odd one out, with only male climbers at a busy crag, and I felt like I had to act. A few months later I found myself a director of the first Women's Bouldering Festival in Fontainebleau, excited and terrified at the prospect of nearly a hundred climbers visiting from all over the world.

On the first day of the event, when the participants had already headed for the rocks, I was held back by some admin work and ended up the last one to arrive at the sandy clearing of L'Éléphant. Seeing one of the oldest, most iconic Fontainebleau locations busy with an international crowd of women suddenly made my eyes well up. It felt very special to flip the gender dynamics of the crag, to witness and experience the difference. I knew nothing about event organising and

I had no idea what I was doing with the festival, but it felt right.

The following year there was a small team of volunteers helping me to run the non-profit organisation which staged the event. Apart from outdoor climbing, we rented a venue and invited professional climbers to give presentations. We had workshops and yoga and wine. I was happy to do something positive in the community, and excited for the next edition of the Festival. We were confident that the third one would be the best yet because we hadn't foreseen the unpredictable: the plague. We downscaled, we put safety measures in place and we waited until the very last moment, not knowing if we'd have an event or not. In the end, we had a small, socially distanced gathering – an unlikely and surreal weekend of celebrating that we were together and that we were alive.

A week after the corona-festival, I did my hardest boulder, but I hadn't achieved my big goal: to climb 8a before my thirtieth birthday. I was nearly thirty-five and had climbed every single grade up to 7c+, but the magical barrier one grade above remained impenetrable. For nearly five years I'd been beating myself up about it, felt insufficient, trained hard, got injured, got anaemic, cried and cursed. And then it all fell away. After mantling the last hold on *À l'Envers*, a little 7c+ roof traverse, I was content. I didn't have to push any more. Whether it was because of five million deaths worldwide or just because I had got older (but most likely not wiser), I was suddenly able to put climbing into perspective.

They say that a watched kettle never boils and that climbing goals are achieved when you stop caring about them too much. For me, it seems that feelings of inadequacy and not being enough were very strong motivators. Now that I've stopped obsessing about an 8a, I've started questioning if I was motivated at all, and if so, why. With great surprise, I realised that perhaps I will never push myself to complete another hard project and that I'm okay with that.

* * *

Odd as it may sound, at the start of the pandemic I got lucky. Unlike millions of people who lost their jobs because of the coronavirus, I had just voluntarily quit nearly all of my assignments to focus on renovating a dilapidated farmhouse in the south of the forest. We moved in, and while Andy took photos and worked on his computer, I demolished and built walls, laid tiles and plumbed toilets. And then all the building stores closed and we were locked up on a building site, with hardly any heating and half a parquet floor.

In a desperate and illogical attempt to slow down the catastrophic spread of the virus in the Île-de-France region, the authorities closed down the Forest of Fontainebleau. Red and white police tape appeared at all car parks, and officers enforced the lockdown with drones circling above the trees. Many local climbers decided to play a game of hide and seek. For me, the idea of law enforcement lurking behind a rock ready to accuse me of spreading the plague seemed only to increase my stress, so I surrendered to the lockdown without a fight.

And after my building supplies ran out, I started writing this book.

I still climb and I will probably do so for as long as I can – but it is no longer the one driving force behind everything I do. Without an overambitious goal in front of me, I would be lying if I said I didn't feel a little lost. But I'm excited to find out what makes me tick, and where I'll go without a clear roadmap.

Perhaps all this is only me fluctuating between the heroic and aesthetic approaches to climbing: having been driven by the achievement, maybe now I'll be in it for the joy of the experience.

* * *

Although Japan was not hit by the pandemic as badly as other countries, in May 2021 Tokyo had extended its state of emergency. Despite the considerable risks of staging a huge international event, calls for the cancellation of the Olympic Games fell on deaf ears. The restrictions were to be lifted at the end of the month, leaving enough of a gap ahead of the postponed event, planned to kick off on 23 July.

Ostensibly, the postponed Games were to be a sign of perseverance in the face of a cataclysm. In practice, a last-minute cancellation would result in multi-billion-dollar losses. As long as the worst-case scenario of a superspreader event could be avoided, the organisers were not going to back out.

Despite unprecedented security measures, issues surfaced before the opening ceremony even took place. From officials fist-bumping members of the public to a shared dining hall serving 45,000 meals daily, it seemed that staging the Olympics could prove to be a game of Russian roulette.[1]

Climbing was scheduled for the first week of August at the Aomi Urban Sports Park overlooking Tokyo Bay. When the athletes walked into the arena, the heat and humidity of the Japanese summer were not on their side. In addition, the stands were nearly empty, with only officials, teams and the press allowed to attend. Along with the convoluted scoring system, these were not the Games that athletes had dreamed of.

The first ever Olympic medals for climbing were to be determined by the multiplication of points earned in speed, bouldering and lead. They were awarded according to standings, and the lowest combined score would win.

The men's competition ended with a surprise. The last athlete to climb on the lead wall was Austrian Jakob Schubert. As he set off on his attempt, Adam Ondra was second in the overall standings. In a nail-biting finish, Schubert climbed past Ondra's high point to the end of the route, winning the lead competition and earning himself bronze overall. This meant that Ondra's score was multiplied by two (corresponding to his second place in lead) and amounted to forty-eight points, knocking him from gold all the way down into sixth. At the top of the table was a score of twenty-eight, a result of first place in speed, and seventh and fourth places in bouldering and lead respectively, earned by Spanish newcomer Alberto Ginés López. The nineteen-year-old became combined sport climbing's first Olympic gold medallist. On the second step of the podium stood American Nathaniel Coleman.

The women's event was no less exciting and even the complex grading system couldn't obscure a dominant performance by Janja Garnbret. Hailed the greatest competitor of all time even before the Olympics, Garnbret's combined score amounted to five: she was fifth in speed and first in both bouldering and lead. In second place was Tokyo native Miho Nonaka, followed by compatriot and the oldest finalist, thirty-two-year-old Akiyo Noguchi.[2]

* * *

As the Olympic torch was put out, Japan was grappling with a surge in coronavirus cases. Officials continued to deny links between the event and growing infection rates, but numerous independent specialists were sceptical. Luckily, the Games did not become the feared superspreader event – but whether that was enough of a reason to justify the risk remains up for debate.

The introduction of new disciplines, as well as the organisers' ambition to lift the audience's spirits during the pandemic, were not enough to prevent viewing numbers falling to their lowest since 1988. The huge time difference between Tokyo and the western world contributed to the poor statistics, with an increase only noted in Japan and Australia. Both NBC and BBC television broadcasts fell short of expectations, but in comparison to previous events, the demand for online streaming grew. How the IOC will adapt to the digital-first reality, and whether 'Agenda 2020' will allow the Games to win over younger audiences, is yet to be seen.

Meanwhile, climbers took to social media to share their experiences. Some, like Shauna Coxsey, were ecstatic, while others had mixed feelings. Alex Megos said that he 'felt a little uncomfortable seeing the lengths everyone was going to and the money federations were spending for only a handful of people to climb an afternoon or two', and 'was beginning to wonder if the athletes really were at the centre of the biggest sports event on Earth.'[3] American Colin Duffy was disappointed with the scoring system, which left him low down the scoreboard ('It is crazy when I think of the three podium finishers, I beat them in two of the three disciplines') and Miho Nonaka said that 'the combined format was really painful'.[4 & 5]

Despite this criticism, climbing has proven itself a valuable asset to the IOC. Accepting the discipline as part of the Paris 2024 Games, the IOC announced that while bouldering and lead would remain combined, speed climbing would become a separate event. In addition, the number of athletes will be expanded from forty to seventy-two.

With climbing being relatively well established in France, it will likely attract a lot of mainstream attention. Beyond the benefit to the athletes, it will be interesting to see the effects of the separation of the three disciplines.

* * *

I watched parts of the broadcast on an old television set at my grandmother's summer cottage. With Poland's speed specialist in the final, Channel One opted to follow the competition. As I thought back to my first forays into rock climbing two decades earlier and my first training venue – a bouldering wall fitted in a sports centre cleaning cupboard – it felt surreal to watch the Olympic climbing live on national TV. Grandma, reclined on a cosy sofa bed, looked over her newspaper at the athletes leaping from one hold to another.

'Look, look now!' My exclamation came a moment too late and Akiyo Noguchi fell off a big green hold. With only ninety seconds left, she opted to take a good rest before the next attempt.

'What are they doing, standing on the mats for so long?' enquired Grandma, and I attempted to summarise the tactics and complexity of a bouldering competition. She adjusted her glasses and looked back down towards her paper. To my dismay, she was clearly disinterested.

'It's not as exciting as when they run up the big wall,' she said in a matter-of-fact way. If bouldering failed to arrest her attention, what chance did lead climbing have? On the other hand, for a lay observer the speed part of the competition was clearly the easiest to follow and the most spectacular. It could be an ironic twist of events if, in the long run, bouldering and lead were to be dropped, while speed – so often ridiculed by the outdoor climbing community – remained an Olympic sport.

Grandma sank back into her reading and I anxiously watched the competition on two screens at the same time. When the national broadcast cut away to the velodrome, I turned to my computer and the weak internet connection for the live stream. To watch it, I had paid for a monthly Eurosport subscription – a baffling move from somebody who ten years earlier had authored a series of anti-Olympic essays. Yet there I was, on the edge of my seat, completely engrossed in the competition.

EPILOGUE

What is climbing, who shapes it and what it is that makes a climber? As the discipline continues to grow, answering these questions becomes increasingly difficult.

For decades, participation numbers were so low that climbing appeared almost homogeneous. Today, it is both a sport and a culture: a fragmented, complex reality shaped by internal and external factors. Although its elitist beginnings fade into the past, they are a part of its history as much as its years of countercultural rebellion. Both inform its present in the same way that the ethics of mountaineering still inform how we climb today. Even at the gym, the trust we put in our belayer is a reflection of the relationship between two climbers navigating a steep snowfield, tied together with a manila rope. Finding our way to the top of a boulder, to validate our ascent we stick to a predefined line and we refer to it by its name and grade as defined by the first ascensionist. Most of all, we follow a certain code of conduct: one which dictates that we only claim summits that we've actually reached, and that doubting others' ascents is regarded as bad style. For a long time, it was this chivalry of sorts, extending from how we treat one another to what holds are allowed on a given route, which used to make a climber – even if these values were subject to change or heated debate.

Today, with sponsors requiring professional athletes to command a social media following on a par with a popstar's fanbase, videos of climbs are posted on the internet almost in real time. (A live transmission of an attempt seems an inevitable progression.) At the top end of the grade spectrum, the practice went from being a perk to obligatory proof of success. Without a video, whether it's an uncut phone recording or a full-blown documentary, questions of an ascent's validity seem to be hanging in the air – one of the many examples of how external factors erode (shape?) our culture.

A cog in the capitalist machine, climbing can be a tool for both those within its culture and those on its outside. With entities such as the IOC and multinational corporations wielding huge budgets, it is likely that these outside forces will exert a dominating influence, impacting at least how climbing is presented to and perceived by mainstream audiences and recreational participants. The shift may seem irrelevant to core, non-professional climbers. Those whose lives revolve around getting out on the rock often don't care about the media. At the same time, my own experience with bouldering destinations proves that we can't escape change.

Only in the last two years, some of the most recently developed Swiss areas went from empty to overcrowded, with rocks covered in gratuitous tick-marks and music blasting from portable speakers. All it took was the publication of new guidebooks.

In France during the summer months, one of the oldest Fontainebleau sectors of Bas Cuvier resembles a desert; vegetation trampled by countless feet marching to and fro; bouldering pads dragged mindlessly on the ground, contributing to the already serious problem of soil erosion. And in the US and Australia, more visitors to sensitive areas result in more conflict with native communities and landowners, more damage to the environment and exacerbated access problems.

The silver lining is that outdoor recreation might become a means of increasing both environmental and social awareness; higher participation numbers can bring more people to engage with subjects they previously ignored. Now, climbing becomes a starting point for a discussion about environmental and restorative justice, as well as sustainability in outdoor recreation and beyond. Similarly, as a discipline that doesn't favour a specific body type, with female and gender-non-conforming athletes performing at the highest level, it adds to the discussion about ending gender-based discrimination.

As a lifestyle, climbing goes far beyond rocks and artificial walls. It can and should be used to take a stance wherever a stance is needed. The adventure sports community is becoming an increasingly strong lobby for the recognition of the climate crisis, and initiatives such as Climb the Hill, Protect our Winters and Recreate Responsibly are all grassroots movements supported by high-profile athletes and affecting change in both the community and, mindless woke-washing aside, hopefully also the industry.

Personally, I'd like to see environmental stewardship, globally or on the micro-scale of the local crag, becoming as ubiquitous as the use of chalk or sticky rubber shoes. The best-case scenario is that climbers will continue to challenge the status quo, and the increased platform we are given will amplify our voices. In a less optimistic version of the future, we will be muffled by the noise of the capitalist machine.

While I wouldn't dare to call anybody to activism, I do believe that we all should honour mentorship, perhaps climbing's oldest tradition. The passage of skills and ethics from one climber to another is the very basis of our community but, as climbing spills beyond itself and into the mainstream, new participants are increasingly introduced to it through media and indoor gyms.

Businesses, professional athletes and influencers should be held accountable to not only share clickbait content, but also climbing's ethics and values. And, appealing as it may seem to withdraw and ignore anything other than the rock under our fingers, core participants should uphold that standard. Yes, it feels awkward to ask people not to climb wet sandstone, but if I want it to be preserved not only for future generations but also for my own old age, I must approach them and explain that the Fontainebleau rock is extremely fragile after it rains. And as the organiser of an international climbing festival,

I must contend with its environmental impact.

Perhaps the most perceptible value of mentorship is on a personal level. Had I benefitted from a support system within the community, perhaps with somebody to tell me they went through the same struggles and that I was going to be okay, it's likely that my Rodellar injury would not have kept me from climbing for more than a decade. The shift from personal to professional relations within climbing, with gym instruction and online coaching becoming an increasingly common means of skill passage, threatens to displace mentorship, but one does not need to exclude the other.

My experience of moving to Sheffield and having my whole life fall into place thanks to the soft cushioning provided by local climbers made me realise that it is the community, and within it the mentorship and other human relations, which is climbing's defining element. To my delight, it is a community that welcomes the socially awkward, non-conforming type also, but it is not without its flaws. I know first-hand that it can be discriminatory, and acknowledging this is the first step to providing a warmer welcome to all those who traditionally were not accepted.

* * *

When I returned to climbing in my mid-twenties, bouldering 8a was still cutting edge. Around the same time, at nine years old and under four feet tall, Ashima Shiraishi became the youngest climber ever to achieve this grade. In the decade which followed, climbing limits were redefined faster than in the earliest days of the sport. With more people drawn in and more research dedicated to training, the discipline is only now beginning to discover its full athletic potential. Young climbers develop in a structured, professional way similar to what has been seen in gymnastics, and outliers of all ages and genders, sometimes parents with full-time jobs, prove that what we consider to be the limits of performance might just be a mirage.

Climbing has now seen the bouldering grade of 9a/V17, a sport

9a+/5.15a flash, and trad 8b+/5.14a. Janja Garnbret proved that training for competition can directly translate to performance on rock, becoming the first woman to flash two 8c/5.14d routes in her first outdoor season after winning Olympic gold. At twelve years old, French phenom Oriane Bertone became the youngest climber to send an 8b+/V14 boulder, once again showcasing children's ability in the sport. And, perhaps more importantly, Francisco 'Novato' Marín climbed his first route graded 8b+/5.14a aged sixty-one. In Fontainebleau, my friend Helen Dudley claimed her first 7c+/V10 boulder aged fifty, potentially making her the second woman in the world, after Lynn Hill, to achieve the grade at this age. (Helen, a mother of two, is now hunting for her first 8a.) Higher off the ground, Alex Honnold's solo of El Capitan's *Freerider* proved that with the right mindset, fear can be controlled as much as elite athletes learn to control their bodies.

At any level, climbing can be a means of searching for and transcending personal limits, but in the era of sedentary lifestyles and climate crisis, the joy of movement and time spent in nature might prove equally, if not more, rewarding. Despite increasing media representation, for most climbers it remains a participatory activity – a lifestyle sport that is about doing it, not watching it. How much we let it shape us and our lives is still a choice we make ourselves.

Two decades ago, Chris Sharma expected the sport's evolution to bring in more 'people doing it for themselves, for the spiritual aspect, enjoying nature and learning about themselves', and perhaps he was right.[1] Witnessing climbing's popularisation, we are more likely than ever to confront the question of why we climb, and the future of the discipline lies in what we make of it.

ACKNOWLEDGEMENTS

Writing a book is something I've wanted to do since I was three years old and my grandmother taught me the alphabet. I can still remember her hand-gesturing cues when I forgot which letter was which. Now that grandma Zofia Reych (I'm named after her) is no longer here to help, I'd like to dedicate this book to her memory, and to the memory of another person no longer with us, Elena Carpignano, who perished much too soon before her time. Those who pass live through those who go on living and through everything we do, and I can't help but feel like both my grandmother and Elena have contributed to the writing of this book.

I very likely wouldn't have written the first sentence without the continuous, unwavering support of Andy Day, my amazing partner, my sweetheart, my sounding board, my first reader, critic, editor, cheerleader, cook and alarm clock. Andy, I love you. Thank you.

My mum and best friend, Małgorzata Reych, has both my deepest gratitude and my love for taking me to the mountains, and for her unconditional support and guidance. And for having the insight to sign me up for an English class when I was three. And for stopping the reading of *Winnie the Pooh* at the most interesting moments, so I'd have to continue on my own. And for every international call since I moved out, some at odd times of the night, some just ten seconds long and others when we talked for hours. Thank you for being the best!

A big thank you also goes to grandma Ewa Ostrowska – a lifelong journalist – for being a wonderful friend and the best writing mentor I could wish for. I honestly don't know how other writers do it without the ability to turn to their grandma with every writing pain and doubt.

I would like to thank my lifelong friends and my newer friends: Ola Stachowska, Agata Ucińska, Magda Malawska, Alice Hafer, Sandra Jonsson and Helene Collin. I am also extremely grateful to Andy's parents, Julian and Sue Day, for their support, advice and editorial comments. To Thomas Couetdic, for his friendship, critiquing my drafts and finding all the typos in the world.

To everybody at Vertebrate Publishing, especially to Kirsty Reade for being the first one to envisage my book on a bookstore shelf.

To Vasily Ponomarenko and Valentina Kurshakova, as well as their granddaughter, Jenya Kazbekhova, for their generosity in sharing with me their time and story.

My thanks and my gratitude go to all of my climbing friends, partners and mentors. To Aleksandra Taistra for showing me that it's sometimes okay to drop everything and just climb. To Johnny Dawes for being a great flatmate and for his beautiful take on climbing, and for good laughs and good food we cooked together. To Liz Fowler and to Dylan Asena for being great climbing partners.

I would also like to thank Julie Angel for always telling me to just grit my teeth and write the damn book. Being able to witness glimpses of her own writing process gave me courage and conviction. Chris McDougall for one very kind comment made a decade ago, making me believe I could really be a writer. Bradley Garrett for his advice about the publishing industry. Tom Randall for his advice about the climbing industry. Dr Dolores P. Martinez for allowing me to write my MA thesis about climbing even though I was supposed to write about Japanese newspapers.

A warm thank you goes to my therapist, Magdalena Siwek. Without her professional support, I wouldn't be able to complete this book in a timely manner and without much drama.

I must thank also everybody who contributed through helping me to find sources or allowing me to use their photos. In the second group, Lena Drapella, Favia Dubyk and Eleanor Lister deserve a special mention. The legendary John Gill has my gratitude and admiration for his indirect help through creating his amazingly comprehensive website, as well as for his kind replies to my emails. Thanks to Henning Peters for sending me the book scans which I needed to write about Wolfgang Güllich, and to Pascal Terray for information about some of the boulders he opened.

If anybody who should be on this list has not been mentioned, it is not for the lack of gratitude but solely through error. Their contribution is most appreciated nonetheless.

GLOSSARY

abseil, to   to descend from a cliff, rock or mountain using a rope sliding through a device attached to the climber's harness or, in older times, wrapped around the body; also known as *rappelling*; see also *Dülfersitz*

adaptive climbing   also known as *para climbing*; climbing, usually competitive, performed by adaptive athletes, i.e. athletes with disabilities

aid climbing   a rock-climbing discipline involving direct use of aid from gear (aiders) attached to the rock and used to support the climber's weight

anchor   a static point of attachment between the rope or the climber and the rock; usually includes multiple points of attachment connected together for safety. Anchors can be permanent (at the top of a sport-climbing route) or temporary (created by the climber with removable gear, as practised in traditional climbing).

arête   a rock or mountain formation involving a sharp, clear-cut ridge or edge

barndoor   a climbing mistake occurring when the external rotating force exerted on the climber's body causes one point of contact with the rock to fail, and the body, usually connected to the rock only by two points of contact, swings away from the rock

belay, to   to control a rope system based on friction to which a climber is attached so that they are held in the event of a fall; in contemporary climbing, harnesses and a belay device are used for safety; historically, the leading climber tied the rope around their waist while the belaying partner threaded the rope around their body to create friction and slow down a potential fall

beta   knowledge of a method used to climb a section of rock; the name might come from Betamax, an old format of video tape

big-wall climbing   climbing on large cliffs involving multiple pitches (lengths of the rope), and sometimes sleeping on the route in a portaledge

biner   short for *carabiner* or *karabiner* (also known as *crab*)

bivvy, to   to sleep outdoors overnight when climbing, often on a vertical route; a bivvy can be planned or accidental; short for *bivouac*

block   a boulder, or a boulder problem, from the French term *bloc*, meaning a boulder; also spelled *bloc*

bolt   a permanent point of attachment fixed in the rock; bolts can be glued (or cemented) into the rock, or secured via an expansion mechanism; usually seen in sport climbing

bomber   describes a reliable, secure point of protection, or a very good hold

bouldering   a climbing discipline performed on small rocks, without a rope; in contemporary times, a bouldering mat (also called a *crashpad*), a large portable mattress, is often used to protect from the frequent falls

boulder problem   a specific way up a boulder (a small rock not necessitating the use of a rope for protection), usually named and graded by the first ascensionist; in recent years sometimes referred to as a *rig*

bridging   a climbing technique involving standing on wide, opposing footholds, usually performed in formations such as a chimney or a dihedral; also called *stemming*, especially in American English

buildering   climbing on buildings; a playful subdiscipline of climbing

carabiner   a type of a shackle, in modern days usually with a spring-loaded gate, used in many climbing gear operations, most commonly to attach a rope to a protection point; also known as *biner* or spelled *karabiner*

chalk   a white powder used to decrease hand sweating and increase friction in rock climbing, usually made from magnesium carbonate ($MgCO_3$); chalk had been used by gymnasts and was introduced to climbing by John Gill

chimney   a rock formation, usually a crack, wide enough for a climber to fit their entire body inside

choss   rock of poor quality, unstable, likely to break under the weight of a climber

competition climbing   a wide range of climbing disciplines involving an event staged to enable direct competition between participants; early competitions were staged outdoors, and gradually moved towards artificial indoor structures

crack climbing   climbing in rock formations involving cracks of various sizes, including narrow fingercracks, off-widths and chimneys

crag   a rocky outcrop, or an area where rocks can be found, frequented by climbers

cragging   the practice of climbing on relatively small rocky outcrops, or in areas where rock can be found; any non-expedition, non-mountain climbing on natural rock can be referred to as cragging

crampon   a device with sharp metal teeth which, attached to the climber's shoe, allows for tackling icy terrain

crashpad   a large portable mattress-like device used in bouldering to protect against frequent falls; also known as a *bouldering pad*, a *crash* or a *bouldering mat*

crimp   a type of a narrow climbing hold on which the climber uses only the tips of their fingers

crimp, to   an action of using narrow climbing hold, usually involving a pronounced bend in the finger

crux   the most difficult section of a climb or pitch

deadpoint   a climbing technique involving a dynamic move towards a distant hold which is grasped at the moment when the body becomes weightless at the top of a dynamic upwards movement

deck out, to   to fall from a climb and hit the ground

dihedral   a rock-climbing formation where two planes intersect, creating a corner

dirtbagging   a lifestyle involving living as cheaply as possible to sustain climbing without the need to earn money for as long as possible; usually involves not having a permanent home but instead sleeping in a vehicle, camping or sleeping rough

double rope   a rope set-up often used in traditional climbing or mountaineering whereby two strands of rope are used together by a leading climber and can be attached to the rock alternating the strands; a double rope reduces rope drag and the risk of a rope being cut by a falling rock or by friction

drag   see *rope drag*

draw   see *quickdraw*

drop knee a climbing technique involving pushing upwards or sideways on a foothold, while the climber's knee faces downwards

dry tooling a climbing discipline in which the participants use ice axes to ascend exposed rock; often necessitated by the nature of mountain climbing (or in mixed climbing), but also performed as a separate discipline

Dülfersitz an antiquated technique used for abseiling or rappelling in which the climber wraps the rope around their body and the resultant friction enables a safe descent; invented by Hans Dülfer or Tita Piaz

figure of eight a knot commonly used by climbers to attach a climbing rope to a harness

first ascent the first time a route is completed; a coveted prize in the climbing world, especially if a route is high in difficulty

flag a climbing technique in which one leg is in contact with the rock while the other one is used as counterbalance

flapper a piece of flapping skin, usually on the finger, often caused by a ripped callous

flash climbing a route or a boulder on the first attempt, without any prior experience of the holds; however, it is permitted to be given information about the route or to watch others complete it

free climbing a kind of climbing in which climbers do not rely on direct aid from gear, which is used exclusively for protection while staying on the rock; progress is exclusively dependent on the climber's body

free solo, to to climb a route without any protection with often potentially serious consequences should the climber fall; chiefly American, in British English referred to as *solo*

free, to to climb a route without the use of direct aid; the term originated at a time when existing free routes were increasingly climbed without the use of aid (this was called a *first free ascent*)

gear any equipment used in rock climbing, but especially used to describe equipment which is used for securing the rope to the rock in trad climbing, or even a place for that equipment, e.g. 'I can't see any gear above me.'

gumby a derogatory term for a novice and inexperienced climber, especially one transitioning from indoor to outdoor climbing

haul, to to pull up bags of gear and supplies, attached to a rope, during a big-wall climb; as climbers are unable to carry their heavy bags when climbing, the equipment is packed in hauling bags and pulled upwards after the climber reaches their belay point

heel hook a climbing technique involving the climber's heel pulling on a foothold

hex a hexagonal piece of gear wedged into a recess or a crack in the rock as a point of rope attachment in traditional climbing

highball a particularly tall boulder problem

hot aches intense pain in extremities caused by the rush of blood into a previously cold part of the body, typically the hands; also known as *screaming barfies*

hueco a hold shaped like a large hole in the rock, from the Spanish word *hueco*, meaning 'hole'

ice climbing a climbing discipline in which climbers ascend frozen waterfalls or ice formed in the mountains with the use of ice axes (also called ice tools or ice picks) and crampons; also a competitive discipline performed in artificial arenas

jam, to a climbing technique in which a limb is wedged into a recess of the rock or a crack, e.g. a hand jam, a fist jam, a foot jam

jug a big and comfortable climbing hold

karabiner see *carabiner*

knee bar   a climbing technique in which the climber uses their knee and foot to wedge the leg between two protruding parts of the rock

lead climbing   climbing with the rope attached to the climber's body from below, placing points of protection on the go

lead, to   leading is a prerequisite to an ascent being valid (as opposed to *top roping*); see also *sharp end*

lifer   a climber, usually not professional, who dedicates their life to climbing

lock off   a climbing move in which the climber pulls down on a handhold until the elbow is bent and low, allowing them to steady the body and reach with the other hand for another, higher hold

mantle   a technique of getting the climber's body over a rock shelf, often performed at the end of a boulder problem

mixed climbing   a climbing discipline in which both ice and exposed rock are climbed within one route

mono   a climbing hold in which only one finger can be placed

nailing   aid climbing, especially at a time when hammering in pitons was a common part of climbing; also known as *pegging*

off-width   a rock crack too wide for the use of hand jams but too narrow for the climber's whole body to fit inside (when it becomes a chimney); off-width climbing requires a specific skill set quite different from other styles of climbing

offset   a type of a climbing gear with a specific, asymmetric shape, used for wedging in a rock crack or a recess to create a point of attachment between the rope and the rock

Olympic climbing   an Olympic discipline introduced during the 2020 Olympic Games in Tokyo consisting of bouldering, lead climbing and speed climbing; briefly called 'sports climbing' by the IOC

one-armer   performing a pull-up with only one arm

onsight   climbing a route without any prior knowledge of it, and no information about the holds, techniques, etc.

overhang   a rock formation steeper than vertical, the opposite of *slab*

peg   piton

pegging   aid climbing, especially with the use of pitons

pinch   a climbing hold which is held between the forefingers and the thumb

pitch   a section of a rock climb done with less than one length of a climbing rope; climbs are often differentiated for single-pitch and multi-pitch climbs, with sport-climbing routes most often being single-pitch

piton   a metal wedge hammered into the rock to create a point of attachment between the rock and the rope, or to be used as an aid point in aid climbing

pocket   a circular hold, usually deep enough to put a section of one or a few fingers inside

poff   a type of resin used (now rarely) in the Fontainebleau region to increase the friction of hand- and footholds; considered detrimental to the rock by most contemporary climbers

portaledge   a foldable shelf usually made of a structure similar to tent poles with a piece of fabric stretched between them; used by climbers to create a shelf on which they can rest, and often sleep, during a multi-day big-wall ascent

pro   see *protection*

project   a climb which a climber attempts multiple times, often over multiple sessions spread over time because of its difficulty

protection   an American English term for a piece of gear used to create a point of connection between the rock and the rope; also known as *pro*

prusik, to   to ascend a fixed rope using prusik knots or other gear

pump   an unpleasant sensation in the muscle, usually forearm, caused by the build-up of lactic acid; the pump can cause the climber to fail, which often happens on routes requiring endurance

quickdraw   a device composed of a short piece of sling and two spring-loaded carabiners, used for connecting the rope to a point of protection (attachment point); also known as *draw*

rack   gear required for an ascent, usually organised on the climber's harness

rack up, to   to organise all gear necessary for a climb on the climber's harness and sometimes also across the chest

rappel, to   see *abseil, to*

redpoint   climbing a route after a number of previous ascents; from the German *rotpunkt*

redpoint, to   to attempt a climb when the climber predicts that a full ascent might already be possible

roof   a rock formation so steep that it is closer to horizontal than to forty-five degrees

rope drag   the force exerted on a lead climber by the rope below them, usually exacerbated by clipping the rope through protection points; the less straight the rope is (with more angles caused by detours for protection points), the greater the drag

route   a recognised path leading up a rock formation, usually named and graded

run out   climbing high above the last piece of gear (protection), facing potentially serious consequences of a fall

run out, to   to climb high above the last piece of protection

runner   a point of attachment between the rock and the rope, created in such a way that allows for the rope to slide through a piece of gear, as opposed to an anchor, which is a static belay

running belay   see *runner*

sandbag   a climb which is harder than expected

sandbag, to   to recommend a climb which is significantly harder than expected

screaming barfies   see *hot aches*

scree   a mass of sharp-edged stones (broken rock pieces) collecting at a base of a cliff, usually seen in the mountains; often forming a *talus*

scum   the action of touching a body part to the rock in order for the friction to give the climber more stability; sometimes a *knee scum*, used to describe a not-very-stable knee bar

second, to   to climb as the second climber in a roped party, enjoying the benefits of a top rope and being belayed from the top by the person who climbed first (led) the route

send, to   to complete a climb, from *to ascend*

sharp end   *to be on the sharp end*, meaning to lead a route; the sharp end indicates the excitement and potential danger associated with leading (as opposed to seconding, or top roping)

single rope   a climbing rope made up of only one strand of rope; most commonly used in sport climbing and competition climbing, where the risks of the rope breaking are very low

sinker   a very good hold, similar to a jug

slab   a rock formation less steep than vertical

sloper   a hold which does not have an incut and usually must be held with a large section of the hand, including the palm, to maximise friction

smear a shallow foothold on which the climber can stand by finding a point of friction between the flat part of the climbing shoe and the rock
soloing in British English, climbing without any protective gear; see also *free solo*
spicy scary; also *necky, interesting*
sport climbing a climbing discipline in which the points of attachment between the rope and the rock are permanently fixed into the rock
spot, to to stand behind or under a person climbing a boulder problem, usually with arms outstretched towards them, to mitigate the potential consequences of a fall
spotter a person performing the action of spotting in bouldering
stemming see *bridging*
talus a slope of amassed scree forming at the bottom of a cliff
tie in, to to attach the rope to a climber's harness or, in the earlier days of climbing, around a climber's body
toe hook a climbing move involving using the top of the climbing shoe to hook under an inverted climbing hold, or over a climbing hold above the climber's head
top out the end of a climb, usually when the vertical section of the rock ends and the climber can stand on top of it on a less steep section
top out, to to reach the end of a climb and stand at the top
top rope when the rope securing a climber is attached above them, meaning that in the event of a fall their body will be held in place; much more secure than lead climbing
toppy see *top rope*
traditional climbing a climbing discipline in which points of attachment between the rock and the rope are not permanent but placed by the climber on the go and removed afterwards either during an abseil or by a seconding climber
traverse a sideways climb
traverse, to to climb sideways
tufa in climbing jargon, a rock formation resembling a vertical tube stuck on to a climbing route, ranging in size from less than an inch to a few feet in diameter. Usually found on limestone. The original, geological use of the term is slightly different
twin rope a rope set-up involving two strands of rope used together; twin rope cannot be separated (unlike a double rope) and its main advantage is lower weight; often used in mountaineering
whipper a large fall arrested by the rope
yo-yo a style of climbing in which a group of people attempt the same climb, but the points of attachment between the rock and the rope of the leader are left in place for the next person climbing, meaning that if the first climber falls after the second bolt, or traditional point of removable protection, the second climber is allowed to keep the rope in these points and enjoy the benefits of a top rope until they bypass the highpoint of the predecessor; antiquated

ACRONYMS

AAC the American Alpine Club, formed in the United States in 1902; also used in the book to refer to the British nineteenth-century Amateur Athletic Club
AAJ the *American Alpine Journal*, the official publication of the AAC, founded in 1929
ABS the American Bouldering Series, predecessor to the Open Bouldering National Championships in the United States
AC the Alpine Club, formed in Great Britain in 1857
AJ the *Alpine Journal*, the official publication of the AC, founded in 1863
BMC British Mountaineering Council, formed in 1944
CC the Climber's Club, a British organisation formed in 1898
ESPN an American international cable sports channel
FA first ascent
FFA first female ascent *or* first free ascent
FFE the French Federation of Climbing, founded in 1985, predecessor to the FFME; the abbreviation comes from its French name (Fédération Française d'Escalade)
FFM the French Federation of Mountaineering, founded in 1942, predecessor to the FFE and FFME; the abbreviation comes from its French name (Fédération Française de la Montagne)
FFME the French Federation of Mountaineering and Climbing, founded in 1987; the abbreviation comes from its French name (Fédération Française de la Montagne et de l'Escalade)
GB Climbing the national governing body of the sport of competition climbing in Great Britain
ICCC International Council for Competition Climbing, founded in 1997 as part of the UIAA; predecessor to the IFSC
IFSC International Federation of Sport Climbing, founded in 2007
IOC International Olympic Committee, founded in 1894
JCCA Junior Competitive Climbing Association in the United States
TOPR Tatra Volunteer Search and Rescue; the abbreviation comes from its Polish name (Tatrzańskie Ochotnicze Pogotowie Ratownicze)
UIAA the International Climbing and Mountaineering Federation, founded in 1932; the abbreviation comes from its French name (Union Internationale des Associations d'Alpinisme)
USA Climbing the national governing body of the sport of competition climbing in the United States; the current name and structure date from 2003, with its first predecessor founded in 1994

GRADE COMPARISON TABLES

The tables include only the contemporary grading systems commonly used in the book.

BOULDERING		
USA (Hueco)	Europe (Fontainebleau)	UK Technical
V0	3	4c
V0	4-	5a
V0	4	5a
V0	4+	5b
V1	5	5b
V2	5+	5c
V3	6a	5c
V3	6a+	6a
V4	6b	6a
V5	6b+	6a
V5	6c	6a
V5	6c+	6b
V6	7a	6b
V7	7a+	6b
V8	7b	6c
V8	7b+	6c
V9	7c	6c
V10	7c+	7a
V11	8a	7a
V12	8a+	7a
V13	8b	7b
V14	8b+	7b
V15	8c	7b
V16	8c+	7b
V17	9a	7b

Notes for sport and traditional climbing table
* sport climbing grades used in Europe
** Yosemite decimal sytem used throughout the US
*** a grade system indicating technical and risk factors used for British traditional climbing

SPORT AND TRADITIONAL CLIMBING

French*	YDS**	British***
	5	
2	5.1	**Mod** *Moderate*
	5.2	**Diff** *Difficult*
3	5.3	
4a	5.4	**VDiff** *Very Difficult*
4b	5.5	**HVD** *Hard Very Difficult*
4c	5.6	**Sev** *Severe* — 3c **HS** *Hard Severe* 4b
5a	5.7	4a **VS** *Very Severe* 5a
5b	5.8	4b **HVS** *Hard Very Severe* 5b
5c	5.9	
6a	5.10a	5a **E1** 5c
6a+	5.10b	5a **E2** 6a
6b	5.10c	
6b+	5.10d	5b **E3** 6a
6c	5.11a	
	5.11b	5c **E4** 6b
6c+	5.11c	6a **E5** 6c
7a	5.11d	
7a+	5.12a	6b
7b	5.12b	**E6**
7b+	5.12c	6c **E7**
7c	5.12d	6c
7c+	5.13a	
8a	5.13b	7a **E8** 7a
8a+	5.13c	
8b	5.13d	7a **E9** **E10** 7a
8b+	5.14a	
8c	5.14b	7b
8c+	5.14c	
9a	5.14d	7b
9a+	5.15a	
9b	5.15b	
9b+	5.15c	
9c	5.15d	

NOTES AND REFERENCES

PREFACE
Notes
1 For an explanation of the differences between solo, free solo and free climbing (as well as other climbing-specific terms), refer to the Glossary on page 256.

CHAPTER 1: FIRST STEPS
Epigraph
'Lying here on the fragrant meadow, on a glorious July day, I felt a sensation so strange to the lowland dwellers: a feeling of inhibited freedom.'
Mieczysław Karłowicz w Tatrach: Pisma taternickie i zdjęcia fotograficzne wydane staraniem zarządu sekcyi turystycznej Towarzystwa Tatrzańskiego, Kraków, 1910. Translated from the Polish original by the author.

Notes
1 The stories of Polish climbers who dominated the great ranges in the post-war period are told in McDonald, B., *Freedom Climbers*, Vertebrate Publishing, 2012.
2 Another book by McDonald is entirely dedicated to Kurtyka: McDonald, B., *Art of Freedom: The Life and Climbs of Voytek Kurtyka*, Rocky Mountain Books Inc., 2017.
3 The grade, amounting to F7c+, is expressed on a Polish scale named after Kurtyka. Nearly three decades later, *Chiński Maharadża* remains a highly technical route suitable only for experienced, physically fit climbers. A solo ascent would still likely earn a mention in the media and warrant the production of a sponsored video.
4 Today the traditional outfits are only worn during major celebrations or holidays, as well as for the tourists. The bale huts were, in earlier times, a shepherd's shelter and a place to smoke sheep cheese; in my lifetime, the huts also became rustic shops, delighting tourists with their salty *oscypek* cheese and a sour, buttermilk-like drink called *żyntyca*.
5 *Images from the Tatras and the Pieniny* (Steczkowska, M., *Obrazkz Podróży do Tatrów i Pienin*, Kraków, 1858) was not intended as a guidebook; however, in the absence of any other publications, the book served as such for a growing group of mountain tourists until the publication of an illustrated guidebook by Walery Eljasz-Radzikowski in 1870. The quoted passage was translated from Polish by the author.

CHAPTER 2: MOUNTAIN GLOOM AND MOUNTAIN GLORY
Epigraph
'History is a series of lies upon which we agree.'
The quote is commonly attributed to Napoleon Bonaparte, although the author did not find its original source. It is often cited in the French media, for example: *Le Figaro*, http://evene.lefigaro.fr/citation/histoire-suite-mensonges-lesquels-accord-12583.php, accessed 12 April 2021.

Notes
1. Petrarch, F., *The Ascent of Mount Ventoux*, written c.1350, https://sourcebooks.fordham.edu/source/petrarch-ventoux.asp, accessed 10 January 2022.
2. The etymology of the very word 'muse' could in fact be connected to the meaning of tower or mountain. Cook, A.B., *Zeus: A Study in Ancient Religion*, Volume 1, p.104, Cambridge University Press, 1914.
3. It feels pertinent here to clarify that the tale this chapter is piecing together is one that forms the background for the not yet nascent sport of mountaineering which was later born and conceptualised as a very European phenomenon. Because of this, we do not talk of fifth-century Chinese landscape painting, or the sacred mountains of Native Americans.
4. The word 'paradise' itself comes from the Persian language and refers to an enclosed garden, usually one surrounding the palace of a king (Mahmoudi Farahani, L. et al., 'Persian Gardens: Meanings, Symbolism, and Design', *Landscape Online* 46:1–19, 2016).
5. The first quote comes from an English traveller, James Howell, describing the Pyrenees (www.ft.com/content/922d07da-9dab-11e1-838c-00144feabdc0, accessed 10 January 2022), and the second was included in Macfarlane, R., *Mountains of the Mind: A History of a Fascination*, Granta, 2003.
6. Macfarlane, R., *ibid*.
7. From the title of a drawing by William Heath, 'Monster Soup commonly called Thames Water' (1828), the British Museum Online Collection, www.britishmuseum.org/collection/object/P_1935-0522-4-121, accessed 10 January 2022.
8. Sublimity as a concept was first talked about in ancient Greece and subsequently Rome, but its meaning was different from that which it assumed in modern times. The *Oxford Classical Dictionary* is a good place to start further reading: www.oxfordre.com/classics/view/10.1093/acrefore/9780199381135.001.0001/acrefore-9780199381135-e-6109, accessed 10 January 2022.
9. The artistic movement was named after a play of the same title, penned by German author Friedrich Maximilian von Klinger, in 1777.
10. Jean-Jacques Rousseau's 'Confessions' quoted in Macfarlane, R., *Mountains of the Mind: A History of a Fascination*, Granta, 2003.
11. Quoted from Walpole's letter written 'From a Hamlet among the Mountains of Savoy, 28th Sept. 1739, N.S. To Richard West, Esq.', www.bartleby.com/209/804.html, accessed 10 January 2022.
12. Burke, E., *A Philosophical Enquiry into the Origin of Our Ideas of the Sublime and Beautiful*, quoted in Open Education Network, https://oen.pressbooks.pub/guidetogothic/chapter/edmund-burke-from-on-the-sublime-and-beautiful-1757/, accessed 10 January 2022.

13. Family letters of Dorothy Wordsworth quoted in Taylor, J., 'The audacious Wordsworth who put mountaineering on the map in the 19th century', *The Independent*, www.independent.co.uk/arts-entertainment/dorothy-william-wordsworth-sister-mountaineering-scafell-pike-lake-district-a8525186.html, accessed 10 January 2022.
14. Coleridge's letter to Sara Hutchinson, quoted in Macfarlane, R., *Mountains of the Mind: A History of a Fascination*, Granta, 2003.
15. *ibid*.
16. Early Romanticism explaining pre-modernity. New research in the field will hopefully soon be conducted by academics working on the subject matter.

CHAPTER 3: MONTY PYTHON'S FLYING CIRCUS
Epigraph
'The Grépon has disappeared. Of course, there are still some rocks standing there, but as a climb it no longer exists. Now that it has been done by two women alone, no self-respecting man can undertake it.'
Étienne Bruhl, French alpinist, commenting on the ascent done by Miriam O'Brien Underhill and Alice Damesme in 1929. Quoted in the *American Alpine Journal*, 2005, digitised at http://publications.americanalpineclub.org/articles/12200509900/Going-Manless-Looking-Back-Forward-and-Inward, accessed 1 March 2020.

Notes
1. *Karta Wspinacza* (Climbing Licence) and *Karta Taternika* (Tatra Climbing Licence) are no longer legally required to climb. Somewhat unbelievably, for decades the Tatra Climbing Licence was successfully enforced, as nearly all climbing in the Polish Tatras falls within the boundaries of a national park. Rangers were readily giving out hefty fines to anybody caught off a marked tourist trail without a valid licence.
2. In Polish it is known by its acronym, TOPR, standing for Tatrzańskie Ochotnicze Pogotowie Ratownicze, which translates to Tatra Volunteer Search and Rescue.
3. V, or 'five' in the Kurtyka scale, equalling 5b in the French scale or 5.8 in the Northern American scale, easy climbing suitable for beginners that can nonetheless feel very scary on the sharp end!
4. In every language and climbing tradition the commands follow a slightly different spiel, with English being a widely accepted standard around the world. The Polish 'Can I go?', 'You can go' and 'Climbing' amount to the English 'On belay' and 'Climbing'.

CHAPTER 4: THE GOLDEN AGE AND OTHER MYTHS
Epigraph
'He is a true apprentice of the craft only when he can say from a full heart Labor ipse voluptas [labour is pleasure].'
Frederick Pollock in 'The Early History of Mountaineering', an introductory chapter to Dent, C.T. and Conway, Sir W.M., *Mountaineering (the Badminton Library of Sports and Pastimes)*, Longmans, Green & Co., 1892.

Notes
1. A pamphlet titled 'Letter from an English gentleman … giving an account of a journey to the glacieres or ice Alps of Savoy' was published by Windham in 1744. It contains an English translation of his letters, originally written in French. The French original of the cited passage reads, '*Il faut s'imagine le lac …* '. However, it is commonly believed that the

popular name of the Montenvers glacier, Mer de Glace, was given to it by Windham in the account of his travels. It might have to do with another description by Windham, given in the same paragraph, and likening the glacier to '*les mers de Groenland*', or 'the seas of Greenland'. In the course of my research I didn't manage to determine whether Windham used the exact phrase '*la mer de glace*' in a different context, perhaps not in writing but in person, or whether attributing the glacier's popular name to Windham is simply incorrect.

2   The dragon encounter was reported by an early palaeontologist, Johann Jakob Scheuchzer (1672– 1733), whose imagination was likely ignited by fossils.
3   Quoted in Gribble, F., *The Story of Alpine Climbing*, Mancha Press, 2017.
4   Information obtained from the official website of the town of Chamonix, www.chamonix.com/vacances/hotel-chamonix.html, accessed 8 January 2020.
5   A Genevan professor of natural philosophy, Horace Bénédict de Saussure (1740–1799), was especially intent upon playing a part in the development. Not only did he attempt the climb himself in 1762, but he also set up a reward for anyone who succeeded, while also covering the expenses for any unsuccessful attempts. De Saussure first travelled to Chamonix in 1760, collecting specimens for the Austrian botanist Albrecht von Haller (the same who authored the idyllic poem '*Die Alpen*'). The young scholar fell in love with the Mont Blanc region and devoted his whole life to extensive travels in the Alps. Despite his scientific interest, De Saussure's writings display a clear emotional attachment to the mountains not unlike that often expressed by modern travellers. Michel-Gabriel Paccard, a member of the first party to scale Mont Blanc, was a close acquaintance of De Saussure. However, to alleviate the conflict between Paccard and his guide, Jacques Balmat, he allowed the latter to claim the entirety of de Saussure's prize.
6   Continental explorers of the Alps included the Benedictine monk Placidus a Spescha, the great pyreneeist Baron de Carbonnières and Professor Peter Karl Thurwieser.
7   *Alpine Journal*, www.alpinejournal.org.uk/Contents/Contents_1951_files/AJ58 1951 Frontispiece-3 Thorington Mt Blanc.pdf, accessed 8 January 2020.
8   McNee, A., *The Cockney Who Sold the Alps: Albert Smith and the Ascent of Mont Blanc*, Victorian Secrets, 2015.
9   *The Times Magazine* quoted in Thompson, S., *Unjustifiable Risk? The Story of British Climbing*, Cicerone Press, 2012.
10 Cost taken from Hansen, P.H., 'British mountaineering, 1850–1914', cited in Unsworth, W., *Hold the Heights: The Foundations of Mountaineering*, The Mountaineers, 1993, recalculated using Ian Webster's estimations (www.in2013dollars.com/, accessed 8 January 2021), amounting to £270 today.
11 Despite his strict Victorian morality, Wills was an early proponent of women's climbing and in later life was frequently accompanied in the mountains by his daughter, who ascended Mont Blanc with him.
12 As per the opinion of Walt Unsworth (*Hold the Heights* …) Wills' book included an exciting passage about the ascent of Wetterhorn, and although it wasn't a first (the guides had misled their clients to believe so) it was one of the first alpinism accounts which treated it as a sporting activity in the spirit of the heroic tradition which focuses on the achievement of an individual rather than the beauty of the mountains.
13 Wills, A., *Wanderings Among the High Alps*, 1858, digitised by Google, https://books.google.fr/books/about/Wanderings_among_the_high_Alps.html?id=xFsBAAAAQAAJ&redir_esc=y, accessed 2 February 2021.
14 Testament to the homophobia of the times is this passage from Newsome, D., *Godliness and Good Learning: Four Studies on a Victorian Ideal*, Cassel & Co., 1961: 'Young men

came to church for spiritual nourishment: they came away perverted. […]; renouncing the love of women, they clung to each other, casting aside all manly reticence by confessing to each other their secret temptations and seeking solace in their own passionate attachments which seemed to a normal, healthy male […] undesirably high-pitched.'

15 Watson, N.J. et al., 2005, 'The development of muscular Christianity in Victorian Britain and beyond', *Journal of Religion and Society*, 7, http://ray.yorksj.ac.uk/id/eprint/840/, accessed 10 February 2020.

16 Roche, C., *Women Climbers 1850–1900: A Challenge to Male Hegemony?*, Department of History, Classics and Archaeology, Birkbeck, University of London. Published online 2 September 2013.

17 Cusik, J., 'Matterhorn conqueror cleared over fatal falls', *The Independent*, 30 August 1997, www.independent.co.uk/news/matterhorn-conqueror-cleared-over-fatal-falls-1248170.html, accessed 2 March 2021.

18 Leslie, S., *The Playground of Europe*, Longmans, Green & Co., 1871, digitised by Google, https://books.google.fr/books/about/The_Playground_of_Europe.html?id=CsFDAAAAYAAJ&redir_esc=y, accessed 1 December 2020.

19 Frison-Roche, R., Jouty, S., *A History of Mountain Climbing*, Flammarion, 1996, in Hollis, D.L., 'Mountain Gloom and Mountain Glory: The Genealogy of an Idea', *ISLE: Interdisciplinary Studies in Literature and Environment*, Volume 26, Issue 4, Autumn 2019, pp.1038–1061, https://doi.org/10.1093/isle/isz0442019, accessed 1 March 2020.

20 From a foreword to Ruskin, J., *Sesame and Lilies*, originally published in 1865, republished in 2002 by Oxford University Press. The 'cutaneous eruptions' Ruskin speaks of are undoubtedly sunburns and frostbites that were almost universally suffered by early mountaineers.

21 In the space of the sixty years that lapsed between the Matterhorn accident and Mallory and Irvine perishing on Everest, the public went from condemnation to glorification and seeing the dead mountaineers as heroes – curiously, this only applied to male climbers, and yet another sixty years later in 1995, the death of British climber Alison Hargreaves sparked outrage again because a woman dared to throw away her life instead of staying with the children.

22 A letter from Ruskin to his father, quoted in Macfarlane, R., *Mountains of the Mind: A History of a Fascination*, Granta, 2003. Emphasis added by the author.

23 Thomas Hardy's heroine in *Far from the Madding Crowd*, Bathsheba Everdene, was a classic, if rare, positive example of a 'new woman'.

24 Proper management often amounted to staying in bed while heavily sedated with opioids. A passage from 1868 by Dr John Burns can serve as an example: 'The patient always must be kept at rest in a horizontal posture. Opiates are to be given if there is much pain and irritation. The food ought to be sparing and anything warm is to be avoided. If necessary the vagina is to be plugged if a great effect has been produced upon the system by the haemorrhage, then strength must be supported by nourishment and cordials and liberal doses of opium will be found of much benefit.' Quoted in Lyster, K., 'The Victorian period: when menstruation was a dangerous disease that could lead to madness', *iNews*, 2020, www.inews.co.uk/opinion/columnists/victorian-period-menstruation-nineteenth-century-130987, accessed 10 January 2021.

25 Crane, J.M. (ed.), *Swiss Letters and Alpine Poems*, Palala Press, 2016, in Roche, C., *Women Climbers 1850–1900: A Challenge to Male Hegemony?*, Department of History, Classics and Archaeology, Birkbeck, University of London. Published online 2 September 2013.

26 Windham, W., *An Account of the Glacieres Or Ice Alps in Savoy, in Two Letters: One from an English Gentleman to His Friend at Geneva; the Other from Peter Martel, Engineer, to the Said English Gentleman (sic)*, 1744, digitised by Google, https://books.google.fr/books/about/An_Account_of_the_Glacieres_Or_Ice_Alps.html?id=6ry9xwEACAAJ&redir_esc=y, accessed 7 October 2020.
27 Windham's guides assured him that in the time of their fathers, the glacier was much smaller than during his excursion and that it had been growing. It reached its peak size in the mid-nineteenth century and started shrinking again after that, a process greatly sped up in recent years by the climate crisis.

CHAPTER 5: THE DESCENDANTS OF GODS
Epigraph
'Mens sana in corpore sano.'
Decimus Junius Juvenalis was a Roman poet. The quote comes from his satires and its original meaning was different from how it is most often used today within the context of good physical health. *Decimi Junii Juvenalis et Auli Persii Flacci Satiræ Expurgatæ*, Wilkins, 1852, digitised by Google, https://books.google.fr/books/about/Decimi_Junii_Juvenalis_et_Auli_Persii_Fl.html?id=3yJPAAAAYAAJ&redir_esc=y, accessed 2 February 2021.

Notes
1 'Philip Barker: 1866 and all that', *Inside the Games*, www.insidethegames.biz/articles/1040094/philip-barker-1866-and-all-that, accessed 11 January 2022, emphasis added by the author.
2 'Ancient Olympic Games', *World History Encyclopaedia*, www.ancient.eu/Olympic_Games/, accessed 3 April 2020.
3 De Coubertin, P., 'The Olympic Idea. Discourses and Essays', *Editions Internationales Olympiques*, Lausanne, 1970.
4 This is best illustrated by the inception of one of London's oldest football clubs, West Ham United, which was founded just after a large strike crippled the Thames Ironworks.
5 The rapid professionalisation of football in the UK resulted in a very different history of the sport from that of many other disciplines. In the business-minded US the general transition from amateur to professional sport occurred much earlier. Universities could boost their budgets through staging athletics competitions, initially in rowing, and particularly talented athletes, regardless of their social standing or race, were admitted to the university to compete for them as amateurs. The education they received was illusory, but it allowed universities to shine through their teams.
6 Perraud, A., 'Racism and sport, a sorry story of modern times', *Mediapart*, 2011, www.mediapart.fr/en/journal/france/130511/racism-and-sport-sorry-story-modern-times, accessed 4 April 2021.
7 'It is indecent that the audience should risk witnessing the shattering of the female body in front of their very eyes. However hardened a sportswoman may be, her organism is not made to endure certain things. Her [emotions] dominate over her muscles.' from *La Revue Olympique, Bulletin Trimestriel du Comité International Olympique*, Imprimerie Albert Lanier, 1901, translated from French by the author.

CHAPTER 6: LONDON, 2011
Epigraph
'It is not the mountain we conquer but ourselves.'
The quote is commonly believed to have been first said by Sir Edmund Hillary, but it is unclear whether it was him who came up with it verbatim. More on the quote's sources can be found at *The Quote Investigator*, https://quoteinvestigator.com/2016/08/18/conquer/, accessed 20 April 2021.

Notes
1. Paying out slack not far from the ground could result in 'decking out' or, in regular English, hitting the ground.

CHAPTER 7: GYMNASTS ON ROCK
Epigraph
'But a line must be drawn somewhere to separate the possible and the impossible, and some try to draw it by their own experience. They constitute what is called the ultra-gymnastic school of climbing.'
Owen Glynne Jones quoted in Thompson, S., *Unjustifiable Risk? The Story of British Climbing*, Cicerone Press, 2012.

Notes
1. 'The First Ascent of Napes Needle', *The Journal of the Fell and Rock Climbing Club*, Volume 3, November 1914, digitised at www.yumpu.com/en/document/read/34300813/number-in-series-8-year-of-publication-1914-fell-and-rock-, accessed 3 October 2020.
2. *ibid.*
3. *ibid.*
4. Thompson, S., *Unjustifiable Risk? The Story of British Climbing*, Cicerone Press, 2012.
5. *ibid.*
6. *ibid.*
7. Crowley, A., *The Confessions of Aleister Crowley: An Autohagiography*, Penguin, 1989.
8. 'The only conquest of Königstein', in *Once a Week*, ed. Dallas, E.S., Volume 1, Issue 7, London, 1868.
9. The first prominent educator interested in physical exercise was Johann Christoph Friedrich GutsMuths, who in 1793 published his *Gymnastics for Youth: Or a Practical Guide to Delightful and Amusing Exercises for the Use of Schools. An Essay Toward the Necessary Improvement of Education. Chiefly As It Relates to the Body*. The manual was translated into English in 1800 and influenced the understanding of the importance of exercise as part of an educational curriculum.
10. *Die Deutsche Turnkunst*, referenced by Gill, J., http://www128.pair.com/r3d4k7/Climbing&Gymnastics1.1a.html, accessed 2 December 2020.
11. Pankotsch, H., *Der Falkenstein: aus der Geschichte eines Kletterfelsen in der Sächsischen Schweiz*, Naisse Verlag, 2001.
12. *ibid.*
13. Thorington, J.M., 'Oliver Perry-Smith, Profile of a Mountaineer', *American Alpine Journal*, 1964, http://publications.americanalpineclub.org/articles/12196409900/Oliver-Perry-Smith-Profile-of-a-Mountaineer, accessed 10 March 2021.
14. *King Lines*, Lowell, J. and Mortimer, P., Sender Films and Big UP Productions, USA, 2007.
15. Thorington, J.M., 'Oliver Perry-Smith, Profile of a Mountaineer', *American Alpine Journal*, 1964, http://publications.americanalpineclub.org/articles/12196409900/Oliver-Perry-Smith-Profile-of-a-Mountaineer, accessed 10 March 2021.

CHAPTER 8: THE PITON DISPUTE
Epigraph
'I do not understand at all how a person could be so cruel as to want to constrain rock-climbing within limits.'
A quote from Ladin guide Giovanni Battista Piaz, known as Tita Piaz, from his article 'Deutsche Alpenzeitung', XI/1, *Mitteilungen*, Nr.14, Oktober 1911; S.89, in 'The collection of essays generally known as the Mauerhakenstreit, the "Piton Dispute", as translated by Randolph Burks, with photographs selected by the translator', www.issuu.com/randisi/docs/mauerhakenstreit_complete_illustrated, accessed 20 October 2020.

Notes
1. A large portion of the information included in this chapter comes from a monograph on Paul Preuss and Emilio Comici by David Smart (for bibliographical note, see Further Reading, p.285).
2. Stephen, L., *The Playground of Europe*, Longmans, Green & Co., 1907.
3. Grohmann, P., *Wanderungen in den Dolomiten*, Fines Mundi GmbH Saarbrücken, Edition Finis Mundi (originally published in 1877).
4. Nieberl, F., Hiebeler, T., 'Das Klettern im Fels' in Smart, D., *Paul Preuss: Lord of the Abyss: Life and Death at the Birth of Free-Climbing*, Rocky Mountain Books, 2019.
5. In the town at the centre of the Italian irredentist movement, any organisation inevitably had a political agenda and the Gymnastic Society was no different. Its aim was to educate its members – both physically and politically – to become model Italian citizens. Influenced by alpine pioneers, the Society used the nearby white limestone of the Rosandra Valley as its training grounds. One of the Society's most influential members was Napoleone Cozzi (1867–1916), a pioneer of guideless mountaineering in the Eastern Alps. Cozzi represented the progressive, heroic faction within Italian climbing and his main rival was Julius Kugy, a bourgeois gentleman who climbed with a guide and stood for the aesthetic values of the mountaineering tradition. Despite their differences, both left a lasting mark on the Gymnastic Society and popularised rock climbing among the Trieste youth.
6. Ascent by Emil Solleder and Gustav Lettenbauer.
7. 'Das Letzte im Fels', a review in *American Alpine Journal*, 1937, http://publications.americanalpineclub.org/articles/12193709801/Das-Letzte-im-Fels, accessed 10 May 2020.

CHAPTER 9: A ROCK SHELF HIGH ABOVE THE BLACK LAKE VALLEY
Epigraph
'I am determined and this gives me a sense of freedom. I am free from everything which is not The Mountain or myself, free from fear and apprehension – because I have no choice left.'
A quote from Wanda Rutkiewicz's autobiography, *On One Rope*, translated by the author. Rutkiewicz, W., *Na Jednej Linie*, ed. Matuszewska, E., Wydawnictwo Iskry, 2010.

Notes
1. *Historia Zakopanego*, ezakopane.pl, https://ezakopane.pl/turystyka/historia-zakopanego/, accessed 10 October 2020.

CHAPTER 10: ON STOLEN LAND
Epigraph
'Being a Native Indigenous person, you come from oppressed people.'
The quote from Lonnie Kauk comes from Kauk, L., Wright, P., 'Magic Line', *Alpinist* 2019, www.alpinist.com/doc/web19s/wfeature-a66-magic-line-lonnie-kauk, accessed 10 June 2021.

Notes
1. Steven J. Holmes.
2. The unprecedented influx of people and the economic stimulus from gold mining quickly led California to become the thirty-first member state of the US. Although it joined the Union as a free state, the Fugitive Slave Act of 1850 meant that African-Americans enslaved in other states could not find safety in California. In addition, a hidden form of slavery existed under the Act for the Government and Protection of Indians, which allowed native children to be taken from their families and native convicts to be used for forced labour. At a time when whites often paid native workers with alcohol, the Act made it legal to enslave and auction native people charged with public drinking, or even loitering. Organised sweeps provided a never-ending stream of free labour. Displaced tribes were forcibly removed to reservations and many could not make a living on the amount of land they were left with. Some retreated further into the mountains and fought the settlers in frequent clashes. When a trading outpost located not far from the present-day Yosemite National Park was attacked and three white settlers killed, a volunteer militia was raised under the name of the Mariposa Battalion. *Discovery of the Yosemite*, Chapter XIV, http://www.yosemite.ca.us/library/discovery_of_the_yosemite/14.html#page_236, accessed 10 March 2021.
3. *Mariposa Gazette* http://www.yosemite.ca.us/library/mariposa_gazette_18550809.html. Another very popular account was soon published by Horace Greeley: *An Overland Journey from New York to San Francisco in the Summer of 1859*.
4. Cothran, B., 'Working the Indian Field Days: The Economy of Authenticity and the Question of Agency in Yosemite Valley', *The American Indian Quarterly*, 34(2), pp.194–223, 2010.
5. Spence, M.D., *Dispossessing the Wilderness: Indian Removal and the Making of the National Parks*, Oxford University Press, 2000.
6. Nelson, A., quoted in Roper, S., *Camp 4: Recollections of a Yosemite Rockclimber*, Mountaineers Books, 1994.
7. ibid.
8. With time, it also morphed into an open-ended scale, with subdivisions ranging from a to d, thus resulting in a scale from 5.10a to 5.15d.
9. Roper, S., *Camp 4: Recollections of a Yosemite Rockclimber*, Mountaineers Books, 1994.
10. ibid.
11. ibid.
12. ibid.
13. Prothero, S., 'On the Holy Road: The Beat Movement as Spiritual Protest', *Harvard Theological Review* 84, no.2, in Johnston, P.J., 'Dharma Bums: The Beat Generation and the Making of Countercultural Pilgrimage', *Buddhist-Christian Studies*, Volume 33, 2013.
14. Kauk, L., Wright, P., 'Magic Line', *Alpinist*, 2019, http://www.alpinist.com/doc/web19s/wfeature-a66-magic-line-lonnie-kauk, accessed 10 June 2021.

CHAPTER 11: HARD GRIT
Epigraph
'The working class, come kiss my ass,
I've joined the Alpine Club at last!'
This is also used as an epigraph in Gray, D., 'The Rise and Fall of the Working Class Climber', *Alpine Journal*, 2007, www.alpinejournal.org.uk/Contents/Contents_2007_files/AJ 2007 142-146 Gray History.pdf, accessed 10 February 2020.

Notes
1. Brown, J., *The Hard Years*, Mountaineers Books, 2001.
2. By Peter Harding (1924–2007). He was at the forefront of development until work took priority over climbing and the top spot of best British outcrop climber became vacant.
3. Skelton, R., 'Manchester's Ardwick Ward Blighted by Poverty and Inequality', *World Socialist Web Site*, www.wsws.org/en/articles/2011/04/ardw-a16.html, accessed 10 December 2020.
4. The perception of the working class as a homogenous entity is as discriminatory as treating any marginalised group as a monolith. Brown's living conditions as a child were much closer to poverty, while for Whillans the main source of difficulty was perhaps his temporary separation from his parents during the Blitz, when children were sent off to safer, rural locations. Biographer Jim Perrin suggests that perhaps the sense of abandonment stemming from this time was behind what later came to be seen as Whillans' aggressive and obstinate character, but the truth of the matter is that, without an intimate knowledge of a person and a psychiatric insight, discerning people's motives and understanding their behaviour is nearly impossible. Writers attempt to do that all the time, but even those who cross paths with their subjects always employ a degree of fiction in creating their portraits. What is true without doubt is that the legend of Whillans as the embodiment of working-class harshness and grit influenced at least two generations of British climbers.
5. *Matinee*, UKC Logbook, www.ukclimbing.com/logbook/crags/roaches_lower_tier-105/matinee-16010, accessed 10 February 2021.
6. Perrin, J., *The Villain: The Life of Don Whillans*, Arrow, 2006.
7. ibid.
8. Perrin, J., *Hard Rock: Great British rock climbs from VS to E4*, ed. Parnell, I., Vertebrate Publishing, 2020.
9. Douglas, E., 'The Vertical Beatnik', *The Guardian*, 2005, www.theguardian.com/sport/2005/mar/06/features.sportmonthly1, accessed 10 February 2020.
10. Thompson, S., *Unjustifiable Risk? The Story of British Climbing*, Cicerone Press, 2012.
11. Jim Perrin interviewed by David Roberts, Banff Centre for Arts and Creativity, 2016, https://youtu.be/s2yStnLKDJY, accessed 10 February 2020.
12. Perhaps Whillans already yearned for these kinds of comforts, as for the 1970 Annapurna expedition he designed his famous 'sit harness' which soon went into mass production, one of the earliest examples of this kind of gear.

CHAPTER 12: STEEL CITY, 2015
Epigraph
'I climb just as hard as anyone. I just do it on easier routes.'
Source unknown.

Notes
1   Pete's Eats is a popular and iconic greasy spoon in Llanberis.

CHAPTER 13: THE POETRY OF MOUNTAINEERING
Epigraph
'This is a pastime epigrammatized by Yvon Chouinard with his customary wit as instant suffering.'
Gill, J., 'The Art of Bouldering', *American Alpine Journal*, digitised by AAC Publications, http://publications.americanalpineclub.org/articles/12196935500/The-Art-of-Bouldering, accessed 10 February 2020.

Notes
1   Quotes and the story of Gill's climbing come from a book by Pat Ament, who for a long time was Gill's bouldering partner, perhaps the only other climber in the world interested in small rocks for their own sake. Ament, P., *Master of Rock: The Biography of John Gill*, Routledge, 1977.
2   At the time of Gill's explorations, bouldering wasn't seen as climbing by the climbing community. In modern climbing lingo, boulder problems can be called 'boulders', 'problems', 'blocs', 'lines', 'rigs', etc., and are considered climbs but of a certain kind, as much as sport climbing, big walling, aid climbing, etc. For more details, see Glossary, p.256.
3   Ament, P., *Master of Rock: The Biography of John Gill*, Routledge, 1977.
4   A couple of years before the Thimble ascent, Gill put up two boulder problems on Red Cross Rock in the Tetons. Both went completely unnoticed despite weighing in at modern-day V8 and V9 respectively, meaning that at the time they were likely the hardest climbs on the planet. (By comparison, the Thimble's route grade of 5.12 equates to 'only' V5 in bouldering money.) It took fifteen years for another climber to surpass Gill's performance – in the mid-1970s in Colorado, Jim Holloway opened three extremely hard boulders which went unrepeated for over thirty years. Inspired by Gill's dynamic movement and much like Gill himself, Holloway was a unique climber way ahead of his time. It wasn't until the 1980s that the rest of the world caught up with the two Americans in their new game of bouldering.
5   John Gill's website, www.johngill.net, accessed 10 February 2020.
6   Laugier, A., in Modica, G., *Fontainebleau: 100 Ans d'Escalade*, Mont Blanc Editions, 2017, translated from French by the author.
7   *Duroxmanie* (6c, with harder variants existing) was opened in the eighties by Pascal Terray, and named after a friend nicknamed Durox who at the time lived the climbing-bum life in the Cuvier car park. Information received from Pascal Terray by email.
8   De Lépiney was the first to climb the route without a rope; roped ascents had been done earlier.
9   There are similar but later photos of Pierre Allain doing outrageous jumps, which suggest that in the pre-war era jumping among the boulders was much more popular than it is today.

10   The current rating system gave it the grade of VIh in the Welzenbach scale coming from the Eastern Alps, which made little sense, and soon Pierre Allain invented the grading system now in use in Bleau and throughout Europe.
11   John Gill's website, www.johngill.net/, accessed 10 February 2020.
12   Author interview: Pat Ament, John Gill: Master of Rock, Vertebrate Publishing, www.v-publishing.co.uk/blog/v-publishing-blog/2018-11-21---author-interview-pat-ament-john-gill-master-of-rock.html, accessed 10 February 2020.

CHAPTER 14: CLIMBING FREE
Epigraph
'It goes, boys!'
Uttered by Lynn Hill after topping out on the first free ascent of *The Nose* of El Capitan in 1993.

Notes
1   The latter had been around only since 1978.
2   These ascents were referred to as FFA, but back then it stood for 'first free ascent', not, like today, 'first female ascent'.
3   Hill, L., Child, G., *Climbing Free: My Life in the Vertical World*, W.W. Norton & Company, 2002.
4   At the same time, it is worth noting that even this new definition of free climbing was entirely arbitrary. While pulling on gear at any point of the climb was considered unacceptable, soft rubber shoes and gymnastic chalk for increased grip became ubiquitous. The latter, first introduced by John Gill, quickly spread throughout the climbing world and even that was not without controversy; in the eyes of the English ace Joe Brown, chalk was as much aid as anything else that the new wave rejected.
5   New ideas were always first propagated by outstanding individuals and when it comes to free climbing Reinhold Messner and Jean-Claude Droyer have to be mentioned as influential in their own right. Another one of its first modern proponents was Belgium-born Claudio Barbier (1938–1977). He ascended to fame over one extremely successful summer in the Dolomites, but equally often climbed on his smaller, home crags. He soon began skipping some points of aid, using them only for protection and marking those he didn't pull on in yellow, giving origin to the French term of *jaunissement*, or yellowing. For a while, it was the synonym of free climbing on the continent, but many years had to pass for the majority of the climbing community to catch up with Barbier's vision.
6   Chouinard, Y., 'Modern Yosemite Climbing', *American Alpine Journal*, 1963, digitised by AAC Publications, http://publications.americanalpineclub.org/articles/12196331900/Modern-Yosemite-Climbing, accessed 10 December 2020. At the time the article was published, existing aid routes weren't exactly a new concept in Yosemite. In fact, they had been a part of the game since 1941 when a route on the Higher Spire was repeated with the elimination of aid on one of its harder pitches. Then, three years later, the whole line was done free. But it wasn't until twenty years later and the arrival of the young Frank Sacherer that free climbing really took off. Sacherer was known for his bad temper and insufferable arrogance, as well as a penchant for climbing at the very edge of what was possible and terrifying his belayers. His career in Yosemite spanned only five seasons and involved thirty free routes: some repeats of existing aid routes, others entirely new. By the time Sacherer left the Valley to pursue his passion for theoretical physics, he left a legacy of a new vision.
7   Roper, S., *Camp 4: Recollections of a Yosemite Rockclimber*, Mountaineers Books, 1994.

8   ibid.
9   Ray Jardine, the inventor of the spring-loaded camming devices which came to be known as 'friends', was one of those who put the most effort into realising this goal, but his vision was an odd one. Instead of following the route exactly, he wanted to create a variation. When it became clear that even that line would be too hard for him to free climb, he bought a chisel and committed what the climbing community almost unanimously considers an atrocity: chipped some holds. Realising his error, he faded away from the Yosemite scene.
10 Hill, L., Child, G., *Climbing Free: My Life in the Vertical World*, W.W. Norton & Company, 2002.
11 ibid.

CHAPTER 15: TO BOLT OR NOT TO BE
Epigraph
'The best climbers in any generation will want to climb harder than anyone has managed before. If necessary, they'll change the rules to achieve that.'
Fawcett, R., Douglas, E., *Rock Athlete: The Story of a Climbing Legend*,
Vertebrate Publishing, 2011.

Notes
1   Douglas, E., *Statement*, Vertebrate Publishing, 2015.
2   Today rated 7c+, at the time of its first ascent by Jean-Pierre Bouvier in 1981, it was the hardest pitch in France. Bouvier is still known in France as 'La Mouche', or 'The Fly', for his diminutive stature. He authored many hard sport lines as well as Fontainebleau boulders. After seeing Moon's redpoint process, Jerry Moffatt managed to achieve his goal of flashing *Chimpanzodrome*. The feat fell on his twenty-first birthday and astonished the French community.
3   Douglas, E., *Statement*, Vertebrate Publishing, 2015.
4   Only the second in the country after Jerry Moffatt's *Oyster*. *Oyster* was perhaps the world's second eighth-grade route after Tony Yaniro's *Grand Illusion* in the US, *Illusion* the more admirable as it was done on gear, meaning trad.
5   Initially 'clip-and-climb' in the US.
6   Much like Claudio Barbier a decade earlier.
7   It was named after a plastic coffee jug at Albert's home where many of the best climbers of the era often stayed. The plastic jug had a red button that had to be pressed for the coffee to flow and its brand was Rotpunkt.
8   At first it was done by hand, long before the cordless drill. Today, glue-in bolts remain the protection of choice on Frankonian rock, while expansion bolts became the standard in most other sport-climbing destinations.
9   Moffatt, J., Grimes, N., *Jerry Moffatt: Revelations*, Vertebrate Publishing, 2009.
10 'The Story of the Indian Face: the UK's First E9 Climb', teamBMC, www.youtube.com/watch?v=JMX4NAw0NSE, accessed 20 March 2020.
11 'Master's Wall' is first written in non-italics as the geographical name of a part of the mountain crag; after Moffatt's ascent the name is treated as a route name and therefore written in italics.
12 Douglas, E., *Statement*, Vertebrate Publishing, 2015.

CHAPTER 16: SWITZERLAND, 2019
Epigraph
'Not everyone feels the need for a baptism of fire, or wants to take part in a direct deed that gives them an immediate feeling of life and death. Yet the jeopardy and the supposed romance are usually overstated, and in fact it's the subtle little things words can never get at that I cling to now. But there was nothing subtle about getting hurt, the flip side of the dream.'
Long, J., *Rock Jocks, Wall Rats, and Hang Dogs*, Fireside, 1994.

Notes
1. It is entirely possible that the author has got both the direction and the name of the mountain wrong.
2. Martina's real name is Alice Martina Biscaglia. To avoid confusion with Alice Hafer I decided to go with Alice Biscaglia's second name.
3. Over twice as long as the world record held by the Basque Kilian Jornet.

CHAPTER 17: THE AGE OF PLASTIC
Epigraph
'Some twenty-two centuries before, the Romans had filled the Colosseum with gladiators, lions, and ill-fated prisoners and slaves. It looked to me as if this crowd were gathered to see a circus maximus of the vertical […].'
Hill, L., Child, G., *Climbing Free: My Life in the Vertical World*, W.W. Norton & Company, 2002e, 1994.

Notes
1. Maurer, E., 'Cold War, "Thaw" and "Everlasting Friendship": Soviet Mountaineers and Mount Everest, 1953–1960', *International Journal of the History of Sport*, 26:4, 2009, digitised by CORE, https://core.ac.uk/download/pdf/79437067.pdf, accessed 10 February 2020.
2. ibid.
3. Foreign travel was not among the liberties enjoyed by Soviet climbers, and in 1987 only the very best athletes were allowed to travel to France for competition – Kurshakova and her husband were not among them. Despite their prowess on the home walls, the Soviet climbers didn't do well in the West – presented with a lead wall, they not only were not accustomed to the level of difficulty but hadn't even seen quickdraws before. 'We only did top-rope speed climbing and suddenly in France it was a lead wall. Our climbers didn't even know how to clip quickdraws.' With surprise, the Russians realised that to do well on the international scene they would have to adapt to the new rules set by the French.
4. The unstated but more likely reason was to make climbing into a cash cow for the private sector and to bring climbing within the realm of state-controlled, organised sports. The authorities began to see the potential in climbing as well as creating more support for the sport; it was a good moment in France when Patrick Edlinger and also Catherine Destivelle became really well known – sport climbing was gaining the attention of the mainstream populace. Co-option like any other movement from the bottom up gets incorporated.
5. Gloria, A., Raspaud, M., 'Émergence des compétitions d'escalade en France (1980–1987). Genèse d'une offre fédérale', *Staps* 2006/1, no.71, www.cairn.info/revue-staps-2006-1-page-99.htm, accessed 10 February 2020.

6   'Le Manifeste des 19', digitised at CAD Climbers, retrieved at http://archive. wikiwix.com/cache/index2.php?url=http%3A%2F%2Fwww.cad-climbers. com%2Ffr%2Fnouvelles%2Fdossiers%2Farticle.php%3Fa%3D22, accessed 10 December 2020.
7   Burgman, J., *High Drama: The Rise, Fall, and Rebirth of American Competition Climbing*, Triumph Books, 2020.
8   ibid.

CHAPTER 18: THE RISE OF A ROCK STAR
Epigraph
'The medium is the message.'
McLuhan, M., *Understanding Media: The Extensions of Man*, MIT Press, 1994.

Notes
1   'Rock Climber Chris Sharma Chases Next "King Line"', All Things Considered, NPR, 2007, www.npr.org/2007/11/01/15825820/rock-climber-chris-sharma-chases-next-king-line, accessed 20 March 2020.
2   Lee, E., 'The Olympics has helped to boost the Peacock streaming platform', *The New York Times*, www.nytimes.com/2021/07/29/business/comcast-nbc-olympics-peacock.html, accessed 20 March 2020.
3   Smith, G., 'Olympics Ratings Slump Forces NBC to Haggle With Advertisers', Bloomberg, www.bloomberg.com/news/articles/2021-07-30/olympics-ratings-slump-forces-nbc-to-haggle-with-advertisers, accessed 20 March 2020.
4   Sowa, J., Wolański, K., *Sport Nie Istnieje*, WAB, 2017.
5   Journal articles were also popular because climbing and mountaineering were initially seen as scientific fieldwork.
6   Mountain Project Forums, www.mountainproject.com/forum/topic/120009866/what-happened-to-eric-perlman-creator-of-the-masters-of-stone-video-series-anyon, accessed 20 February 2020.
7   *La Dura Dura*, Lowell, J., Sender Films and Big UP Productions, USA, 2012.

CHAPTER 19: 'AGENDA 2020'
Epigraph
'In brief, sport, born of truly popular games, i.e. games produced by the people, returns to the people, like "folk music", in the form of spectacles produced for the people.'
Bourdieu, P., *Sport and Social Class*, 1978.

Notes
1   Including independent athletes representing the Individual Olympic Athletes (IOA) team.
2   'London 2012: UK public says £9bn Olympics worth it', BBC, 2013, www.bbc.com/sport/olympics/23434844, accessed 10 December 2020.
3   From 1988 the IOC made all professional athletes eligible for participation.
4   Chang, C., 'How the Olympics Lost Millennials', *The New Republic*, https://newrepublic.com/article/136096/olympics-lost-millennials, accessed 10 February 2020.

5   Wheaton, B., Thorpe, H., 'Action Sport Media Consumption Trends Across Generations: Exploring the Olympic Audience and the Impact of Action Sports Inclusion', https://researchcommons.waikato.ac.nz/bitstream/handle/10289/13712/sport%20and%20comm%20paper%20with%20edits.pdf?sequence=5&isAllowed=y, 2018, accessed 10 October 2020.
6   Bridges, P., 'Boycott the Olympics: the IOC Needs Snowboarding More Than We Need Them', *Snowboarder*, www.snowboarder.com/featured/boycott-the-olympics-the-ioc-needs-snowboarding-more-than-we-need-them/, 2014, accessed 10 February 2020.
7   Leigh, E., 'The Revolution Will Be Televised – How Snowboarding Is Dominating the Olympics', *On Board Mag*, https://onboardmag.com/features/talking-points/olympics-revolution-will-be-televised.html, 2018, accessed 20 February 2020.
8   Olympic Agenda 2020, International Olympic Committee, https://olympics.com/ioc/olympic-agenda-2020, accessed 20 February 2020.
9   Mission Statement, the UIAA, https://theuiaa.org/about, accessed 20 February 2020.
10 'Survey finds Olympic, elite athletes struggling financially', *USA Today*, https://eu.usatoday.com/story/sports/olympics/2020/02/24/survey-finds-olympic-elite-athletes-struggling-financially/111365842/, accessed 20 February 2020.
11 'IFSC Signs Four TV Right Deals Ahead of Sport Climbing's Olympic Bow', *Sport Business*, www.sportbusiness.com/news/ifsc-signs-four-tv-rights-deals-ahead-of-sport-climbings-olympic-bow/, accessed 20 December 2021.
12 Wheaton, B., Beal, B., '"Keeping It Real": Subcultural Media and the Discourses of Authenticity in Alternative Sport', *International Review for the Sociology of Sport*, 2003.
13 Wheaton, B., Thorpe, H., 'Action Sport Media Consumption Trends Across Generations: Exploring the Olympic Audience and the Impact of Action Sports Inclusion', https://researchcommons.waikato.ac.nz/bitstream/handle/10289/13712/sport%20and%20comm%20paper%20with%20edits.pdf?sequence=5&isAllowed=y, 2018, accessed 10 October 2020.
14 It is sometimes said that a sport becomes commercialised when companies selling products not directly associated with the sport start using it in their marketing by, for example, sponsoring athletes: think rock climbing in a bank ad or a professional climber sponsored by a sugary-beverage company.
15 Adam Ondra: 'My opinion on the Olympics is still very critical', *OnBouldering.com*, https://onbouldering.com/adam-ondra-my-opinion-on-the-olympics-is-still-very-critical/, accessed 12 December 2021.
16 Becker, T., 'Climbing and Olympics Hotly Debated: "We Should Stick to Our Roots"', www.ispo.com/en/markets/adam-ondra-climbing-olympics-we-should-stick-our-roots, accessed 12 December 2021.
17 Grohmann, K., 'Tokyo 2020 to be rescheduled to no later than summer 2021 – IOC and Japanese organizers', Reuters, 2020, www.reuters.com/article/us-olympic-coronavirus-olympics-ioc-idUSKBN21B1ZP, accessed 20 February 2020.

CHAPTER 20: BLEAUSARDE WITH AN E
Epigraph
'Over half a lifetime of climbing is stamped on my body, from crowded toes and undainty knuckles to overdeveloped back and elongating spine. It seems that what we think, what we feel and what we do changes us in ways both physical and less visible.'
Steph Davis quoted on her sponsor's website, 2012, quoted in Reych, Z., 'Climbing Women and Niche Media: Beyond Alternative Femininities', SOAS, UK, 2013.

Notes
1. Iki, M., 'Staff, Athletes in Constant Fear of Infections at Olympic Village', *The Asahi Shimbun*, 2021, www.asahi.com/ajw/articles/14401618, accessed 8 September 2021.
2. Bassa Mawem, who qualified in eighth place for the men's final, would have been the oldest finalist but he couldn't compete due to a bicep injury.
3. Megos, A., on his Instagram page, www.instagram.com/p/CVZ9x-9MPep/, www.instagram.com/p/CTSrOIKlZK9/, accessed 2 January 2022.
4. Dart, T., 'Climbing is a hit at the Tokyo Olympics – but does it reward the best athletes?', *The Guardian*, www.theguardian.com/sport/2021/aug/05/climbing-scoring-tokyo-2020-olympics-adam-ondra, accessed 2 January 2022.
5. Nussey, S., 'Olympics-Climbing-Sport Overcomes Format Limitations to Reach New Heights', *Reuters*, https://www.reuters.com/lifestyle/sports/review-olympics-climbing-sport-overcomes-format-limitations-reach-new-heights-2021-08-08/, accessed 2 February 2022.

EPILOGUE
Notes
1. Fraser, C., 'Zen and the Art of Climbing: Santa Cruz native Chris Sharma is redefining the limits of his sport: bouldering', MetroActive Features, 2007, www.metroactive.com/papers/cruz/09.27.00/sharma-0039.html, accessed 20 September 2020.

FURTHER READING AND RECOMMENDED VIEWING

CHAPTER 2: MOUNTAIN GLOOM AND MOUNTAIN GLORY
Further Reading
Hollis, D.L., 'Mountain Gloom and Mountain Glory: The Genealogy of an Idea', *ISLE: Interdisciplinary Studies in Literature and Environment,* Volume 26, Issue 4, Autumn 2019, pp.1038–1061, https://doi.org/10.1093/isle/isz0442019
Macfarlane, R., *Mountains of the Mind: A History of a Fascination,* Granta, 2003.
Nicolson, M.H., *Mountain Gloom and Mountain Glory: The Development of the Aesthetics of the Infinite,* Weyerhaeuser Environmental Classics, 1997
Thompson, S., *Unjustifiable Risk? The Story of British Climbing,* Cicerone Press, 2012.

CHAPTER 4: THE GOLDEN AGE AND OTHER MYTHS
Further Reading
Carrington, D., 'Two-thirds of glacier ice in the Alps "will melt by 2100"', *The Guardian,* 9 April 2019, https://www.theguardian.com/environment/2019/apr/09/two-thirds-glaciers-alps-alpine-doomed-climate-change-ice, accessed 5 March 2021.
Dowling, C., *The Frailty Myth,* Random House, 2008.
Roche, C., 'Women Climbers 1850–1900: A Challenge to Male Hegemony?', Department of History, Classics and Archaeology, Birkbeck, University of London. Published online: 2 September 2013.
Unsworth, W., *Hold the Heights: The Foundations of Mountaineering,* The Mountaineers, 1993.

CHAPTER 5: THE DESCENDANTS OF GODS
Further Reading
Brownelle, S. (ed.), *The 1904 Anthropology Days and Olympic Games: Sport, Race, and American Imperialism,* University of Nebraska Press, 2008.
Chatziefstathiou, D. and Henry, I., 'Hellenism and Olympism: Pierre de Coubertin and the Greek Challenge to the Early Olympic Movement' in *The Olympics. A Critical Reader,* ed. Griginov, V., Routledge, 2010.
Young, D., *A Brief History of the Olympic Games,* Blackwell Publishing, 2004.

CHAPTER 7: GYMNASTS ON ROCK
Further Reading
Pilley, D., *Climbing Days*, Harcourt Brace, 1935
Thompson, S., *Unjustifiable Risk? The Story of British Climbing*, Cicerone Press, 2012.

Recommended Viewing
King Lines, Lowell, J. and Mortimer, P., Sender Films and Big UP Productions, USA, 2007.

CHAPTER 8: THE PITON DISPUTE
Further Reading
Smart, D., *Emilio Comici: Angel of the Dolomites*, Rocky Mountain Books, 2020.
Smart, D., *Paul Preuss: Lord of the Abyss – Life and Death at the Birth of Free-Climbing*, Rocky Mountain Books, 2019.

CHAPTER 10: ON STOLEN LAND
Further Reading
Blakemore, E., 'California's Little-Known Genocide', History, 16 November 2017, https://www.history.com/news/californias-little-known-genocide, accessed 2 February 2022.
Maranzani, B., '8 Things You May Not Know About the California Gold Rush', History, 24 January 2013, https://www.history.com/news/8-things-you-may-not-know-about-the-california-gold-rush, accessed 2 February 2022.
Roper, S., *Camp 4, Recollections of a Yosemite Rockclimber*, Mountaineers Books, 1994.
Spence, M.D., *Dispossessing the Wilderness: Indian Removal and the Making of the National Parks*, Oxford University Press, 2000.

Recommended Viewing
Valley Uprising, Mortimer, P., Rosen, N. and Lowell, J., Sender Films, USA, 2014.

CHAPTER 11: HARD GRIT
Further Reading
Brown, J., *The Hard Years*, Mountaineers Books, 2001.
Parnell, I. (ed.), *Hard Rock. Great British rock climbs from VS to E4*, Vertebrate Publishing, 2020.
Perrin, J., *The Villain: The Life of Don Whillans*, Arrow, 2006.

CHAPTER 12: STEEL CITY, 2015
Further Reading
Dawes, J., *Full of Myself: Johnny Dawes*, Johnny Dawes Books, 2011.

Recommended Viewing
Stone Monkey: Portrait of a Rock Climber, Williams, H., Hughes Film, UK, 1988.

CHAPTER 13: THE POETRY OF MOUNTAINEERING
Further Reading
Ament, P., *Master of Rock: The Biography of John Gill*, Routledge, 1977.
Gill, J., 'The Art of Bouldering', *American Alpine Journal*, 1969, digitalised by AAC Publications, http://publications.americanalpineclub.org/articles/12196935500/The-Art-of-Bouldering
John Gill's website, https://www.johngill.net/, accessed 10 February 2020.

CHAPTER 14: CLIMBING FREE
Further Reading
Hill, L. and Child, G., *Climbing Free: My Life in the Vertical World*, W.W. Norton & Company, 2002.

CHAPTER 15: TO BOLT OR NOT TO BE
Further Reading
Dawes, J., *Full of Myself: Johnny Dawes*, Johnny Dawes Books, 2011.
Douglas, E., *Statement*, Vertebrate Publishing, 2015.
Fawcett, R. and Douglas, E., *Rock Athlete: The Story of a Climbing Legend*, Vertebrate Publishing, 2011.
Moffatt, J. and Grimes, N., *Jerry Moffatt: Revelations*, Vertebrate Publishing, 2009.

Recommended Viewing
The Story of the Indian Face: the UK's First E9 Climb, teamBMC, https://www.youtube.com/watch?v=JMX4NAw0NSE, accessed 20 March 2020.

CHAPTER 17: THE AGE OF PLASTIC
Further Reading
Burgman, J., *High Drama: The Rise, Fall, and Rebirth of American Competition Climbing*, Triumph Books, 2020.
Destivelle, C., *Rock Queen*, Hayloft Publishing, 2015.

CHAPTER 18: THE RISE OF A ROCK STAR
Recommended Viewing
E Pericoloso Sporgersi, Nicod, R., France, 1985.
King Lines, Lowell, J. and Mortimer, P., Sender Films and Big UP Productions, USA, 2007.
La Dura Dura, Lowell, J., Sender Films and Big UP Productions, USA, 2012.
La Vie au Bout des Doigts, Janssen, J.P., France, 1982.
The Real Thing, Tucker, S., UK, 199.
The Story of the Indian Face: the UK's First E9 Climb, teamBMC, https://www.youtube.com/watch?v=JMX4NAw0NSE, accessed 20 March 2020.

INDEX

A

À l'Envers 240
AAC see *Amateur Athletic Club* or *American Alpine Club*
Abraham, George and Ashley 73, 222
Abratzky, Sebastian 76–77, 182
Academy Awards 9, 226
Action Directe 187, 190
advertising 214, 221–222, 234
aesthetic vs athletic approach to climbing 24, 48, 75, 241
Ahwahnee 113, 115
Ahwahneechee 113–117, 125–126, 172
aid climbing 78, 91–92, 94, 115, 119, 169, 173, 182
Aiguille du Jardin 206
Aiguille du Midi 202–204
Albert, Kurt 182–183, 188–189
Allain, Pierre 161–162
Allen, John 153
Almaty, Kazakhstan 229
Alpine Club (UK; see also *American, Austrian, German, Italian* and *Swiss Alpine Club*) 38, 46–47, 61, 69, 72, 74, 95, 127, 130, 131, 157
Alpine Journal 41, 72
Alpine Times 87–88
Alpini 90, 117
Alpinist 126

Alps 6, 22, 23, 25, 42–45, 47, 48, 50–51, 59, 66, 69, 72, 75, 79, 83–85, 88, 90, 91, 95, 98, 112, 115, 128, 135, 161, 162, 164, 169, 170, 206, 214
Altaussee 83, 89
Amateur Athletic Club (AAC) 55–56
amateurism 47, 55–56, 60, 66–67, 228
Ament, Pat 165
American Alpine Club 164, 168, 175–176, 216
American Alpine Journal 94, 170
American Bouldering Series (ABS) 218
Andrich, Anvise 95
Annapurna 136
antisemitism 85, 88
Antonovich, Ivan 209
Aomi Urban Sports Park 242
Appalachian Mountain Club (AMC) 112
Arête du Diable 50
'Artificial Aids on Alpine Routes' 87
Astroman 174
Athens 55, 57, 58
Austrian Alpine Club (Alpenklub) 46, 84, 85
German and Austrian Alpine Club 79, 87
Austro-Hungarian Empire 84, 90
Avignon 17

B

Bachar, John 174, 222
Bad Schandau (previously Schandau) 78, 81
Baker, Mary 26
Ballenberger, Thomas 182
Balmat, Jacques 40–41
Bardonecchia 208, 213–216, 236
Bas Cuvier 247
BBC 6, 243
Bela Lugosi is Dead 151
Bell, Gertrude 49
Bergsport 86
Berkeley 216
Bernardini, Bruna 97
Bertone, Oriane 250
Biscaglia, (Alice) Martina 199, 205–207
Black Hills National Forest 155
Black Lake Valley 99–110
Black Pearl 197–198, 204
bleausard 162–164
Bonington, Chris 135
Boulder Rock Club 218
bouldering 4–5, 74, 145, 152–153, 155–165, 197, 217–218, 219, 223, 233, 235–236, 239, 242–245, 247, 249–250
Bourdieu, Pierre 228
Bridwell, Jim 172–175, 217
British Empire 22, 41
British Mountaineering Club 75, 101

Broad Stand 27
Brookes, Dr William Penny 54–59
Brown, Joe 127–128, 130–137, 150–151, 172, 184
Bruhl, Étienne 30
Buchenhain 86
Buhler, Oskar 183
Bulgaria 1–2, 205–206
Burke, Edmund 24–25
Burke, Scott 177
Burnet, Thomas 22–23

C

Caldwell, Dean 170–171
Caldwell, Tommy 8–9, 11, 177, 223
California Gold Rush 113
Cambridge 22, 73, 75
Oxbridge 128, 135
Camp 4 (Yosemite) 124, 125–126, 171–172, 174
Campanile Basso 86, 96
capitalism 59, 88, 116, 191, 221, 247, 248
Carmichael, Bob 215
Carpignano, Elena 199–206
Carrion, Obe 223, 225
Cathedral Peak 113
Caucasus 80, 209–210
CBS 215, 229
Cemetery Gates 128
Cenotaph Corner 127–128, 131–132
Chai Vasarhelyi, Elizabeth 9
chalk, introduction of 158, 211, 248
Chamonix 38–42, 45, 50–53, 69, 84, 101, 161, 199–200, 202–203, 205–206, 232
Change 225
Changing Corners 176–177
Channel One 244
Charlet-Straton, Isabella 49

chimney sweep 74, 76, 77
Chimpanzodrome 180
Chin, Jimmy 9
Chouinard, Yvon 155, 170, 173
Christianity 18, 20–21, 23, 38, 56, 85
see also *Muscular Christianity* and *Valley Christian*
Cima di Riofreddo 91–92
Cima Grande di Lavaredo 93–96
Cima Piccola 95
Cimon della Pala 95
Civetta 91–92
City Rock 217
Clan des Rochassiers 160–161
Clarion Ramblers 129
class 28–29, 42, 45, 46–47, 49, 54–55, 58–59, 67, 72, 77–79, 86, 121, 127, 129, 130–131, 134–135, 188, 221–222
Cliffhanger 173, 190, 217
Climb the Hill 248
Climb Time 217–218
Climbers' Club 74
Climbers' Club hut 144, 147–149
Climbing Competitions 209
climbing gyms/walls 6–7, 9–10, 63, 163, 211, 215–218, 223, 248
Climbing Works 143
Mile End Climbing Wall 63, 65, 100, 139
'Climbing with Women' 85
Climbing Works 143
Clogwyn Du'r Arddu 184–186
Club Alpin Français (CAF) 160
Coeur de Lion 151
Cold War 12, 209
Coleman, Nathaniel 243
Coleridge, Samuel Taylor 26–28
Comes the Dervish 151
Comici, Emilio 90–97

communism 12, 13, 208–209, 210
Confessions 73
competition climbing 4–7, 9–10, 44, 140, 176, 209, 212–218, 220, 232–233, 235–236, 242, 244–245, 250
controversies 4–5, 23, 45, 72, 74, 88, 168, 170, 176, 181–182, 186, 188, 230, 235–236
Cook, Thomas 67
Coolidge, W.A.B. 45
coronavirus 6, 236, 238–243
Cortina d'Ampezzo 93
Coubertin, Baron de 57, 60–61, 228, 235
Coxsey, Shauna 11, 225, 236, 243
cragging 169, 180
Crimea 209–212
Crimean War 41
Crowley, Aleister 73–74, 159
Crystal Palace 55
Cuvier Est 161

D

Dame Jouanne 160
Das Klettern im Fels 88
Das Letzte im Fels 94
Davis, Steph 238
Davos 79
Dawes, Johnny 141–149, 151–154, 186–187
Dawn Wall 8–9
Day, Andy 100–110, 139–140, 193, 241
Decimus Junius Juvenalis 54
Demon Rib 128
Der Falkenstein 78, 79
Der Mönch 78
Destivelle, Catherine 213–215
Diavolezza 79
'Die Alpen' 23
Dimai, Guiseppe and Angelo 93–94, 96
Dinas Cromlech 127, 148

INDEX

Dinorwig quarry 150
Dnipro (Dnipropetrovsk) 209–211
documentaries 9, 222–225, 226
Dolomites 83, 84–85, 86, 90, 91, 95, 168, 169
Dombai 209
Dove Cottage 68
Downward Bound 171
Drei Zinnen (Tre Cime) 93, 95–96
Dresden 80–81
Dudley, Helen 250
Duffy, Colin 244
Dülfer, Hans 85
Dülfersitz 85, 102
Duroxmanie 161

E

Eastern Bloc 12, 212
Eckenstein, Oscar 74, 159, 168
Edelweiss 81
Edlinger, Patrick 13, 212, 214, 216
Egyptian Hall, Piccadilly 42
Eichorn, Jules 115
Eisenberg, Emmy 85
Eiter, Angela 225
El Capitan 8–9, 111, 121, 123–124, 170–171, 174, 175, 177, 206, 222, 250
El Sendero Luminoso 195
El Toro 195
Elbe Valley 79, 86, 182
environmental issues 2, 20–22, 66, 112, 229, 247–249
Es Pontàs 220
ESPN 6, 217, 231
Eternal Flame 189
ethics, climbing 44, 61, 68, 77, 80, 82, 87, 95, 115, 119, 122, 158, 168, 170, 173, 176, 181–184, 186–188, 213–214, 246, 248
Eurosport 245

F

Fabjan, Giordano 92
Falkensteiner 81
Farquhar, Francis 112, 115
fascism 90, 92–93, 96, 229
Fat Man's Agony 28
Faus, Isabelle 225
Fawcett, Ron 179, 184–185
Fehrmann, Rudolf 80–82
Fehrmann's Dihedral 87, 96
Field Days (Yosemite) 116
File 137
films 8, 9, 81, 143, 153, 173, 190, 193, 215, 217, 220, 222–225
Findlay, Hazel 225
Fischer, Ernst 78
'Five Ladies' 51
Flatanger 225
Fontainebleau 159–164, 223, 238–241, 247, 248, 250
Fowler, Liz 137–138, 143–152
Frankenjura 30, 182–183, 188–191
Frédy, Charles Pierre de see *Coubertin, Baron de*
free climbing 80, 82, 88, 91, 92, 120, 168–170, 172, 174, 175, 177, 181–183, 188, 211, 223
Free Solo 9
Freerider 9, 250
French Climbing Federation (FME) 212
French Federation of Mountaineering and Climbing (FFME) 213
French Mountaineering Federation (FFM) 212
French Revolution 41, 58
Frenzel, Heinrich 78
Fresno River Reservation 113
Frick, Hermann Johannes 78
Full of Myself 140

G

Garnbret, Janja 7–8, 243, 250
Gąsienicowa Valley 99
gear inventions and innovations 74, 85, 117, 121–122, 168, 169, 172, 180, 183
gender gap and (in)equality 26, 28, 30, 32, 35, 36, 44, 46, 49–51, 95, 172, 175, 184, 192, 214–215, 225–226, 230, 239, 248, 249
Geneva 38–40, 42
German Alpine Club 94
German and Austrian Alpine Club 79, 87
German General Sports Exhibition 86
Gill, John 155–159, 163–165
Ginés López, Alberto 242
Glowacz, Stefan 214, 236
Gobright, Brad 193–196, 205, 206
Godoffe, Jacky 158, 216
Goethe, Johann Wolfgang von 24
Gogarth 136, 144, 146, 204
Gosaukamm 83, 89
Goûter Route 51
grading systems 74, 91, 120, 163, 181–182, 190–191, 243
Grand Illusion 167
granite 2–3, 8, 9, 13, 16, 31, 52, 100, 117, 122–123, 155, 159, 166, 171, 183, 194, 197, 202, 210, 213
Gray, Thomas 24–25
Greece 54, 56–57
Greek gods 19, 56
Greek Theatre 216
Grépon 30
gritstone 128, 131–134, 137, 140, 152, 183
Grohmann, Paul 84
Guardian 135
Guide Through the District of the Lakes 68–69
guides and guiding 15, 39–47, 50, 83, 85, 93, 96, 98, 114, 130, 168, 205, 214
Güllich, Anette 189, 190

Güllich, Wolfgang 187–191, 214
Gunks see Shawangunks
gymnastics 7, 55, 60, 66–82, 84, 88, 90, 92, 156–159, 164, 175, 211, 233, 249

H
Hachioji 5, 236
Hafer, Alice 139, 153, 193–196, 205, 206–207
Half Dome 111, 120–121
Haller, Albrecht von 23
Hamilton, Mrs 49
Hard Rock 134 (book), 223 (film)
Harding, Warren 120–124, 168, 170–171, 173, 174, 222
Harrington, Emily 225
Harvard Mountaineering Club 112
Haskett Smith, Walter Parry 69–73, 128
Hastings, Stevie 151
Havergal, Frances 51
Hayes, Margo 158, 225
Heights, The 146
Hering, August 78
Higgar Tor 137–138
Higher Cathedral Spire 115
Hill, Lynn 158, 166–167, 173, 175–177, 208, 214–215, 217, 250
Hillary, Sir Edmund 62
Himalaya 12, 135, 152, 209
homophobia 43, 75
Honnold, Alex 8–9, 226, 250
Hubble 190
Huber, Alex 9
Hueco scale 163
Hukkataival, Nalle 225
Hutchings, James 114

I
IFSC (International Federation of Sport Climbing) 4–5, 10, 233–236
Imitator 144
Indian Face, The 187
indigenous peoples (see also Ahwahneechee) 60, 111, 113, 125
Industrial Revolution 59, 66, 68, 129, 130
industrialisation 21, 22, 129, 191, 208
Innsbruck 5
International Climbing and Mountaineering Federation (UIAA) 232–233
International Federation of Sport Climbing (IFSC) 4–5, 10, 233–236
International Olympic Committee (IOC) 4–6, 10, 58, 60–61, 220, 231–233, 235, 243–244, 247
Italian Alpine Club 95
Ivy Sepulchre 127–128

J
Jacobson, Aidan 195–196
Jahn, Friedrich Ludwig 77
Jones, Owen Glynne 66, 72–74
Jorgeson, Kevin 8–9
Journal of the Lakes 24
Jura (Polish; see also Frankenjura) 30, 32, 37

K
K2 99
Kaisergebirge 86
Kangchenjunga 99, 135
Karakoram 12
Karb Pass 102
Karłowicz, Mieczysław 12
Karpaty 13
Kauk, Lonnie 111, 126
Kauk, Ron 111, 174, 188, 190, 222
Kazbekova, Jenya 209
Kern Knotts Crack 73
Kerouac, Jack 124–125
Kinder Scout 129, 131
 Mass Trespass 129
King Lines 81, 220
King Swing 122
Kingsley, Charles 43
Kirkus, Colin 131
Klettersport 86
Klimmer, Martin 79
Königstein Fortress 76
Kościelec 102
Kroening, Amy 196–199, 204, 206–207
Kugy, Julius 94
Kurshakova, Natalya 212
Kurshakova, Valentina 209–212
Kurtyka, Wojciech 12

L
L'Angle Allain 162
L'Arête des Cosmiques 202–203
L'Éléphant 239
La Dura Complete: The Hardest Rock Climb In The World 225
La Dura Dura 224–225
La Fissure Wehrlin 161
La Joker 163
La Prestat 161
Ladin 93, 98
Lake District 24–28, 68–74
Late Night 217
Latest in Rock Climbing, The 94
Lauener (Alpine guide) 43
Laycock, John 128
lead climbing 4–5, 233, 236, 242–245
leisure, climbing/sport as 25, 29, 55, 59, 78, 78, 160–161, 208–209
Leonard, Dick 115
Lépiney, Jacques de 161

INDEX

Letterman, David 217
LGBTQ+ climbers 75, 225, 248
licences (climbing) 31–32
limestone 13, 30, 32, 63–65, 84, 86, 88, 179, 181–183, 186, 195, 197, 218, 220, 224
Lingmell 69
Little Meadow Valley 15
Llanberis 127, 137, 146, 148, 150
London 21, 39, 40, 41, 42, 46, 55, 57, 61, 62–65, 72–73, 230
Long, John 166, 173–174, 190, 192
López, Alberto Ginés 242
Lost Arrow Chimney 119
Lost Arrow Spire 118, 168
Lowe, Greg 215
Lowe, Jeff 215–216
Lowell, Brett 223
Lowell, Josh 223, 224

M

Macfarlane, Robert 21
Mallorca 219–220
Manchester 128, 130, 135
Mandlkogel 89
Manifesto of the Nineteen 213
Marín, Francisco 'Novato' 250
Markneukirchen 79
masculinity and machismo 43–44, 48–50, 55, 91, 95, 172, 181, 217
Master's Wall 184–186
Masters of Stone 222
Matinee 133
Matterhorn 44–45, 94
Matthews, C.E. 47
Mayfiend, Peter 217
McHaffie, James 151
McLuhan, Marshall 219
media coverage 6, 8, 10, 13, 28, 67, 92, 94, 123, 135, 170–171, 189, 191, 214, 215, 216, 219, 220–223, 226, 229–232, 236, 243, 244–245, 246, 247, 248, 250

Megos, Alex 243
Mer de Glace 53
Merry, Wayne 122
Meyer, Maud 49
Midnight Lightning 111, 174
Midwest Bouldering Tour 218
Mile End Climbing Wall 63, 65, 100, 139
Milton, John 20
misogyny 30, 33, 35–37, 49–51, 60, 85, 95, 172, 214–215
Moffatt, Jerry 179, 184, 185–186, 189, 213–214, 223
Mönchsteiner 81
Mont Blanc 40, 42, 46–47, 49, 50, 51, 161, 222
Mont Oreb 202
Mont Ventoux 17–18
Montenvers 38–39, 51–53
Moon, Ben 179–181, 184, 186, 189, 190, 223
Moore, Dr John 39
Morning Post 68
Mount Olympus 18, 19
Mountain Gloom and Mountain Glory 29
Mountaineering 47
Mountaineering Club Rustig 80
Mountains of the Mind 21
Much Wenlock 54, 57
Muir, John 112–115, 173
Mummery, Mary 50
Munich Academic Alpine Section 85
Muscular Christianity 43, 48, 50, 54
Mutiny Crack 152

N

Napes Needle 69–71
Napoleon 17, 58, 77

National Geographic 9
National Olympian Committee (NOA) 55
National Socialist Party 82
nationalism 47, 58, 77, 90, 93, 215
Native Americans 110, 113–117, 126, 158
Nazism 77, 82, 162, 229
NBC 221, 243
Needles Highway 155–156
Nelson, Ax 118–119
neoclassicism 56
Neruda, Maud 49
Netflix 8
New Republic, The 230
New York Times 167
Nicolson, Marjorie Hope 29
Nieberl, Franz 88
NOA (National Olympian Committee) 55
Noguchi, Akiyo 7, 237, 243, 244
non-binary climbers 225, 248
Nonaka, Miho 243, 244
Norway 225
Nose, The 123, 175, 176–178

O

O'Brien, Miriam 112
Ociepka, Kinga 35
Oliana 224
Olympia 56
Olympic Games 4–6, 10, 54–61, 228–237
  ancient Olympics 55–56
  Much Wenlock 54–55, 57
  modern revival (Athens 1859) 55, 57
  modern era (1896–2016) 60, 61, 221, 228–232, 235
  Tokyo 2020 (in 2021) 4–6, 10, 235–237, 241–245

how climbing became an Olympic sport   4–5, 10, 232–236
'Agenda 2020'   231–232, 235, 243
Beijing 2022   229
Paris 2024   244
costs   228–229, 235, 242
controversies   228–229
media   229–231, 234
Ondra, Adam   8, 9, 223–225, 236, 242
Opening Gambit   150
Osman, Dan   222
Oxbridge   128, 135
Oxford   69, 72

P

Paccard, Dr Michel-Gabriel   40–41
Pamir   12
Paradise Lost   20
Paragot, Robert   163
Parisella's Cave   179–180
Parker, Julia   126
Path Under the Firs   14
Paulet, Charles   22
Peak District   100, 132–133, 137, 140, 152
Pen Trwyn   179–180, 182, 186
Pen-y-Pass   75
Perlman, Eric   222
Perrin, Jim   134
Perry-Smith, Oliver   81–82
Pete's Eats   151
Petrarch, Francisco   17–19
Pfalz   187–188
Philosophical Enquiry into the Origin of Our Ideas of the Sublime and Beautiful, A   24–25
physical education and training   57–59, 61, 67, 77, 90, 137, 156–158, 161, 164–165, 174, 177–178, 188–189, 209, 211, 223, 235, 249
Piaz, Tita   83, 85, 86, 88, 93, 98
Pigeon, Anna   49, 50
Pigeon, Ellen   49, 50
Pirna   78–81
Piz Badile   45
Planta de Shiva   225
Playground of Europe, The   46, 51
Pococke, Richard   39–40, 52
Poland   12–16, 30–37, 100–110, 211, 236, 244
Polish Alpine Association   101
Polish Mountaineering Association   31
Pollock, Sir Frederick   38, 47
Ponomarenko, Vasily   209–211
portaledges   119, 169
Potrero Chico   206
Powell, Mark   122, 124
Preuss, Lina   83
Preuss, Mina   86–87, 96
Preuss, Paul   83–89, 91, 94, 96–97, 168
professionalisation   44, 48, 55, 67, 124, 210, 214, 218, 222, 228, 233, 249
Protect our Winters   248
psicobloc   219–220
Puccio, Alex   225

Q

Quarryman   151

R

racism and ethnicity (see also Ahwahneechee and indigenous peoples)   28, 60, 85, 88, 93, 116, 125–126
Rainbow Slab   151
rambling   73, 129, 132
Rampage   223
Recreate Responsibly   248
Redhead, John   185–186
Refuge du Montenvers   53
Relly (friend of Paul Preuss)   86–87, 96
Renaissance   56
Rennak, Scott   217–218
Restant du Long Rocher   160
Reych, Małgorzata (Zofia's mother)   12–16
Riera, Miguel   219–220
risk   19, 21, 25, 45, 48, 83, 88, 156, 164, 181, 183, 187, 193, 219
Roaches, the   132
Robbins, Royal   120–123, 157, 168, 171, 172–173, 174
Robins, Pete   151
Robinson, Bestor   115
Rock and Ice   134
Rock Climbing in the English Lake District   73
Rodden, Beth   223
Rodellar   63–64, 249
Rogora, Laura   225
Roman Empire   20, 56, 77, 90, 208
Romanticism   24, 25–26, 43, 57, 66, 75, 159
Roof-Climber's Guide to Trinity, The   75
Roper, Steve   123, 173
Rosandra Valley   92
rotpunkt   183
Rousseau, Jean-Jacques   23–25, 48
Royal Society   39
Rudatis, Domenico   94
Rugby School   57–59
Ruskin, John   47–48, 74
Rutkiewicz, Wanda   99

S

Sabourin, Lor   225
Sacherer, Frank   172
Sacred Theory of the Earth, The   23
Sadie   140–141, 143, 153
Safety Third   193

Salathé, John   117–120, 168
Sandahl, Brooke   176–177
sandstone   76, 78–80, 159, 161, 187, 248
Saussure, Horace Bénédict de   41
Savoy   39–40
Saxon Climbers' Federation   81
Saxon Switzerland Mountain Association   79
Saxon Switzerland National Park   78
Saxon–Bohemian railway
Saxony   76–82, 182
Scafell Pike   26–28, 69
Schandau (now Bad Schandau)   78, 81
Schubert, Jakob   242
Schuster, Oscar   79–80
scientific advances and exploration   21, 22, 38–41, 47
Scolaris, Marco   234, 235
Scrambles Amongst the Alps   45
Sentinel Rock   119–120
Separate Reality   188
Sharma, Chris   81, 220, 223–224, 226, 234, 250
Shawangunks   111, 166–167
Sheffield   100, 139–143, 184, 249
Shiraishi, Ashima   225–226, 249
Sierra Club   112, 115, 117, 119
Sierra Nevada   113, 115, 120
Silence   8, 225
Skrajny Granat   105
Smith, Albert   41–42, 46, 47, 222
'sneakers wars'   229
Snowbird's Cliff Lodge   215–216
snowboarding   231
social media   28, 194, 226, 231, 243, 246
Some Shorter Climbs   128
Sorbonne Congress to Revive the Olympic Games   58

speed climbing   4–5, 211, 212, 233, 235, 236, 242–245
Spigolo Giallo   95
Spinotti, Ricardo   91–92
sponsorship   48, 189, 212, 214, 216, 218, 222–223, 226, 229, 231, 233, 246
sport climbing   4, 19, 31, 181–182, 185, 187, 205, 225, 233, 242
Stallone, Sylvester   190
Statement of Youth   181–182, 186
Steck, Allen   119
Steczkowska, Maria   15
Stephen, Leslie   46–47, 51
Stone Love   223
Stone Monkey   153
Stonemasters, the   173–175
Strawberries   184–185
Summit, The   75
Sunday Express   135
Swiss Alpine Club   79
Swiss Notes   51
Switzerland   78–80, 82, 117, 182, 192–207, 211

T

Taistra, Ola   35
Täschhorn   50
Tatra mountains   13–16, 31, 100–110
Taugwalder, Peter   45
Technical Master   153
television   6, 7, 8, 135, 171, 213, 215, 217, 221, 229, 230, 234, 243, 244–245
Theodosius the Great   56
Thimble, the   155–157
Tokyo 2020 (in 2021)   4–6, 10, 235–237, 241–245
Tormented Ejaculation   185
Totenkirchl   86–87
Trango Towers   189
trans climbers   225
transport, development of public   42, 67, 68, 101, 129, 160–161

Tre Cime   93, 95–96
Trentino   90
Tribout, Jibé   213, 216
Trieste   90, 93
Tröger, Gustav   78
Twll Mawr   151

U

Ufer, Otto Ewald   78
UIAA (International Climbing and Mountaineering Federation)   232–233
Underhill, Robert   112, 115
University of Georgia   158
University of Texas   157
USA Climbing   6, 233
USSR   208–212, 228
USSR Mountaineering Federation   212
Utah   215

V

Valle Stretta   213
Valley Christian   122, 123, 171
Vallon-Pont-d'Arc   213
Vandals   167
Varale, Mary   95
Vector   135
Vertical Kilometre   200–203
via ferrata   13, 106
Via Normale   86–87, 96
Vienna   83, 84, 86, 89

W

Wähnert, Johannes   78
Wales   73, 127, 132, 137, 143–152, 159, 179–180, 184–186, 204
Walker, Lucy   49
Wall and Roof Climbing   75
Wall of Early Morning Light   170–171
Wall Street   189
Walpole, Horace   24, 25

Wanderings Among the High Alps   43
Wanderlust (climbers' association)   81
Warsaw   12, 14, 65, 110
Wasdale   69–70, 72
Wasdale Head Inn   69, 72–73
Wehrlin, Jacques   161
Welzenbach grading system   120
Westbay, Billy   174
Wetterhorn   45–46
Whillans, Don   127–128, 132–137, 172
Whitmore, George   122
Whymper, Edward   45
Wills, Alfred   42–43, 45–46
Wills, Lucy   42–43
Windham Sr, William   38–40, 52
Winkler Tower   85
Winthrop Young, Geoffrey   74–75
Women's Bouldering Festival   239–240
women and climbing   26, 30, 32, 46, 49–51, 60–61, 85, 95, 112, 172, 214–215, 225
Woods, Daniel   225
Wordsworth, Dorothy   26–27, 68
Wordsworth, William   26, 28, 68–69
World Championships (see also *Youth World Championships*)   8
  Hachioji 2019   5, 236
  Innsbruck 2018   5
World Cups   6, 8, 216
World Fair   60
World War I   80, 98, 101, 128
World War II   82, 101, 117, 130, 208, 228

X
X Games   217, 231
XXX Ottobre   90

Y
Yaniro, Tony   167–168, 222
Yellow Crack Direct   167
yo-yoing   167, 183, 188
Yosemite Decimal System (YDS)   120
Yosemite Valley   6–7, 8–9, 95, 111–126, 157, 169–177, 190, 206
  Ahwahnee   113, 115
Youth World Championships
  Basel 1992   211
  Innsbruck 2017   5
YouTube   225, 234

Z
Zakopane   14, 101
Zermatt   44–45, 69, 84, 101
Zeus   19, 56